TV GOES TO HELL
AN UNOFFICIAL ROAD MAP OF
SUPERNATURAL

Edited by
Stacey Abbott
& David Lavery

ECW

Published by ECW Press
2120 Queen Street East, Suite 200, Toronto, Ontario, Canada M4E 1E2
416-694-3348 / info@ecwpress.com

Library and Archives Canada Cataloguing in Publication

Lavery, David, 1949-
TV goes to hell : an unofficial road map of Supernatural / David Lavery, Stacey Abbott.

ISBN 978-1-77041-020-6
Also issued in electronic formats:
978-1-77090-034-9 (EPUB); 978-1-77090-035-6 (PDF)

1. Supernatural (Television program : 2005-). I. Abbott, Stacey II. Title.

PN1992.77.S87L38 2011   791.45'72   C2011-902812-3

Developing editor: Jennifer Hale
Cover design: Cyanotype
Cover images: road © Clint Spencer / iStock; angel © Mike Wiggins / iStock
Typesetting and production: Rachel Ironstone
Printing: Thomson-Shore   5   4   3   2   1

Printed and bound in the United States

ECW PRESS
ecwpress.com

To our families

Contents

Acknowledgments vii

Introduction Then: The Road So Far (Stacey Abbott) ix

"Bon Jovi rocks . . . on occasion": Comedy and Music

Rabbits' Feet and Spleen Juice: The Comic Strategies of TV Horror (Stacey Abbott) 3

Two Greasers and a Muscle Car: Music and Character Development in *Supernatural* (Stan Beeler) 18

Skin Mags and Shaving Cream: Sam and Dean on the Fringes of Time and Place

Purgatory with Color TV: Motel Rooms as Liminal Zones in *Supernatural* (Lorna Jowett) 33

Rebels, Rogues, and Sworn Brothers: *Supernatural* and the Shift in "White Trash" from Monster to Hero (Aaron C. Burnell) 47

Renegades and Wayward Sons: *Supernatural* and the '70s (Simon Brown) 60

"Jerk . . . bitch": Representations of Gender and Sexuality

The Road to Lordsburg: Rural Masculinity in *Supernatural* (Lorrie Palmer) 77

Angels, Demons, and Damsels in Distress: The Representation of Women in *Supernatural* (Bronwen Calvert) 90

"Go be gay for that poor, dead intern": Conversion Fantasies and Gay Anxieties in *Supernatural* (Darren Elliott-Smith) 105

The Gospel According to Chuck: Narrative and Storytelling in *Supernatural*

"That's so gay": Drag, Camp, and the Power of Storytelling
in *Supernatural* (James Francis, Jr.) 119
"There's a ton of lore on unicorns too": Postmodernist
Micro-Narratives and *Supernatural* (David Simmons) 132
Breaking the Mirror: Metafictional Strategies in *Supernatural*
(Alberto N. García) 146

"What's the lore say?": Exploring Folklore & Religion

"There's nothing more dangerous than some a-hole who thinks he
is on a holy mission": Using and (Dis)-Abusing Religious and
Economic Authority on *Supernatural* (Erin Giannini) 163
"I am an angel of the Lord": An Inquiry into the Christian
Nature of *Supernatural*'s Heavenly Delegates (Jutta Wimmler
and Lisa Kienzl) 176
Televisual Folklore: Rescuing *Supernatural* from the Fakelore Realm
(Mikel J. Koven and Gunnella Thorgeirsdottir) 187

Cruel Capricious Gods: Auteurs, Fans, Critics

Sympathy for the Fangirl: Becky Rosen, Fan Identity, and
Interactivity in *Supernatural* (Brigid Cherry) 203
Crossing Over: Network Transition, Critical Reception, and
Supernatural Longevity (Karen Petruska) 219
Plagiarism or Props?: Homage to Neil Gaiman in Eric Kripke's
Supernatural (Laura Felschow) 230

Epilogue Now: The Road Ahead,

or the Chapter at the End of This Book (David Lavery) 245

Seasons 1–6: *Supernatural* Episode Guide (Stephanie Graves) 253
Notes 273
TV and Filmography 286
Contributors 290
Bibliography 295
Index 316

Acknowledgments

The editors would like to thank each of the contributors to this book who made our job such a pleasure because of their passion for the series and their professionalism as scholars. It was wonderful sharing *Supernatural* with you throughout this process. We would like to thank everyone at ECW for all of their hard work producing this book. In particular we owe our deepest gratitude to our commissioning editor Jennifer Hale for recognizing the significance of *Supernatural* and taking a chance on the project and the show by producing this pop culture academic book. Thanks also for all of her editorial advice which made this book all the stronger.

Stacey Abbott:
I would like to thank Karen Myers for putting me on the road to this book by giving me my first *Supernatural* DVD and convincing me it was worth giving the show a chance. Special thanks go to my co-editor David Lavery for encouraging me to take the next step of this journey by convincing me that despite my manic work schedule we should edit this book together. I am indebted to Stan Beeler for recording and sending me DVDs of season 6 when the series' UK broadcast was

delayed. Finally, my most heartfelt thanks go to my husband Simon Brown, who has been my constant companion on this journey and who has been a source of love and support throughout an extremely hectic year.

David Lavery:
My always brilliant (in the British and American sense of the word) co-editor Stacey Abbott introduced me to *Supernatural*, and without that conversation as we walked the dark streets of Istanbul, my imagination would be so much poorer and this book probably would not exist, so my warmest thanks go to her. Special thanks, too, to Stephanie Graves, who wrote our episode guide and probably knows The Brothers much better than I.

Introduction
Then: The Road So Far
Stacey Abbott

Normal people, they see a monster and they run,
not us. No, no, no we search out things that want to
kill us, yeah, huh, or eat us. You know who does that?
Crazy people. We are insane.
Dean ("Yellow Fever")

Hunting ghosts, demons, and monsters and staving off the Apocalypse may make Sam and Dean Winchester crazy, according to Dean, but it is that very premise that enabled *Supernatural* to build up a loyal fandom eager to come back for more. The show began its broadcast on the wb (before the network merged with upn to become the cw) on September 13, 2005, and was conceived as a hybrid of the horror and road movie genres. The show mixes American urban legends with a *Route 66* (cbs, 1960–1964)[1] formula that focuses on two brothers traveling across the U.S. in a 1968 Impala, looking for their demon-hunting father while fighting ghosts and monsters. While the pilot episode sets up the back story about their mother's mysterious death and their father's mission to hunt all manner of supernatural beings, the second episode, "Wendigo," establishes the show's formula when Dean explains to Sam that he thinks their father left them his journal — his guide to "everything he knows about every evil thing" — in order to pick up where he left off: "you know, saving people, hunting things. Family business." The episode ends with Sam and Dean taking to the road, in *Route 66* fashion, to find their next hunting job. Along the way, however, the show becomes so much more.

Looking back at *Supernatural*'s first five years, the series not only draws upon the iconography and conventions of the road movie genre on an episodic level, but its entire narrative arc is constructed as a journey. This journey begins when Sam and Dean accept their father's mission and ends when Dean drives the Impala into Stull Cemetery — not to stop the confrontation between Lucifer and Archangel Michael, now inhabiting the bodies of Sam and their half-brother Adam, but to be with Sam at the end regardless of the consequences ("Swan Song," 5.22). This epic narrative trajectory is called to mind in "Two Minutes to Midnight" (5.21) as Sam and Dean, surrounded by fellow hunter Bobby, fallen Angel Castiel, and demon-ally Crowley, prepare for their next mission:

> Dean: Good luck stopping the whole zombie apocalypse.
> Sam: Yeah. Good luck killing Death.
> Dean: Yeah.
> Sam: Remember when we used to just hunt wendigos? How simple things were?
> Dean: Not really.

Throughout the first five seasons, Sam and Dean hunted ghosts, vampires, shapeshifters, witches, werewolves, demons, ghost ships, haunted trucks, and pagan gods. They lost their father, traveled back in time to meet their mother, found and lost a brother, drank loads of beer, died and came back to life, and died and came back to life again. They went to Hell and Heaven. They met angels, Lucifer, Death, and

God. They appeared in reality ghost-hunting show *Ghostfacers!* and, scariest of all, went to a *Supernatural* fan convention. It has been a hell of a journey and a journey to Hell.

Supernatural is part of a longer journey through the horror tradition, building upon what has come before, but taking the genre further and making it darker. The show's monster-of-the-week premise bears a clear connection with *The X-Files*, which itself was influenced by *Kolchak: The Night Stalker* (1974–1975). Executive producer and director Kim Manners, along with executive producer/writer John Shiban and director David Nutter, worked previously on *The X-Files*, with Manners in particular bringing to *Supernatural* the aesthetic language of TV horror which he established in such memorable *X-Files* episodes as "The Calusari" (2.21), "Grotesque" (3.14), and "Home" (4.2). The expressionist lighting iconically used in *The X-Files* has been transformed in *Supernatural* into a grungy chiaroscuro.[2] The visual similarities are enhanced by the fact that both shows were filmed in Vancouver, lending them a similar Pacific Northwest aesthetic. Furthermore, the writers for *Supernatural* repeatedly acknowledge the legacy of *The X-Files* through knowing references to the earlier show while also highlighting their differences, including Dean's ironic comment that "*The X-Files* is a TV show. This is real," just as they were about to face a shapeshifter with a preference for classic horror movie monsters ("Monster Movie," 4.5). The show's initial narrative pursuit of knowledge about the demon who killed the Winchesters' mother and his hidden agenda for Sam calls to mind Mulder's obsessive pursuit of answers about his sister's disappearance.

The X-Files is not the only genre TV show that has influenced *Supernatural*. The series also demonstrates a substantial influence from *Buffy the Vampire Slayer* and *Angel*, a connection that is reinforced by the casting of *Buffy/Angel* actors Amber Benson (Tara) and Mercedes McNab (Harmony) as vampires and the hiring of Ben Edlund, a writer for *Angel*, in 2006.[3] The story of the Winchesters, a family of demon hunters who know the truth about the existence of the supernatural, is highly reminiscent of *Buffy* as it explores the weight of this knowledge and the responsibility that comes with it. Like Buffy, Sam and Dean struggle with their destinies and responsibilities, largely because they possess the knowledge about "what's really going on" and must therefore protect those who don't at the expense of their own ambitions or desires. Buffy does accept her destiny as the Slayer, although she changes the rules about what being a Slayer means. Sam and Dean, on the other hand, deny their fate to be vessels of Archangels Lucifer and Michael as they enact their holy war and instead choose "team free will" ("Song Remains the Same," 5.13), regardless of the consequences. This takes them on a much darker road than the one Buffy had to travel.

While Sam is often described in the first few seasons as the Chosen One, he is more like Angel than Buffy in that he walks an ambiguous line between good and evil. He both releases Satan from his cage and sacrifices himself to put Satan back. As Bobby points out to Dean, "Sam's got a darkness in him . . . but he's got a hell of a lot of good in him too" ("Two Minutes to Midnight"). It is this ambiguity of evil that makes *Supernatural* reminiscent of *Angel*, for a major strand of the series focuses on the characters — particularly Dean — learning that the supernatural landscape is not as clear-cut as they would like to believe. Vampires can be peaceful and victims of renegade hunters, angels can be "dicks," demons can be allies, and heroes can give in to weakness — Sam when he becomes addicted to demon blood and Dean when he agrees to become a torturer in hell in order to be released from his own torment. The series deliberately sets out to cloud and question moral distinctions.

Furthermore, in contrast to *Buffy* and *Angel*, the conclusion of *Supernatural*'s major mythological arc is dark and tragic. While the climaxes to *Buffy* and *Angel* are somewhat open-ended, they are also uplifting. With the Hellmouth closed and Buffy no longer the only Slayer, Buffy faces an exciting but unknown future, while *Angel* closes in mid-battle, with Team Angel forever continuing to fight the good fight. Sam and Dean's final victory, however, is conclusive but melancholic. Both brothers make the ultimate personal sacrifice to save the world: Sam throws himself into Hell in order to trap Lucifer, and Dean agrees not to risk releasing Lucifer by trying to rescue Sam. By concluding the five-year narrative arc in this manner, the series reflects upon the real personal cost of being a hero, not glorifying it but rather conveying the painful reality of sacrifice for the greater good, as Dean expresses in this final exchange with Castiel:

> Dean: [God] brought you back. But what about Sam? What about me? Where's my grand prize? All I got is my brother in a hole.
> Castiel: You got what you asked for, Dean. No paradise. No Hell. Just more of the same. I mean it, Dean. What would you rather have? Peace or freedom? ("Swan Song")

Castiel's words reverberate with a cynicism about heroic sacrifice. No great victory or reward for Dean, just the pain of loss and the freedom to choose. Even the episode's conclusion, in which Dean is reunited with his love interest Lisa and her son, is a subversion of classic narratives where the restoration or preservation of the family is the ultimate goal. Here the restoration of the nuclear family is not a happy ending but is presented as pained and empty, a hollow substitute for the loss of Dean's real family — his brother. TV horror has never been so dark; the journey from pilot to "Swan Song" has shown us that this show is about more than urban legends, ghouls, ghosts, demons, and monsters. In the tradition of the best of the horror genre, it was about family — not the idealized nuclear family but the messy, dysfunctional-yet-loving reality of family. As Bobby explains to Dean, "Are you under the impression that families are supposed to make you feel good? Make you an apple pie, maybe? They're supposed to make you miserable — that's why they're family!" ("Lucifer Rising," 5.22)

The development of *TV Goes to Hell* has been a journey as well, beginning on the streets of Istanbul as I convinced David Lavery to watch *Supernatural*. I thought the man who had written some of the earliest academic books on *Supernatural*'s key predecessors — *Twin Peaks*, *The X-Files*, and *Buffy* — should love this show . . . and he did. Along the way, audiences for the show have grown alongside burgeoning academic interest in the series and TV horror in general. This book brings together fandom and scholarship by drawing upon a diverse range of scholars, all of whom are fans of the series (what Matt Hills would describe as the "scholar-fan"), expressing their engagement with the show through analysis while considering the place of *Supernatural* within broader discourses on folklore, religion, class, gender, music, genre, authorship, and fan studies. The range of topics covered in this book illustrates the complexity of the show. While contemporary academic discussions of quality TV rarely include programs that fall within telefantasy genres (i.e., science fiction, fantasy, and horror), let alone a show on the CW with a target demographic of 18- to 34-year-old women, *Supernatural*, like the horror predecessors discussed above, is a testament to how telefantasy can often push the boundaries of narrative, genre, and aesthetics. This book is therefore an attempt to unravel the many layers of meaning within *Supernatural* and explore *how* the series pushes the boundaries of television.

The chapters included focus upon on the first five seasons, for as Kripke explained, "I *did* set out [to] tell a five-season storyline. Quite frankly, I never expected [the show] to make it to five years. But now that we're in our fifth year, I have every intention of ending the story with a bang and not drawing it out or watering it down" (Ausiello).

And end it with a big bang he did. While the show continued into a sixth Kripke-less season helmed by Sera Gamble (discussed in David Lavery's epilogue to this book), the first five years offer a coherent narrative featuring challenging storytelling, complex character development, moral ambiguity, complicated depictions of gender and sexuality, and transgressive representations of family and religion. The aim of this book is, therefore, to reflect back upon the five years that took Sam from college to Hell and Dean from life on the road to a traditional family before concluding with a few thoughts about season 6 and the show's life post-Kripke.

On paper it might seem out of place to begin a book on a horror series like *Supernatural* with chapters on comedy and music but amidst the horror and the Apocalypse, Sam and Dean regularly listen to classic rock and occasionally drift into bouts of practical joking. These moments often present the lighter side of life on the road but, as the chapters in "'Bon Jovi rocks . . . on occasion': Comedy and Music" demonstrate, the show's often uplifting use of music and comedy does not distract from the series' darker themes, but rather serves them. Comedy and music are used to advance the plot, develop characterization and themes, and portray the Winchesters as under attack within a world that is spiraling out of control.

In addition to the show's predilection for classic rock, one of the qualities that distinguishes *Supernatural* from other tales of heroism is that while the Winchesters might be fighting a grand battle between good and evil, they are doing so from the margins of society. Denied a traditional upbringing after the death of their mom, Sam and Dean save the world, but they do so from the road. "Skin Mags and Shaving Cream: Sam and Dean on the Fringes of Time and Place" brings together different explorations of how the Winchesters haunt the periphery of mainstream culture through their transient lifestyle. These chapters locate *Supernatural* within an alternative form of Americana defined by motels, bars, road-side cafés, and poor white trash, all of which stands in opposition to the "white picket fence" lifestyle promised by the American Dream.

Sam and Dean may not fit into mainstream society, they may not get the girl, and they may be denied a "normal life" but it is their male-centered image of masculinity, as well as their brotherly relationship, that has captured the interest of a large portion of the show's audience (as evidenced by the countless fan forums often divided between Team Sam and Team Dean). The show, a curious hybrid of horror, western, and melodrama, is macho, action-oriented, and, despite Dean's frequent requests to avoid "chick-flick moments," driven by the deep-seated love that the brothers feel for each other and their father. The chapters in "'Jerk . . . bitch': Representations of Gender and

Sexuality" seek to unravel the show's seeming ambivalent relationship with issues around masculinity and feminism, as well as its underlying homoeroticism. This section will address how *Supernatural* is situated within evolving discourses on masculinity and homosexuality, while also questioning the place of women — usually identified as girlfriends, mothers, victims, demons, and bitches — within Sam and Dean's predominantly male world.

⚔ Storytelling has always been a central focus of *Supernatural*. Folklore and urban legends are, after all, a form of oral storytelling. This preoccupation was brought to the forefront with the introduction of Chuck Shurley, the writer of the *Supernatural* novels later revealed to be a prophet writing the Winchester Gospels. The chapters in "The Gospel According to Chuck: Narrative and Storytelling in *Supernatural*" are, therefore, a response to the show writers' textual deconstruction of narrative by examining the diverse and often postmodern storytelling strategies used in episodes such as "Tall Tales" (2.15), "Mystery Spot" (3.11), and "The Monster at the End of this Book" (4.18). From camp to folklore to intertextuality, *Supernatural* invites audiences to think about the relationship between the episodic and seasonal narratives, how stories are constructed, the role of performance, and how audiences read *Supernatural* in relation to other texts including music, film, and other television programs.

From wendigos to angels, from werewolves to Lucifer himself, the heart of the series is its lore. Kripke admits that it was his desire to explore urban legends and folklore that inspired him to write *Supernatural*, and the series quickly expanded into a narrative arc building toward Armageddon. The section "What's the lore say?" will consider how *Supernatural* draws upon and rewrites folklore while also provocatively engaging with and critiquing religious dogma through its representation of angels and its transition from an urban-legend-of-the-week narrative to an apocalyptic religious war.

Finally, a series that includes characters such as Chuck Shurley, the author of the Supernatural series of cult fantasy books, and Becky Rosen, *Supernatural*'s number one fan and writer of Sam/Dean slash fiction, is inviting discussions of the show in relation to its production and reception. The chapters in "Cruel Capricious Gods: Auteurs, Fans, Critics" therefore do just that by considering the response to the show's representation of its fans by its fans, the impact and influence of the critical response to *Supernatural*, and how the show negotiates notions of authorship. While most fans would agree that this is Eric Kripke's show, the chapters in this section demonstrate that a wide range of creative voices have contributed to the show's success, therefore complicating traditional notions of the single author.

If the chapters that follow are a consideration of the Road So Far, then David Lavery's epilogue that concludes the book will consider the Road Ahead for *Supernatural* as it emerges from its apocalyptic narrative arc and enters its sixth season. In true road movie fashion, however, for Sam and Dean, and the countless fans who follow them every week, the journey never ends. This book is a part of that journey.

And so, as Sam and Dean would say, it's time to hit the road.

Part 1

"Bon Jovi rocks . . . on occasion"

Comedy and Music

Rabbits' Feet and Spleen Juice
The Comic Strategies of TV Horror
Stacey Abbott

I lost my shoe.
Sam ("Bad Day at Black Rock")

I'll man the flashlight.
Dean ("Yellow Fever")

In "Bad Day at Black Rock" (3.3) and "Yellow Fever" (4.6) Sam and Dean come under the influence of magical forces that not only threaten to kill them but yield slapstick comic moments that one does not expect to see in a show that presents itself as horror. In "Bad Day at Black Rock" Sam loses a "lucky" rabbit's foot and is cursed with bad luck, which causes him to fall over, lose his shoe down a sewer, catch on fire, get shot, and sit in a chair, unable to scratch his nose for fear of the dire consequences that may follow. In "Yellow Fever," while Sam is squirted with spleen juice when observing an autopsy, Dean catches "ghost sickness" from the corpse. This contagious virus, according to Sam, causes its victims to "get anxious, then scared, then really scared, then your heart gives out," reducing Dean to the comic "fraidy cat" role more typical of Lou Costello in *Abbott and Costello Meet Frankenstein* (1948) or Bob Hope in *The Cat and the Canary* (1939). Dean becomes afraid of heights, speeding, junk food, teenagers, cats, Yorkshire terriers, and even carrying his own gun, choosing to "man the flashlight" instead. It's classic slapstick at its finest.

Other television shows that can be described as TV horror, such as *Buffy the Vampire Slayer* (1997–2003), *Angel* (1999–2004), *The X-Files* (1993–2002), and *Doctor Who* (2005–), similarly contain both comic moments and episodes, but these series are more overtly characterized by their genre hybridity, allowing for a greater expectation of comedy within their particular matrix. *The X-Files* brings together science fiction, conspiracy thriller, procedural series, melodrama, comedy, and horror, while *Buffy* is a hybrid of the teen genre, horror, melodrama, romance, and, occasionally, musical. Lorna Jowett has argued that *Angel* "slips from one [genre] to another and thus retains multiple associations that help frame its narrative or emphasize its themes" ("Plastic, Fantastic?" 176), while Matt Hills has argued that the new *Doctor Who* is "more generically flexible and multiple than its predecessors" (13).

Supernatural is, of course, also a hybrid series, mixing horror and the road movie with melodrama, but unlike the other shows mentioned above, it privileges horror as its dominant generic mode, visually and narratively. The first season clearly establishes the show's horror credentials with monster/urban-legend-of-the-week storylines, regular blood and gore, and near-weekly allusions to classic examples of the horror genre, including *The Ring* (1998), *Don't Look Now* (1973), *The Shining* (1980), and *Poltergeist* (1982). It is only once the horror genre conventions are established that the show begins to infuse comic moments into otherwise dramatic episodes or incorporate comedy episodes into its seasonal narrative arc. Much of the humor on display in *Supernatural* is generated by the show's intertextuality and postmodern narrative interplay, as demonstrated in "The Monster at the End of This Book" (4.18), in which Sam and Dean discover the *Supernatural* series of books that chronicle their every mission. When they meet the writer of these novels, Carver Edlund[1], a.k.a. Chuck, he is shocked to discover that his literary creations are real and horrified by what he has put them through:

> Chuck: I toyed with your lives. Your emotions for . . . entertainment.
>
> Dean: You didn't toy with us, Chuck. Okay? You didn't create us.
>
> Chuck [turning to face Dean with a horrified look on his face]: Did you really have to live through the bugs?
>
> Dean: Yeah.
>
> Chuck: What about the ghost ship?
>
> Dean: Yes. That too.
>
> Chuck: I am so sorry. I mean horror is one thing but to be forced to live bad writing. . . . If I would have known it was real I would have done another pass.

The humor of this scene is derived from Chuck's reference to "Bugs" (1.8) and "A Red Sky at Morning" (3.6), episodes that Erik Kripke has openly criticized as examples of bad writing on the show (Knight, *Supernatural: The Official Companion Season 1* 50–51; *Season 3* 45). This postmodern approach to the show is discussed in detail by Alberto N. García on pp. 146–160 in this volume. I am interested in those comic episodes that use physical or slapstick humor and draw out from Jensen Ackles and Jared Padalecki decidedly comic performances that undermine their more conventional heroic personas and seem, on the surface, to be at odds with the show's horror identity.

Despite their seeming opposition in style and content, horror and comedy do share a great deal in common. They are both affective genres built upon the emotional effect they have on their viewers, evoking fear and laughter respectively. They also share many thematic similarities and preoccupations. Both genres regularly undermine social or cultural conventions, transgress accepted gender roles, and exploit, for comic or horrific effect, the body out of control. They both exist within a liminal space in "between the set rules of society" (Horton 5). Andrew Horton argues that "a work that is identified in a way as comic automatically predisposes its audience to enter a state of liminality where the everyday is turned upside down and where cause and effect can be triumphed over and manipulated" (5). Horror similarly operates within a space in which the rules of the natural world and society are overturned through the existence of ghosts, vampires, and other monsters, as well as human serial killers or slashers. Furthermore, both genres are preoccupied, as Pete Boss argues, with presenting the body in "profuse disarray" (15). Andrew Tudor argues that "whether set to the task of conveying the peculiar fascination of monstrousness or simply portraying the horrific violence practiced by movie monsters upon their victims, bodies are inevitably to the fore in horror movies" (25). Comedy is similarly preoccupied with the body under attack, whether that be a pie in the face, a pratfall, or the coyote falling off yet another cliff in his never-ending pursuit of the road runner. As Lorna Jowett argues in "Biting Humor: Harmony, Parody and the Female Vampire," theory explains the similarities between comedy and horror "in terms of the carnivalesque, the grotesque, or transgression and subversion. Horror films have often contained humor and there has been a long tradition of horror-comedy (like *Shaun of the Dead*, 2004) and comedy-horror (such as *Dracula: Dead and Loving It*, 1995). Horror on television operates rather differently than on film and, perhaps, draws on humor more consistently to achieve its effects and success with its audience" (17–18).

Here Jowett highlights the difference between TV and cinematic horror, generally attributed to the restrictions upon the representation of violence and the body on television, as well as the positioning of television within the domestic space, which can affect how viewers engage with their programs. These fundamental differences have meant that creators of TV horror must reconfigure the conventions and aesthetics of the genre to suit the industrial and cultural specificity of television.[2] Part of this reconfiguration involves the interrelationship between humor and horror, designed to enhance horror effects and the exploration of the genre's cultural preoccupation with the notions of good and evil, the body in disarray, and the abject. As Jowett points out, serial television offers greater opportunity for character nuance and development and enables "more scope to use both comedy and horror as ways of offering new stories or angles on a familiar premise and cast" (18). The aim of this essay will, therefore, be to explore how the comic is used in *Supernatural*, not to diffuse the genre and make it more acceptable for mainstream television, but as a strategy for the construction of TV horror and in the representation of the monstrous hero.

Physical vs Verbal Comedy

Despite the series' dark overtones, *Supernatural* is a very funny show that places particular emphasis on verbal humor. Its dialogue is replete with innuendo, sarcasm, comic insults, and witty retorts, delivered in almost equal parts by demons and hunters. As Jana Riess has argued with regard to *Buffy the Vampire Slayer*, verbal "humor not only entertains but also signals which of the characters is in control" (42). In *Supernatural*, demons such as Alastair and Ruby are prone to humorous verbal exchanges with Sam and Dean as a means of asserting their power. In this they have much in common with villains from contemporary horror films such as Freddy Krueger in *Nightmare on Elm Street* (1984) and Hannibal Lecter in *Silence of the Lambs* (1991), both of whom are assigned a macabre wit that grants them absolute authority. Similarly, each of the hunters in *Supernatural* uses sarcasm as a means of asserting machismo in the face of evil and overwhelming odds. For instance, Gordon uses sarcasm to taunt Sam. Aware of Sam's concern for the peaceful vampire Lenore, Gordon pulls out a knife to kill her and then reassures Sam by telling him "I just sharpened it so it's completely humane" ("Bloodlust," 2.3). In "When the Levee Breaks" (4.1), after Dean swears his allegiance to Heaven, Bobby asks him, "Correct me if I'm wrong. You willingly signed up to be the angel's bitch? . . . I'm sorry, do you prefer sucker?"

However, it is Dean in particular who repeatedly uses "joking" as a means of asserting his control over the people and situations around him. For instance, when Sam questions Dean on his taste in music, Dean tells him, "Driver picks the music, shotgun shuts his cakehole" ("Pilot," 1.1). In "The Benders" (1.15) Dean is tied up and questioned by a group of red-neck *Texas Chainsaw Massacre*–inspired hunters and undercuts their attempt to threaten him with a series of comic one-liners that play on this hillbilly stereotype: "If I tell you, promise not to make me into an ashtray"; "It's not nice to marry your sister"; and "Eat me . . . no no no wait, you actually might." In "A Very Supernatural Christmas" (3.8), Dean is chastised for swearing while being bled by a pagan god, to which he responds, "I'm going to fudging kill you." Finally, he repeatedly undercuts the angel Uriel's authority by nick-naming him "Junkless." Dean uses humor to take control of a situation, convey his confidence in the face of danger and horror, and undercut any opposing forces, be they demon, pagan god, or angel. Humor is a sign of Dean's heroism.

The series, however, also uses humor to speak to Dean's *need* to be in control and to distance himself from others. In "Route 666" (1.13) former girlfriend Cassie tells him "whenever we get, what's the word, close — anywhere in the neighborhood of emotional vulnerability — you back off or make some joke or find any way to shut the door on me." Dean retreats, or attempts to retreat, behind humor as a form of emotional protection. For instance, in "On the Head of a Pin" (4.16), when Dean is forced to question and torture Alastair, the demon who tortured him in Hell, Dean attempts to use humor to convey his confidence, despite his misgivings about the situation. When Alastair asks Dean if he thinks he'll "see all your scary toys and spill my guts," Dean quips, "Oh, you'll spill your guts one way or another. I just didn't want to ruin my shoes." The delivery of this line feels forced and is spoken without Dean's cocky smile or aggressive tone. Rather than putting Dean in control of the situation, this weak attempt at humor comes across as an act to cover up his fear about reliving his experience as a torturer, and it is notable that Dean remains silent throughout most of the remaining torture sequence. Instead it is Alastair who keeps up the regular comic banter, undermining Dean by responding to each of Dean's physical torments with a series of comic retorts. After Dean removes a blade from the demon's abdomen, Alastair, still spitting blood, responds with "it's your professionalism that I respect," and after Dean pours salt down Alastair's mouth, Alastair comments, "Something's caught in my throat . . . I think it's my throat." While Alastair may be the "victim" in this sequence, his comic wit tells us that he is clearly still in control.

In contrast, physical comedy is often about a lack of control, particularly control of the body. If one looks at the slapstick comedy of the Keystone Cops, Jerry Lewis, or Jim Carrey, the humor comes from depicting of the human body as out of control, prone to pratfalls, accidents, and bodily contortion. As Nöel Carroll argues in "Notes on a Sight Gag," slapstick "comedy was generally less a function of [narrative] structure than of the transgression of social inhibition about the proper way in which to treat the human body" (26). The body out of control is the heart of the genre, as embodied by Charlie Chaplin being pulled through the cogs of a machine in *Modern Times* (1936) or Jim Carrey transformed into a cartoon character by donning a magical mask in *The Mask* (1994). If verbal comedy is used in *Supernatural* primarily as a means for Sam and Dean to maintain control, physical comedy is used to wrest control from them. For instance, in "Hell House" (1.17) Dean initiates a battle of practical joking that escalates as the episode progresses. These practical jokes do not advance the episode's narrative but rather offer comic moments to convey the brothers' sibling rivalry. Dean stuffs a spoon down the sleeping Sam's mouth; Sam raises the volume on Dean's car stereo, making him jump when he turns it on; Dean puts itching powder in Sam's underwear; Sam puts crazy glue on Dean's beer bottle. The humor is generated by the brothers undermining each other's cool image by causing each other physical discomfort. Sam squirms and scratches, while Dean complains that he "barely has any skin left on [his] palm." While they playfully mock each other, however, their heroic image largely remains intact.

In contrast, in "Tall Tales" (2.15), the boys' sibling rivalry begins to chip away at the brothers' image by attacking their dignity through physical comedy, for, as Alan Dale argues, "the essence of a slapstick gag is a physical assault on, or collapse of, the hero's dignity" (3). In this episode, Sam and Dean, who have been bickering from the start, recount different aspects of their case to Bobby, but in doing so they portray the other brother in a ridiculous manner. In Sam's story, Dean is seen drunkenly slurping shots called Purple Nurples, cavorting with a peroxide blonde named Starla, and stuffing chocolates in his mouth until his cheeks bulge — all a grotesque exaggeration of Dean's insatiability. In Dean's narration, Sam is presented as prissy and overly sensitive as he lectures Dean on the importance of the case and later tells one of the witnesses of these strange events, "I know this all has to be so hard. . . . but I want you to know that I'm here for you — you brave little soldier. I acknowledge your pain." Sam's words are even taken away from him in Dean's memory as Sam tells Dean, "This is an important investigation. We don't have any time for any of your blah, blah, blah . . . blah, blah, blah, blah. . . ." While it is revealed that it is a trickster who is fueling their rivalry, it is Sam and Dean who, through their narration, wrest agency from each other and launch a comic assault on each other's physical image. While the comic gags in "Hell House" are narrative digressions, "Tall Tales" integrates these physical gags into the show's broader narrative and thematic arcs, as it highlights the tension between the brothers and begins to present Sam and Dean's bodies as under attack. It is through this notion of bodily attack that the series' use of comedy interacts with the show's horror genre preoccupations.

Comedy & Horror: The Body Under Attack

While there are many ways of defining the horror genre, narratively, thematically, and aesthetically, one key characteristic is the presence of monsters, be they supernatural or human. *Supernatural* is firmly placed within the horror genre because of its monster-of-the-week narratives, in which Sam and Dean combat ghosts, vampires, were-wolves, shapeshifters, devil dogs, ghouls, and demons. Noël Carroll argues that a monster is frightening because it is "regarded as threatening and impure," and that impurity refers to anything that is "categorically interstitial, categorically contradictory, incomplete, or formless" (*Philosophy of Horror*, 32). Carroll's concept of impurity relates to Julia Kristeva's concept of abjection, which she defines as anything that "disturbs identity, system, order. What does not respect borders, positions, rules. The in-between, the ambiguous, the composite" (4). Barbara Creed has further argued that the horror genre is a significant "illustration of the work of abjection" for it is filled with images of abject bodily liquids including sweat, vomit, pus, tears, and blood (10), and the genre's concept of the monster is built around the notion of blurring the boundaries between living/dead, animal/human, good/evil, natural/supernatural, inside/outside the body (10–11). The body in particular is the focus for horror because any attack upon the body is an attack upon the self. As Matt Hills and Rebecca Williams argue, "by challenging cultural norms of the bounded self and body, abjection depicts selves in states of physical disintegration and mental/spiritual 'possession'" (204). The horror genre challenges our concept of the self, whether that of the individual or society as a whole, by placing it under attack.

Comedy is similarly awash with images of the abject. The comic persona of Jerry Lewis blurs boundaries between adult/child and male/female, while the long history of cross-dressing comedians from Fatty Arbuckle to Robin Williams blurs gender boundaries. As William Paul has argued, gross-out comedy is engulfed in abject bodily liquids including vomit, urine, feces, and semen. The dog semen–filled éclair–eating scene in National Lampoon's *Van Wilder* (2002) is a notable example of how the gross-out comedy is both comic and grotesque, simultaneously provoking laughter and the gag reflex. Both horror and comedy, then, use abjection as a means of exploring the body under attack, and *Supernatural* draws upon this notion of abjection as a means of integrating comedy within the show's horror matrix.

In addition to the presence of monsters, the series' preoccupation with the abject is conveyed through the blurring of physical and spiritual boundaries. The depiction of demons and angels as possessing the bodies of human hosts emphasizes the permeability of the body by showing its violent invasion by a cloud of black smoke in the case of demons and an engulfing white light for angels. Moreover, the co-existence of demon and human, of two souls, within the same body undermines an understanding of a bounded individual self. Victims of demonic possession regularly explain to Sam and Dean that they were aware of what their bodies were doing but had no control of the actions of their shells. Demons and angels cross bodily borders by changing human hosts, with demons Meg, Alastair, and Ruby repeatedly appearing to Sam and Dean in different bodies. In doing so, the show undercuts the perception of the body as contained and complete. Finally, the manner in which both demons and angels discuss the humans they possess presents the body as abject waste — the human body is simply a disposable container into which they pour their spirits. The angel Zachariah describes Dean as Michael's "vessel" or "receptacle," Dean refers to the prospect of becoming Michael's vessel as being "an angel condom," and the demons deem their human hosts "meat suits." The use of the term "meat" in particular reduces humanity to the corporeality of the body, emptied of a soul, making it highly abject for, as Kristeva explains, the body without a soul equates the body with physical waste. The term "meat" also ties the series to the meat movie, a category of horror film that treats the body as waste by depicting its destruction in graphic detail (e.g., *Night of the Living Dead* [1968], *The Hills Have Eyes* [1977], *The Texas Chainsaw Massacre* [1974]).

More than anything, however, it is Sam and Dean who themselves represent the show's engagement with abjection, for while possessing the faces of all-American boys and strong virtuous heroes, Sam and Dean repeatedly blur the boundary between hero, victim, and monster, making them, in Carroll's terms, "categorically interstitial" and therefore impure. In this manner, the series engages with what Hills and Williams describe as "elaborated abjection":

What we are terming "elaborated abjection" is, then, abjection that does not merely represent the collapse of cultural classifications such as dead/alive, inside/outside, or self/other, but which instead challenges established generic and narrative classifications (i.e. . . . . whether characters are clearly defined as good/evil, or as monsters/victims). (214)

While Sam and Dean are hunters who fight on the side of good, it is also revealed that Sam is infected with demon blood that gives him superhuman powers fueled by his increasing blood addiction, making him a creature other hunters try to destroy. Chuck tells Sam that in his vision of the battle with Lilith, Sam was "like full on Vader. Your body temperature was 150, your heart rate was 200. Your eyes went black" ("Sympathy for the Devil," 5.1). Sam blurs the lines between human and demon. Similarly, Dean is sent to Hell and tortured by Alastair until agreeing to take up the blade and become the torturer — as Alastair tells Dean, "I carved you into a new animal" ("On the Head of a Pin"). Dean's spirit is later pulled out of perdition by Castiel and thrust back into his body, in its grave, forcing him to dig his way out like a vampire or zombie. Dean is both victim and monster. Both brothers regularly cross the threshold between life and death. They have repeatedly died and come back to life and have escaped the confines of their bodies by crossing into the spirit realm ("In My Time of Dying," 2.1; "Death Takes a Holiday," 4.15), dreams ("Dream a Little Dream of Me," 3.10), and Heaven ("Dark Side of the Moon," 5.16). As a result the brothers not only live an existence that is untraditional but are themselves coded as victims and monsters, as expressed in this scene from "Death Takes a Holiday":

> Sam: Look I don't want 'em to die either, Dean, but there's a natural order.
> Dean: You're kidding, right?
> Sam: What?
> Dean: You don't see the irony in that? I mean you and me . . .

we're like the poster boys for the unnatural order. All we do is ditch death.

Sam: Yeah, but the normal rules don't really apply to us do they?

Dean: [laughs] We're no different than anybody else?

Sam: I'm infected with demon blood. You've been to Hell. Look, I know you want to think of yourself as Joe the plumber, Dean, but you're not. Neither am I. The sooner you accept that, the better off you're gonna be.

Dean: Joe the plumber is a douche.

In addition to being presented as abject because they are "categorically interstitial," Sam and Dean are also depicted as physically abject as their bodies fall under attack from monsters, ghosts, demons, and angels. The show regularly presents Sam and Dean as bearing the scars of physical attack in the form of scratches, gashes, burns, and bullet holes. More importantly, Sam and Dean are repeatedly violated by demons and angels alike, and their resistance to this, as well as their supposed fate as Lucifer and Michael's "meat suits," expresses their anxiety about the loss of their own identity and free will. The battle they are fighting is a battle to protect the self, and to do so is to protect the boundaries of their bodies. It is often in the comic episodes that the most violent of these attempts to wrest control from Sam and Dean are enacted. In "Bad Day at Black Rock" Sam is cursed with catastrophic bad luck, and in "Swap Meat" (5.12) he is forced to swap bodies with a 17-year-old boy. In "Yellow Fever" Dean is infected with a disease that transforms him into an hysteric before inducing a heart attack, and in "The Curious Case of Dean Winchester" (5.7), he is transformed into his 80-year-old self and must confront the horrors of his aging body. In both "Swap Meat" and "Curious Case," the Winchesters are forced into different bodies that attack them from within. Dean, thinking he's having a heart attack, discovers that his 80-year-old self suffers acid reflux when he eats a bacon cheeseburger, while Sam finds himself vomiting up his toast after discovering that he has been placed in a body that is allergic to wheat gluten. In "Mystery Spot" (3.11), the brothers are ripped from linear time when they are made to relive (or re-die) the same day over and over again while new identities are forced upon them in "It's a Terrible Life" (4.17). These cataclysmic attacks upon their bodies and souls are treated as comic.

This use of comedy might, of course, be seen as a means of undermining the horror for mainstream television. I would argue, however, that it actually facilitates a more extreme representation of Sam and Dean as abject. Hills and Williams suggest that in TV horror, substitutes are often found to stand in for the graphic images of abjection that are characteristic of cinematic horror. Comic exaggeration is, therefore, used as a "symbolic translation of full-blooded representations of abjection" difficult to present on prime-time television (208). Here comedy is used to express the full horrors of the horror genre, for it is through the comic performances of Jared Padalecki and Jensen Ackles, breaking from their well-established characterizations, that the show is able to convey the extent of Sam and Dean's abject transformation. In "Bad Day at Black Rock" and "Yellow Fever," Padalecki and Ackles each deliver extreme performances that undermine their characters' traditional personas and transform their behavior, mannerisms, and physicality.

As Sam's bad luck takes hold in "Bad Day at Black Rock," he becomes clumsy and hapless, spilling his coffee, knocking over a waitress' tray in a restaurant, and, in a bravura pratfall, falling to the ground as he and Dean chase a suspect from the restaurant, skinning his knees in the process. Sam is reduced to the kid brother image that he has been so keen to escape. This child-like persona is reinforced by the episode's composition as he is repeatedly framed in the background while Dean dominates the foreground. Any attempts to move forward and play a more assertive role in the action result in further mayhem as he trips over an electrical cord and falls to the ground, steps in gum and ends up losing his shoe down the sewer, or catches fire. Padalecki's physical performance further emphasizes Sam's transformation from fearless hunter to dejected child as he slumps his shoulders, casts his eyes downward, and generally sulks when Dean leaves him behind in a motel.

While Padalecki's comic performance is all about restraining Sam and reducing his hulking image to that of a child, Ackles' performance in "Yellow Fever" is larger than life. Initially, the symptoms of the virus present themselves subtly. Dean becomes increasingly cautious, crossing the street to avoid a group of teenagers, observing the speed limit, and not making a left-hand turn into oncoming traffic. He is unsettled by an interviewee's predilection for pet lizards and snakes, conveying his anxiety with nervous twitches and wide eye movements. As the virus progresses, however, Ackles' performance becomes more exaggerated and increasingly comedic. As they search for the ghost that generated the virus, Dean cowers behind Sam, jumps at every noise, and screams hysterically when startled by a cat. This scream is humorous not only because it is atypical of Dean, but because of the extremity of the performance. In an interview for the cw, Ackles explained that he was instructed to scream for as long as he could and he gave it his all (Ackles, *Supernatural 4*). This over-the-top performance culminates in Dean running hysterically from a small Yorkshire Terrier that is wearing a pink bow, telling a homeless man along the way, "Run. It'll kill you."

In both episodes, comedy is generated by the contrast between our expectations of Sam and Dean and their uncharacteristic behavior. This contrast is made possible by the seriality of television, where we are made intensely familiar with these characters only to have that familiarity undermined for comic effect. As a result the comedy conveys the violating transformation of the boys from heroes to hapless victims, unable to defend themselves and confronted by dark and dangerous forces. As a result, these episodes appear to be light in tone, but they have a dark undercurrent. Furthermore, the extremity of Padalecki's and Ackles' performances drives home the level to which Sam and Dean have been made abject. While Zachariah gives Dean stage-four stomach cancer and removes Sam's lungs, and Castiel carves an Enochian Sigil into their ribs ("Sympathy for the

Devil"), these violent and internalized attacks upon their bodies are implied rather than made visible. What is made visible are Sam and Dean, their hapless bodies devoid of control, scratching, twitching, running, falling, jumping, and screaming with increasingly hysterical abandon. The comic strategies of *Supernatural*, therefore, do not sanitize TV horror but convey in graphic detail the abject horror of Sam and Dean, their bodies and their souls presented in "profuse disarray."

Two Greasers and a Muscle Car
Music and Character Development in *Supernatural*
Stan Beeler

> And so we finally stumbled onto the formula
> by saying it's about two greasers and a muscle car,
> but the canvas that they're on are demons and angels
> and battles and the Apocalypse. . . .
> *Eric Kripke, Comic-Con interview with Maureen Ryan*

Eric Kripke originally conceived of *Supernatural* as a "horror movie of the week" that would depend only marginally upon the two brothers, Sam and Dean Winchester, for continuity. However, as the series progressed, Kripke realized that the character development of the Winchester brothers had become far more important to the audience than the monster of the week. The selection of classic rock (from about 1968 to 1980) — used both diegetically and non-diegetically — is one of the most important tools employed by the series writers to identify the characters and pace the action of the episodes. Although the series incorporates a traditional orchestral non-diegetic soundtrack by Jay Gruska and Christopher Lennertz that serves to cue the audience to an emotional response to on-screen events, the incorporation of popular music that was not created for the show is of particular interest to this essay.

Although one might expect that popular music in contemporary television would be selected from material already familiar to a specific demographic and target audience, anachronistic musical elements are, in fact, not uncommon. Dennis Potter's *The Singing Detective* may have established the technique, but Jamie Brittian and Brian Elsley's series *Skins* and Tom Kapinos' *Californication* both incorporate music that is up to 30 years older than their contemporary settings. *Supernatural* is an especially effective example of this technique as the anachronistic music is used to evoke the spirit of two greasers in a muscle car speeding across the landscape of demon-haunted Middle America. The nuances of their characters and situation are enhanced by music from the 1960s and '70s in a way that would not be possible if a more contemporary soundtrack had been chosen.

Although there is some effort to leaven the series' soundtrack with occasional examples of more contemporary popular songs, *Supernatural* is rife with music that seems to have been selected from mix tapes compiled in the 1970s. Many episodes take their name or their theme from hard-rocking classics that were popular before Eric Kripke or any of the series' stars were born.[1] Of course, the older characters, like John Winchester, have a diegetic age that would make the music appropriate. The series is diegetically anchored in contemporary America, although there are a few time-traveling excursions and the occasional flashback that introduce the lead characters to an historical period that is more appropriate to the soundtrack. For example, "In the Beginning"(4.3) and "The Song Remains the Same" (5.13) feature Dean and then Sam traveling back to the time when their parents first met. These episodes use the same admixture of popular music and non-diegetic original music as the episodes set in contemporary America. However, in these episodes the popular music from the 1970s is appropriate to the time and place of the action and is not foregrounded as a signature of Dean's particular taste as it is in other episodes. It is used to anchor episodes in the past, whereas, the anachronistic music used throughout the rest of the series evokes a certain historical spirit and aesthetic ambiance that matches the geriatric muscle car — a 1967 Chevy Impala — that serves as the home locator for the Winchester brothers. That is, the car and chronologically consistent music anchor the show to an anachronistic mood with the same regularity that establishing shots of identifiable location items are used in other television series. This is particularly important in a series that does not have a regular setting or location. In *Supernatural* the car and music combination serves as what Sara Gwenllian-Jones refers to as a series node; a home location that provides a focus for the adventures in each episode.[2] When the brothers travel from place to place in the continental U.S. the location transitions are often accomplished through a shot of them driving off in their car with the signature classic rock music running as a diegetic background to their discussions. The spirit of this music provides thematic direction and the lyrics may often be interpreted as obvious commentary on the plot.

The choice of music over 30 years old is remarkable in that it does not literally indicate the time-frame of the series or even the age of the protagonists. However, we may find some clue to the unusual selection of music when we look more closely at the role that the music plays in character development of the two young protagonists of *Supernatural*. One might argue that the statement "two greasers and a muscle car" is not quite accurate, since Dean Winchester is the only true greaser in the series. Sam, although he follows his brother through the adventurous experiences of wreaking tough-guy vengeance upon demonic hosts, never really buys into the aesthetic experience of fast cars and classic hard-rock to the same degree as his older brother. He lacks the underlying unshakable confidence in the rectitude of his own choices — both aesthetic and moral — that enable his sibling to adopt the lifestyle of his father's generation with enviable panache. Sam is a creature of today's world — tempted by convenience, compromise, and contemporary music — while his brother has the unshakable adherence to his own moral code (and musical selections) that one might expect in an Old Testament prophet. This underlying disparity between the two brothers is evidenced by Sam's early attempts to develop an independent life through higher education and a career outside of the demon-hunting world. The tension between the brothers is represented by their disagreements over music. We must assume that Sam's tastes in music are closer to that of the target audience, although they are not given extensive expression in the series soundtrack. Like the car and the unwavering dedication to the mission, the music is an expression of Dean's spirit.

In the series' pilot, Sam is drawn back into the peripatetic life of demon hunting — at first in an effort to help Dean find their father, John Winchester — then to avenge the murder of his girlfriend, Jessica Moore. In a few brief days Sam is transformed from a happy young man looking forward to a future law career and a stable relationship to a bitter and confused person who has regressed to a state that closely resembles his childhood. Events conspire to bring him back to a rootless life, living in a series of cheap hotels and driving across America in an aging car, dedicated to a mission and listening to a soundtrack chosen by his older brother. Very early on in the series, as the characters of the protagonists are being developed, this change in Sam's status is exemplified through the use of music as a metaphor. While Sam is looking through his brother's music collection vainly trying to find something more to his taste, Dean clearly states his understanding of their relationship:

> Sam: Seriously, man, you have to update your cassette tape collection.
> Dean: Why?
> Sam: One, they're cassette tapes! And two, Black Sabbath, Motörhead, Metallica! It's the greatest hits of mullet-rock.
> Dean: House rules, Sammy. Driver picks the music, shotgun shuts his cake-hole. ("Pilot," 1.1)

The non-diegetic lead-in music to this exchange is the 1973 Allman

Brothers Band hit "Ramblin' Man," and the diegetic exit music as Dean pops in a tape and drives away is the 1980 AC/DC song "Back in Black." Both songs are germane to the plot as well as clearly defining the anachronistic musical aesthetic of the series. "Ramblin' Man" extols the virtues of a rootless wandering lifestyle and provides a logical introduction to a short recap of Dean's experience as a demon hunter living on fast-food purchased through credit-card fraud. "Back in Black" was written to celebrate the life of AC/DC's deceased lead singer Bon Scott, so the "live hard and die young" ethos of the piece permeates its lyrics. One should note that neither song is given enough air time in this episode for an uninformed audience member to gather much more than a general impression of the narrative connections, but an aficionado of the musical genre would be able to infer a great deal.

Most of the anachronistic music selected for the series is upbeat, with rapid tempos, prominent drum beats, and numerous overdriven guitar solos.[3] There are occasional exceptions, but in general the music provides an appropriate background to the intense and violent action of the series. The power of the music is enhanced by the editorial decision to cut to the beat[4] during many action sequences. A prominent example of this is found in "Lucifer Rising" (4.22). The episode begins with a recap of the salient plot elements from previous episodes under the heading "The Road So Far," done in the form of a montage, cut to the beat of Kansas' 1976 hit single "Carry On Wayward Son." The triumphant yet wistful progressive rock classic plays against a visual selection that tells the tale of Sam and Dean's disagreement over the proper way to avoid the impending Apocalypse.

Classic rock music serves as a channel of private communication between the series' creators and a certain spectrum of its cult fandom. Dean is, in fact, represented as the ideal musical expert who would be able to interpret the multiple references that permeate the show. In "Sex and Violence" (4.14) he has a friendly contest of musical knowledge with Nick Monroe, whom he believes to be an FBI agent assigned to the same case that the brothers are investigating. Dean begins the game by mentioning "Nobody's Fault but Mine" which Monroe identifies as a Led Zeppelin "cover of a Blind Willie Johnson tune." Monroe responds by asking Dean to identify "You Shook Me," which Dean indicates is a Zeppelin cover of another blues classic. There is a level of irony in this exchange as Monroe is actually a succubus who usually appears as a woman to his victims and entices them to commit murder through sexual attraction. In this case he seduces Dean with male camaraderie and feigned admiration of his taste in automobiles and music. Not only do the creators regularly use snatches of classic rock to enhance the plot and mood of the narrative, the series also abounds with textual references to the music. Both brothers, for example, often use as aliases the names of musicians from Dean's favorite groups. Cult fans derive a great deal of pleasure from their ability to catch these obscure references.

Further textual references to the music central to the conception of the series are to be found in episodes that borrow their titles from the hits of the '60s and '70s. For example, the following *Supernatural* titles come directly from music:

Supernatural Episode Title	Performer	Date
"Houses of the Holy" (2.13)	Led Zeppelin	1975
"Born Under a Bad Sign" (2.14)	Albert King	1967
"Folsom Prison Blues" (2.19)	Johnny Cash et al	1968 live version
"The Kids Are Alright" (3.2)	The Who	1965
"Dream a Little Dream of Me" (3.10)	Cass Elliot	1968 version of Ozzie Nelson's 1931 recording
"Time Is on My Side" (3.15)	Rolling Stones	1965 version of 1963 song
"When the Levee Breaks" (4.21)	Led Zeppelin	1971 version of a 1929 song

These selections are primarily in the hard-rock or blues-rock genre, although the Johnny Cash and Cass Elliot pieces fall somewhat outside of the primary genre preferences. Though the titles of the episodes are usually thematically related to the diegesis of the episodes, the genre of the music, at least on this level, is not necessarily of the highest significance. For example, the episode entitled "Time Is on My Side" (3.15) is concerned with a villainous physician's search for immortality played against the background of Dean's remaining few weeks of life before the demonic bargain he made in the season 2 finale "All Hell Breaks Loose, Part 2" (2.22) runs out. The title puts an ironic spin on the events of the narrative, as time is definitely working against Dean. He has bargained away the balance of his own life in order to resurrect his brother and awaits the return of the demon to fetch him to Hell. Like most of the episodes that use musical references as their titles, "Time Is on My Side" uses no eponymous music in the soundtrack. Musical references in episode titles serve to maintain the superficial look-and-feel of '60s and '70s music without actually referencing the core of the music's sound or even — for the most part — the lyrics. If this were the only use of anachronistic music in the series, it would be reduced to a simple puzzle solved by an easily acquired knowledge of the pop charts or access to a search engine. However, as we have seen, the use of music in the series is not limited to textual references.

In fact, the series' creators have used the cultural impact of popular music as a broad palate designed to communicate a number of subtle shadings to the representation of characters and plot. An important aspect of this is the fact that all references to popular music in the series are, indeed, not strictly linked to the classic hard rock selections. While *Supernatural*'s creators are careful to link the anachronistic music to demon-hunting activities, when victims of various supernatural threats are depicted, they are sometimes represented with contemporary diegetic music. For example, in "Bloody Mary" (1.4) a teenage girl who has just flippantly invoked the name of the Bloody Mary demon is shown parading around in her underwear while the song "Sugar, We're Goin' Down" by Fallout Boy plays in the background.

While this song is close in genre and instrumentation to much of the music that is used to characterize the brothers, its period of origin — 2005 — is used to indicate to the audience that the girl is a victim. Contemporary hard rock and metal music are popular choices for the soundtracks of horror films and this scene exhibits many of the tropes that characterize the horror genre, including the use of contemporary rock as a background to her attack, defiance of the supernatural threat, and, of course, partial nudity. Joseph Tompkins, in a discussion of the horror film *Freddy vs. Jason* (2003), indicates that

> the soundtrack also works to manage our experience of Freddy and Jason more generally, aurally tagging these two franchises to fit a certain market niche. So, while we enjoy another slice 'em and dice 'em episode in the Freddy and Jason chronicles, we're encouraged to associate the metal music we hear with the spectacular viewing pleasures of horror; at the same time, the soundtrack becomes the locus for an effective practice of content management, where film and music industries are able to swap their respective properties in order to repurpose extant material and diversify potential markets. (66)

Tompkins' somewhat cynical view of horror film music is that it is shaped to fit a demographic exactly and exploit cross-marketing opportunities for the multimedia corporations that produce films in the genre. Although there are numerous examples of extended narrative television series applying this marketing strategy to the soundtracks of their series, one has the impression that *Supernatural*'s use of back-catalog classics would not be conducive to either large scale cross-marketing opportunities or targeting a demographic already familiar with the music.[5] A CD entitled *Supernatural: Original Television Soundtrack — Seasons 1–5* was released in 2010, but it is comprised of original music composed for the series. The '60s and '70s popular music does not appear on the CD, and one might speculate that this is for copyright reasons.

In contrast to the example from "Bloody Mary," the popular music soundtrack that forms the backbone of the series' rationale is subtly different from the music of theatrical release horror films. After all, the original fans of most of the popular music used in the series would be in their 50s by the time *Supernatural* aired and therefore not in the demographic sweet-spot preferred by the cw, *Supernatural*'s home network. Dawn Ostroff, President of Entertainment for the cw, states in an interview: "Our target audience is 18–34 women." The cw's preference for a female audience means that character development is often given precedence over the visceral impact of raw violence, and the classic rock soundtrack, because of its existing cultural implications, is better suited to nuanced shading of characters. Unlike the horror film, which tends to attract a primarily young male audience, character development in the eminently televisual *Supernatural* is of paramount importance, and the music is used to enhance the audience's understanding of the principal characters rather than to simply augment the experience of the series' admittedly violent visuals. According to Tompkins, the horror-metal soundtrack of theatrical release horror films is aimed at a pre-existing audience that enjoys the music and the films. The soundtrack tends to unify the separate experiences and develop co-dependent markets of metal-horror fans. *Supernatural* provides music whose initial audience has probably moved on from horror films to other forms of entertainment, yet it develops a rather nostalgic air that can be appreciated by a more mellow demographic than the teenage boys who flock to horror films. Although contemporary heavy-metal and classic rock both work very well as background for the intense action and violence that characterize horror films and *Supernatural*, for many audience members, classic rock carries a somewhat different emotional association.

As Simon Frith suggests, "Genres initially flourish on a sense of exclusivity; they are as much (if not more) concerned to keep people out as in" (88). Contemporary heavy metal often functions as an intergenerational barrier, excluding parents with a wall of sound, while classic rock can serve as common ground between a younger audience and their elders. *Supernatural*'s core audience, while appreciative of the powerful emotional appeal of both classic rock and contemporary heavy metal, is more likely to welcome the parental associations that come with Dean's taste in music. The fact that the show is usually enjoyed in the home rather than in a public setting dominated by a youthful peer group may also have some effect upon the choice of music for *Supernatural*.

The interaction of Sam and Dean is an example of the female-friendly experience of *Supernatural*. Dean serves as a bad boy, "love 'em and leave 'em" personality, while Sam is presented as a more conservative potential romantic partner. The brother's differing tastes in music bring home this difference in what we may consider effective melodramatic technique. Sam's alternate taste in music is exemplified in "Lazarus Rising" (4.1) when Dean, newly returned from the dead, sits behind the wheel of his beloved car again:

> Sam: I assume you'll want to drive.
>
> Dean: [Laughing, takes the keys] I almost forgot. Hey, Sweetheart, you miss me? [Sits behind the wheel and stares] What the Hell is that?
>
> Sam: It's an iPod jack.
>
> Dean: You were supposed to take care of her, not douche her up! [He turns on the car and as "Vision" by Jason Manns[6] bursts from the speakers, he rips the iPod out and flings it into the back seat.]

In contrast to Sam's more mainstream tastes, Dean is completely immured in the goals and lifestyle of his father. He drives his father's antique muscle car, he listens to music that is appropriate to his father's generation, and he carries and consults his father's leather-bound notebook with the devotion usually reserved for holy scriptures. In many ways, Dean is a patriarchal cliché. The series writers develop a backstory over the course of the show in which Dean is represented as a boy who must take over parental responsibility for his younger brother while his father is away hunting the evils of the world. Like many children who are forced to assume responsibility for their siblings at an early age, Dean follows the template of his father as closely as possible. The Winchester family becomes insular, unable to compare their behavior with other families because their "mission" precludes normal interaction with others.

In "A Very Supernatural Christmas" (3.8) the brother's abnormal childhood is represented in a series of flashbacks to Christmas Eve in 1991. The two boys are spending Christmas Eve alone in a hotel room, while waiting for their father to return from a hunting trip. Sam asks his brother why their lives are so different from other children:

> Sam: Dad's gonna be here, right?
> Dean: He'll be here.
> Sam: It's Christmas!
> Dean: He knows. He's gonna be here. Promise!
> Sam: Where is he, anyway?
> Dean: On business.
> Sam What kinda business?
> Dean: You know that. It's all stuff.
> Sam: What kind of stuff?
> Dean: Stuff!
> Sam: Nobody ever tells me anything!

Dean spends the rest of this Christmas Eve attempting to reassure his brother that their father's choice of lifestyle is appropriate. Although this episode does not incorporate classic rock directly, it poignantly demonstrates Dean's reliance upon their father as a source of wisdom, guidance, and protection. The music that drives the action in the series is a tragic reminder that Dean — and to a lesser extent, Sam — are locked into a lifestyle that their father developed in his own youth and passed on to his children.

As the series develops the characters of the two brothers, it is revealed that Sam is not a completely passive soldier in his brother's two-man army. Sam begins to rebel against Dean's unwavering rejection of all things demonic and by season 4 he develops an addictive relationship with Ruby — one of the minions of Hell. Sam's attitude toward the struggle against evil is more utilitarian (Schmidt 4.13) while Dean remains firmly ensconced in a mindset that is dominated by his desire to preserve family traditions (Schmidt 4.14). Dean's taste in music (and automobiles) reflects his perception that his father's youth was some sort of golden age.

Despite Dean's penchant for the hard-rocking end of the spectrum of '60s and '70s music, there are occasional instances in which the classic music is more about thought and feelings than action. A pertinent example of this may be found in "Abandon All Hope" (5.10).[7] The first popular song that we hear is the mellow 1972 R & B hit "Everybody Plays the Fool," running as diegetic background music while the demon Crowley watches video recordings of a fascist demonstration and pours himself a scotch on the rocks. The Winchester brothers break into Crowley's home, and he gives them the Colt — a specially developed gun able to kill demons — so they can execute Satan. Although they are rather nonplussed by this turn of events, the brothers collect their confederates and plan their next move. The scene transitions to the bar where the Winchesters and their colleagues are discussing strategy is accomplished with the video-editing technique known as a J-Cut (in which the soundtrack for the next scene is heard before the visuals shift). Before the video image changes from Crowley's home we hear music that belongs to the bar scene that follows. The music that signals the change in scene is Carlos Santana's 1970 version of Tito Puente's "Oye Como Va." The music is non-diegetic and lasts for four minutes, fading in and out to strategically link the dialogue and images of an emotional leave-taking. The fact that "Oye Como Va" is selected for such a long segment of background music is quite significant for a number of reasons. The gentle Latin rhythm of the music is egregious in its deviation from the usual hard-rocking selections that characterize the series. Moreover, the version selected is from *Abraxas*, an album named for a quotation from Hermann Hesse's novel *Demian*. Hesse — and to some extent Carlos Santana — typify the mystic tendencies of '60s and early '70s pop culture. They provide a neo-romantic repackaging of Eastern mysticism in a form attractive to an American audience. Abraxas was a demon/god figure from Gnostic mysticism introduced to European culture by Hesse's mentor Carl Jung. Although the connection may at first seem somewhat tenuous, the music is in complete accord with the later seasons of the series in that it seems to follow an essentially Gnostic cosmology with a relatively complex system of divinity, demons, and angels that transcends the doctrines of most contemporary Christians. By using "Oye Como Va" in this episode, the series creators have provided the fan audience another puzzle that is accessible only to an elite audience.

Dean's attachment to period music is part of a hermeneutic game that the series creators play with the audience. As Lisa Schmidt discusses, the interaction of *Supernatural*'s creators with its fan communities is quite remarkable. Not only do the writers embed characters representing the fan community in their narratives, they also use a host of references that are only accessible to cult fans. Although she did not specifically deal with the use of musical references to enhance the interpretive experience, she does, however, correctly indicate that *Supernatural* may be categorized as a melodrama in that it uses music to express the emotional lives of its characters. The fact that much of this musical communication is couched in terms of 30-year-old popular music means that it not only fits the definition of melodrama, but it also serves as closed reference system for cult fans.

Part 2

Skin Mags and Shaving Cream

Sam and Dean on the Fringes
of Time and Place

Purgatory with Color TV
Motel Rooms as Liminal Zones in *Supernatural*
Lorna Jowett

In the movies, the motel is usually a temporary stop en route to somewhere else. The motel (or hotel) offers a transitional space where the protagonist experiences a crisis of identity — when the crisis is resolved, the protagonist moves on. A television show, though, might be predicated on an endless journey, following protagonists who travel across the country, rarely stopping for long, never establishing a home. In such shows, life on the road defines characters as well as structuring narrative. *Route 66* (1960–1964), an early example, is cited by *Supernatural* creator Eric Kripke as an influence ("Pilot" commentary). *The Incredible Hulk* (1978–1982) combined the road format with a superhero story and *The X-Files* (1993–2002) featured FBI agents based in Washington who traveled across the U.S. to investigate paranormal events. *Supernatural* draws on these earlier shows, combining horror, the fantastic, and the road genre to present ever-moving protagonists in the Winchester brothers, Dean and Sam, and their mission of "saving people, hunting things."

Dean and Sam not only cross physical space to investigate the supernatural, they also pass between different dimensions (literally when

Dean goes to Hell and then returns), and (via hauntings from the past) between times, so liminal zones feature frequently. Motels are non-places, between places, "purgatory with color TV," as Katherine Lawrie Van de Ven suggests (235) and the motel rooms the Winchesters stay in replicate other sites where borders between the supernatural and the mundane blur.[1] Motel rooms in *Supernatural* have an aesthetic function: signifying Anytown, USA, they are generic but distinctively American, providing visual flourishes in the generally dark, washed-out landscape of the show. When the Trickster traps Dean and Sam in a TV land fantasy ("Changing Channels,"5.8), this grittiness is exaggerated by the brightness of the "sitcom" motel room compared with the "real" motel room — it is the same room with the same décor but one pops with color, the other is dull and slightly worn. Furthermore, as spaces for both exposition and emotion, motel rooms also serve a plot function, enhancing their thematic significance: the Impala may be the Winchesters' "home," as the season 5 finale suggests, but life in motel rooms has shaped who they are. Van de Ven notes, "trading in the purgatorial gray areas of identity, hotel/motel films provocatively employ marginal, transitory spaces to speak to experiences of complexity or uncertainty" (236–237). *Supernatural*'s motel rooms are key sites of uncertainty, even contradiction, that relate as much to the brothers' identity as to supernatural phenomena.

Distance

Because of their nature as stopping places, motels, "[e]ven when located in the middle of a city . . . are outside its community," Van de Ven comments (237), and therefore they do not quite adhere to society's rules. Moreover, Steven Cohan and Ina Rae Hark observe that the road movie is popular "in periods whose dominant ideologies generate fantasies of escape and opposition, as in the late 1960s" (2). Motel rooms in *Supernatural*, simultaneously generic (often with standard furniture and facilities) and individualized (at times with spectacularly unique décor), demonstrate how the road genre has, as Cohan and

Hark note, "obvious potential for romanticizing alienation as well as for problematizing the uniform identity of the nation's culture" (1).

Motels in popular culture are often dubious moral ground, a gray area disrupting black and white moral codes. Characters check in under false names, use motel rooms for illicit sexual encounters or drug taking, and bodies (unidentified or otherwise) are often found in them. The anonymity offered by interchangeable roadside facilities like motels is also ideal for harboring fugitives. Dean and Sam survive on the road under false names (usually drawn from Dean's favorite pop culture), subsisting on fraudulent credit cards. In several episodes they are actively pursued by law enforcement (see, for example, "The Usual Suspects," 2.7, or "Jus in Bello," 3.12). The anonymity of the small motel is highlighted in *Supernatural* by the way there never seem to be any other guests, and the brothers are rarely interrupted by housekeeping.[2] There are some pragmatic reasons for this anonymity (the rooms are filmed on set, not on location), nevertheless the Winchesters — or any motel residents — are detached from larger American society.

This detachment can be read positively or negatively. Van de Ven suggests that motels "enable . . . subjects to distance themselves from their past, from society, and from its moral values" (241), this distance allowing for behavior that would never be contemplated in society proper. Thus the Winchesters are violent vigilantes, and Sam's reliance on demon blood to increase his power is presented as a metaphor for both illicit sex and dangerous drug addiction of the type frequently associated with seedy motel rooms. On the other hand, the road is often presented as "an alternative space where isolation from the mainstream permits various transformative experiences," as Cohan and Hark observe (5). *Supernatural*'s engagement with ghosts, demons, and angels certainly offers transcendence, and Dean and Sam are presented as heroes whose experiences transform them. A televisual example of the road genre, the show folds together the Western hero and the lawless frontier with the alienation of film noir. Melissa N. Bruce draws on Mark Osteen's analysis of "film noir 'automobility,'" which "offers the apparent freedom to become anyone, anywhere, but . . . perpetually ends in the solidification of the main characters' role as social outcasts," as "Dean and Sam are consistently aware" (3.3). In other words, the potential freedom of the road (of America itself?) is false: the protagonists are marked as outside the law and outside society, hence the brothers' consistent comparison of their lives with other people's more "normal" existence. "Normality," however, is also presented as both desirable and stifling.

In early seasons this ambivalence is emphasized through Sam, who rebels against his family by returning to mainstream society. During the pilot episode he is studying at Stanford, living with a steady girl-friend, and about to be interviewed for law school. The specter of this normal life haunts the brothers' partnership initially because it offers a fallback position that Dean does not have. Yet this version of Sam's life, like the scenes of the Winchester family before Mary is killed, and the visions Dean is given of what might have been ("What Is and What Should Never Be," 2.20; "It's a Terrible Life," 4.17) are stereotypical, even hyperbolic, and suggest that from the start the show is highly conscious of playing with iconic images and ideals. Helen Wheatley argues that horror television show *Millennium*'s (1996–1999) rather saccharine version of the protagonist's family life works to counter the horrors depicted (188). Here, however, ideas of home and family resonate strongly because of, not despite, the brothers' isolation from "normal" versions of these comforts and bring elements of the soap opera or family melodrama to *Supernatural*'s genre mix.

As a consequence of not having a home, Sam and Dean have very few personal possessions, another possible counter to mainstream American society. Despite Sam's assimilation into the mainstream before his return to the family business, his only notable possession is a laptop (contributing to the college boy persona). A recent news article describes some young professionals following a "cult of less," purging themselves of possessions and keeping only what can be transported via digital technology (see Danzico), and Sam is part of that demographic. Most of the personal items we see in *Supernatural* belong to Dean. Almost all of these are inherited (literally or meta-phorically) from their father, John: the Impala, Dean's leather jacket, John's journal, the arsenal in the car trunk, and Dean's amulet (origi-nally intended as a gift for John, "A Very Supernatural Christmas," 3.8, see below). The majority of Americans are not living like Dean Winchester or the 20-somethings Matthew Danzico describes, but increased travel and job insecurity are eroding long-term residence in traditional communities. The recent success of the movie *Up in the Air* (2009) demonstrates how resonant this anxiety is for audiences.

From the mid-20th century, popular fictions have posited the targeting of men as consumers of anything from hair products to furniture as a destabilization of traditional masculine identity (see novels and films like *American Psycho* or *Fight Club*[3]). Jamie Chambers describes the Winchesters as blue collar make-do hunters who simply "get by using what little they have" (166). Arguably, like Tyler Durden's manifesto in *Fight Club*, this suggests a (mythical) return to masculinity unencumbered by domesticity and mainstream consumption. *Supernatural*'s protagonists do not aspire to a salary, a disposable income, a house and its contents (the white-collar life Sam could have had), but treasure a few items handed down from father to son. It is certainly easy to read the show in this way. But the road narrative, with its breakdown of the family unit and apparent potential for "free" masculinity, according to Cohan and Hark, never-theless results in "destabilization of male subjectivity and masculine empowerment" (2). The motel rooms the Winchesters inhabit strip them down to an essentialized (masculine) state, but they also enclose and threaten that identity.

Proximity

The very anonymity of the motel is destabilizing. As Van de Ven elabo-rates, the motel room "is theoretically designed to be universal . . . to embrace any individual identity into its structure, but this is a slippery kind of individuality, in which the hotel/motel room's own mode of anonymity or sameness creates the possibility for individual space" (238). For the Winchesters, choosing this anonymity as a permanent way of life threatens their sense of self. Sam has the option of a regular job, but Dean's whole life is about being a hunter.

The motel rooms are, moreover, an important plot device, offering convenient settings for exposition scenes as the brothers discuss their latest case, as well as enforcing close quarters living that intensifies their relationship (characteristic of the road genre). Jules Wilkinson identifies three different kinds of space common to serial television: "private space, such as a bedroom (or prison cell); a semi-public space, such as a living room in a sitcom or workplace (think squad room or hospital doctors' lounge); and a contained public space, like the Bronze (*Buffy the Vampire Slayer*), or Central Perk (*Friends*)." Noting "The Winchesters have access to none of these," she adds, "They do not have access to spaces in which to develop relationships with other people . . . because this show is all about Dean, Sam — and the Impala" ("Back in Black" 200), which emphasizes the close, even claustrophobic, nature of the relationship. The motel room, however, functions as at least two, if not all three, of these spaces in *Supernatural*. It is bedroom, living room, and workspace, blurring the boundaries of public and private.

A motel room offers a private haven for an individual but is inhabited by many consecutive travelers.[4] The door can shut away the outside world, but its privacy is open to interruption. In "Free to Be You and Me" (5.3) when the angel Castiel unexpectedly materializes in Dean's room, Dean admonishes him, "We talked about this — personal space!" but there is little personal space in *Supernatural*. The permeability of the motel room is an extension of the vulnerability of the family home in the show (and in U.S. horror generally since the 1970s).[5] Family homes are sites of invasion and terror, not safe havens, as the pilot episode makes clear from the prologue, when it shows Mary Winchester being killed in Sam's nursery by the yellow-eyed demon. From this point, the Winchesters lack a permanent home. If no space is safe from supernatural forces (and this includes our own bodies), then a temporary motel room is as good as any, as the conclusion of *Poltergeist* (1982) also demonstrates.

The motel room as bedroom raises specific issues about private space. FBI agents Mulder and Scully in *The X-Files* always have separate rooms when traveling, keeping their personas professional while allowing small glimpses into more private territory. As brothers, the Winchesters share a room. Cohan and Hark note that the male buddy formula and enforced intimacy of road movies can be problematic for mainstream media (9), yet *Supernatural* offers a diegetic justification: as brothers, Dean and Sam *are* intimately related. This family relationship enables greater than usual engagement with emotion for a horror/action show with male leads. They are able to fight, make up, and admit their love for each other because they are family. Bruce argues that the liminality of the road genre also facilitates this: "Neither Sam nor Dean has ever truly had access to the 'normal' society that enacts the strict gender binaries viewers are accustomed to" (3.1). She suggests, as others have, that the Impala, "a visual space that is typically masculine," is used "as a device through which to filter the more intensely emotional moments that characterize television melodrama and the Winchester brothers' relationship" (1.1). Motel rooms also operate regularly as sites for emotional exchanges, as examined in the following sections.

Family is valorized by the brothers and the show, yet the lack of private or domestic space (and female family members) challenges standard representations of the American family and of heterosexual masculinity. The show consciously plays with the nature of the brothers' intimacy: other characters often assume they are a gay couple when they ask for a shared room (as in "Playthings," 2.11). During an early episode ("Something Wicked," 1.18), Dean is asked, "A king or two queens?" on checking in at the motel, and is forced to reply, "Two queens," while during "Point of No Return" (5.18), Zachariah states that the brothers are "psychotically, irrationally, erotically co-dependent." Wincest fan fiction (depicting incestuous sexual relationships between the brothers) demonstrates both the level of intimacy apparent in the televisual representation of the relationship and just how far outside regular society it can be pushed. By season 4, the show even references this when the Winchesters find out about Wincest fanfic in "The Monster at the End of This Book" (4.18). Extreme intimacy between the characters is possible only because of their lifestyle as itinerant hunters, sharing motel rooms and living in unusually close proximity to each other.

Shared motel bedrooms complicate sexuality on other levels too. Life on the road apparently offers the ultimate freedom: random sexual encounters with minimal responsibility. Dean initially appears to be characterized in this fashion. However, he has formed a more serious relationship with Cassie ("Route 666," 1.13), and may even be the father of Lisa's son, Ben, though she insists he is not ("The Kids Are Alright," 3.2; see also "99 Problems," 5.17). John had another son in the course of his travels, though Dean and Sam only meet their half-brother after his dead body is taken over by a ghoul ("Jump the Shark," 4.19). Thus the road's sexual freedom is reframed according to the central motif of family, underlining tensions between family responsibility and the life of a hunter.

The claustrophobic nature of that life, and the necessity for secrecy (Cassie and Dean's relationship ends after he tells her what he really does in "Route 666"), also set limitations on Dean and Sam's sex lives. Both have sexual encounters, but sharing a room makes this difficult, just as their itinerant life ensures that such encounters will be brief. They are unlikely to bring a sexual partner back to their shared room, though in "The Magnificent Seven" (3.1) Sam waits in the car while Dean has sex in the motel. Here, Sam's tolerance is explained by his knowledge that Dean will die soon and "deserves" some fun. In the Trickster's fantasy sitcom ("Changing Channels"), Dean is caught with a buxom blonde in the room when Sam returns expecting him to have been researching. Played for laughs, in both the shift from the show's usual style and its parody of the sitcom, this seems in-character for Dean, and yet such scenes are rare except to make a specific point. It is Sam who is more frequently shown having illicit sexualized encounters in motel rooms, though sex is displaced onto demon blood drinking (see, for instance, "Criss Angel Is a Douchebag," 4.12).

All these aspects limit the brothers' construction of individual identities. The motel rooms are a visualization of closeness. Their obvious similarities (the same set) are never quite disguised by the distinctive décor (the same set dressed differently), suggesting that the brothers cannot escape the enclosing familiarity of family, their distinguishing features just set dressing. The Winchesters are one unit, demonstrated by the ease with which characters and viewers refer to them as the Winchesters, the brothers, the boys. The road promises space, freedom, and distance from social norms, but Dean and Sam end up back in the same small motel room, close and enclosed in a wild distortion of the ideal, loving, all-American family (or the totally involved romantic couple).

Time

The motel room's ability to blur boundaries between public and private, distance and proximity, is linked to the show's blurring of past and present. Its use of "Then" and "Now" to distinguish "previously on" recaps from new material suggests clear boundaries, but fantasy elements create liminal temporal zones. If supernatural forces exist, then so does a whole alternate history of the USA. The emphatically small town, provincial, if not rural, settings of *Supernatural* situate the phenomena the Winchesters investigate (like the characters) as outside the mainstream of U.S. society, generally depicted as urban or suburban. Origins in either established folklore or urban legends position the supernatural as part of folk culture. The road genre, according to Cohan and Hark, "does not oppose so much as bring together the modernity of transportation on the 20th-century road and the traditions still historically present in the settings that the road crosses" (3), and *Supernatural* demonstrates this in the 21st century. The rooms the brothers stay in have wi-fi, but the motels, bars, and diners shown are mom-and-pop businesses, not global franchises. The small-town motel is embedded in national and local history: Chester H. Liebs notes that motels often cash in on nearby historic attractions, benefiting "from the reservoir of romantic ideas the public held regarding a historic site or geographic region" (50). This sometimes features in *Supernatural*: Milan, Ohio, is "Birthplace of Thomas Edison" ("Long-Distance Call," 3.14), and more generally motel décor is inspired by the region it is supposedly located in: polka band posters in Wisconsin ("Nightshifter," 2.12), flamboyant décor for "Sin City" (3.4) to chime with the decadent Las Vegas atmosphere. Regional specificity is denoted, but the provincial settings are also representative, as Warner Brothers executive David Janollari comments (in Fernandez): "It allows you to feel on a week-to-week basis that the show is very real, that it could happen in your home town or anywhere in the USA." The local histories uncovered in *Supernatural* both uphold and subvert the ideal of small-town America. Just as the roadside architecture provides "a cultural landscape that is quintessentially American" (Liebs xiii), research into the supernatural uncovers broader national histories of racism ("Route 666"), serial killers ("No Exit," 2.6; "The Benders," 1.15), or religious belief ("Faith," 1.12; "Houses of the Holy," 2.13), angel lore (seasons 4 and 5). In one sense, then, the alternative supernatural history of the country is not far removed from its received history — it is often a history of violence.

The Winchesters' motel room is where research into this history takes place. Arguably their motel rooms do not function as living rooms, since the brothers have no life beyond hunting, but they are workspaces where information is drawn from tabloid newspapers, websites, and John's journal. During "Long Distance Call," Dean even finds a clue in the "motel pamphlet rack," and in early seasons these materials are displayed on the walls of their rooms (like police incident boards). Bobby Singer often helps out with research, and his role as surrogate father is linked to his role as mentor. Other hunters provide an alternative work-family or community: they are "keepers of the lore, the ones who remember what others have forgotten or who believe in what others scoff at as old wives' tales or urban legends" (Swendson

252). Sites like the Roadhouse provide meeting places for this alternative family, but a sense of community is based on shared knowledge of supernatural lore and history, not on geographic proximity.

This slippage between myth and history, and between individual, community, and national histories, takes another turn in later seasons with the discovery that Dean and Sam's adventures are becoming a new American myth. In "The Monster at the End of This Book," they find that prophet Chuck is publishing their lives as a "fictional" series of books; "Sympathy for the Devil" (5.1) introduces its strong fan base; and in "The Real Ghostbusters" (5.9) the brothers visit a *Supernatural* fan convention (one of the few episodes featuring a hotel, not a motel, presumably for reasons of size).

Episodes and flashbacks also uncover the family history of the Winchesters themselves. Two episodes have even sent one or both into the past ("In the Beginning," 4.3; "The Song Remains the Same," 5.13), though neither alters the tragedy that caused John to become a hunter and take his sons on the road. If the small-town landscape dotted with motels offers an alternative to mainstream urban American life, then the Winchester history offers an alternative to the standard American family. The Winchesters are all male, and the itinerant hunter lifestyle enables an archetypal escape from feminized domesticity that U.S. fiction has enacted in such classic novels as *Moby-Dick* (1851) and *Huckleberry Finn* (1884). Constant travel means that their family history is dispersed geographically across the U.S. Yet the recurring locus of the motel room stands in for the domestic, and Liebs notes how motels promote themselves as a home away from home (45). Further, the motel room can become a liminal temporal zone that offers glimpses into the brothers' past. "It's only valuable to go back in the past if it can tell you something about the present," says Kripke ("In the Beginning" commentary), and thus some episodes weave together past and present, flashbacks adding emotional weight to family relationships in the present.[6] This strategy is introduced in "Something Wicked," when the brothers investigate a mysterious illness affecting young children. As Dean recalls the same thing once happening to

Sam, flashbacks uncover the Winchester brothers' own childhood, when they were often left without adult supervision or protection in a dingy motel.

In this episode, Fitchburg, Wisconsin, advertises itself as "a place to call home," but the shtriga responsible for the crisis there is one of many supernatural monsters that invade the home and prey on families. The elongated handprint it leaves on windowsills emphasizes how easily the "safe" boundaries of home are permeated. Here, a boy, Michael, his brother, Asher, and their mother run the motel the Winchesters check into, a live-in job that literally turns the motel into their home. Yet for young Dean and Sam, the motel room John leaves them in is far from home-like (flashback motel rooms are always grimmer than present-day ones), so much so that Dean goes out to "get some air," leaving Sam vulnerable to the shtriga's attack. This is the "unfinished business" that prompts John to send Dean on this job, and throughout the episode Dean struggles with guilt for neglecting Sam and for hesitating to use the shotgun he was left with, believing that the shtriga could have been killed then, rather than sent underground to resurface later. The cyclical nature of the attacks — clusters every 15 or 20 years since the 1890s — connects past and present, just as Michael's sense of responsibility for little brother Asher (who falls victim to the shtriga) parallels Dean's feelings for Sam. This motel is the site for a major working through of anxieties related to the brothers' way of life, both the danger inherent in hunting, and a lack of family stability.

In *Supernatural*, national holidays, like the home, are not sites of idealized family togetherness. Drawing on melodrama and horror, both are more often filled with tension, violence, and threat. "A Very Supernatural Christmas" follows a series of mysterious abductions, twinned with an unfolding view into the Winchesters' Christmas Past. "Something Wicked" gave Dean's perspective; here Sam recalls Christmas Eve in 1991, waiting in yet another motel room, as Dean tries to reassure him that John will be back for Christmas. As Kripke says, the changed opening titles for this episode put "on the trappings of a really cheery traditional Christmas special" ("A Closer Look"). Yet the "spirit of Christmas" is challenged immediately: the first victim is violently dragged up the chimney in the opening minutes, watched by a young child, while pagan blood sacrifice, insistent observation of commercialism and excess, and a debate about the non-Christian origins of the festival follow.

The emotional core of the episode, though, is the brothers' argument in the present about whether they should celebrate Christmas. When Dean comments that they had "some great Christmases," Sam angrily responds, "Those weren't exactly Hallmark memories for me." Dean's desire for Christmas is explained by his deal with the crossroads demon: Sam asks him why, when he hasn't "talked about Christmas for years," he is "Bing Crosby all of a sudden," and he replies, "Yeah, well, this is my last year." Sam is reluctant to celebrate with Dean, as this will acknowledge his brother's impending death. Moreover, Christmas is associated with his own loss of innocence. Sheltered from the truth by Dean and John, in 1991 Sam finally finds out that monsters are real (but Santa is not) and that John is a hunter. Again, the motel room in both time-streams is the site for emotion surrounding family and hunting. In the present, the ongoing argument is left hanging with a two-shot: Dean and Sam each sit on a twin bed, facing straight ahead. (Typically, the characters do not look at each other while expressing emotion.) The twin beds visualize emotion in the flashback motel room too, the brothers divided while Sam reveals that he has looked in John's journal and keeps pressing until Dean admits that it is all true. When Sam breaks down at this discovery, Dean moves to sit on the bed beside him, physical closeness signaling solidarity if not comfort.

John never appears in this episode, emphasizing the bond between the brothers that has formed in his absence. After young Dean tries to provide a tree and gifts for Sam (unsuccessfully, having stolen them from a nearby house without checking if they were "chick" presents), Sam gives him the gift meant for their father, the amulet Dean wears throughout the series, saying, "Dad lied to me, I want you to have it."

Although this is a moment of trust and sharing, Sam's face remains in shadow, suggesting that their relationship is touched by the darkness Dean has exposed, forever banishing Sam's innocence. Back in the present, having dispatched the pagan gods responsible for the grisly abductions, Sam decides to go along with Dean's desire to celebrate Christmas. There is a brief scene of gift giving (which includes "skin mags and shaving cream" from the Gas Mart) and a festive toast with eggnog, and the episode closes with the camera pulling back through the motel window to take in festive lights around the frame, their colors reflected in the hood of the Impala that is parked outside. Yet this apparently upbeat ending is undercut by the hesitation after the toast, eventually filled by Sam asking if Dean wants to watch the game. Neither really knows how to have a family Christmas.

Stopping Place?

The liminality expressed in the motel room allows *Supernatural* to be read in complex and contradictory ways, as masculinist (if not misogynist), queer, metatextual, and anti-capitalist. The motel room signifies distance from mainstream society and its ideals of home and family. But it is also a means to depict uncomfortable proximity. This closeness can be stifling, and Dean's habit of leaving the room to "get some air" dates to an early age, as seen in "A Very Supernatural Christmas." It can be invasive, neatly verbalized when Sam tells Dean during "The Magnificent Seven," after unintentionally interrupting him having sex in the motel room that there are "part[s] of you I never wanted to see." The repetitive series of motel rooms figures the brothers' journey (through time and space), a cycle that unspools continuously, the rooms linking past and present.

Rebels, Rogues, and Sworn Brothers
Supernatural and the Shift in "White Trash" from Monster to Hero
Aaron C. Burnell

After the death of his wife, John Winchester deserts any form of traditional community, entering instead into a space that exists outside of the American paradigm of class. He uses violence, misdirection, and arcane knowledge in attempts to find vengeance for his wife's death, which inadvertently positions him as a hero within the suburbs where these supernatural terrors often reside. Likewise, he teaches his sons how to survive through these means and then how to inhabit the same role. In this new form of identity construction, we can see remnants of the Hollywood Western's "class struggle [. . . that] is primarily a struggle over the identification of the social individual with either the power of the capitalist class or the struggles of the multitude" (McGee 236). By being grifters(/hunters), the Winchesters, like the cowboy, can neither fully align themselves against the capitalistic work force nor the imagined community of suburbia. They can exist neither as complete monsters nor as total heroes. Instead, they are something in between: they are "white trash."

From the gruff frontiersmen of manifest destiny as independent trailblazers to the Beverly Hillbillies as laughable yokels, poor whites have existed on the periphery of middle-class American culture as imagined and conceptualized objects. The way in which these lower-class bodies are presented is often through monstrous imagery. Genres such as horror have illustrated how the men and women who exist on the fringes of dominant culture function as an outlet for the fears, anxiety, and abjection that exist within the collective middle-class imagination when confronted with whites who do not fit within the assumed norm of social class. Julia Kristeva theorizes abjection as a kind of push-and-pull dance of desire and disgust. While the middle class is appalled by those who have yet to "pull themselves up by their bootstraps" as they imagine they themselves have done in some form or another, the middle class is simultaneously filled with a curious desire to witness the seemingly surreal and "authentic" world of "white trash."[1]

White trash, like many forms of identity, is a concept that is diffi-cult to define. Any time a list of qualities is deemed to be the definitive demarcation of anything from an identity to a genre, examples will emerge that do not fit. Therefore, it seems much more applicable to consider white trash not as a schema of things one is or is not but rather as a specific part of the discourse of American class dynam-ics. Despite the use of designations such as "upper-," "middle-," and "lower-class," the American class system is ambiguous and without concrete markers, thus blurring the line between what is white trash and what is working class. If we are to imagine American class as a gradient, these two identities would be very close to one another. However, they are not synonyms despite the fact that they are often used as such. The designation of "working class" fits within the cultur-ally approved narrative of class. While working-class persons have less cultural capital than members of the middle class, they have a place within the discussion of American class. White trash persons, though, are removed from the American conception of class. Not only is their cultural capital within the dominant American class system non-existent, which places them in a liminal position of existence, but the very use of the word "trash" marks these subjects as contaminants.

With this idea of liminality in mind, we can see how hunters as a culture and, more specifically, Sam and Dean Winchester, exist as white trash. They exhibit not only aesthetic cues that can be read as either white trash or working class (such as their wardrobe, which consists of boots, flannel shirts, and torn jeans), but they hold no cultural capital that can be translated for their own identity group nor exchanged with dominant cultural capital.

Annalee Newitz and Matthew Wray explain that white trash creates the white Other (168). Othering, or the process of intellectually and culturally marking a group as non-dominate or abnormal, is critical to white identity. Dominant whiteness, the whiteness that brings to mind privilege, defines itself not as something it is but rather as something it is not. Whites are not slaves. Whites are not savage. Whites are not poor. White trash functions as an Other to dominant whiteness, because white trash shows what whiteness should never be. I plan to use Eric Kripke's *Supernatural* to explore the apparent shift from shameful monster to prideful hero that seems to occur by appearing to subvert the monstrosity of white trash and creating a mythology in which the abject white trash are heroes who very literally save the day. Despite this seemingly progressive stance, *Supernatural* instead upholds the traditional narratives of white trash by highlighting and, in some ways, privileging the monstrosity that is often viewed as intrinsic to white trash.

Monsters Hunting Monsters: The Winchesters as "White Trash"

The Winchester brothers have a large and devoted fan base that consists primarily of relatively young women. (See the essay by Cherry later in this volume.) The cw, the channel that airs *Supernatural*, openly states that it targets the demographic of women from 18 to 34. If the commercials that air alongside cw programming and the advertising plugs that pepper the cw website can be used as an indicator, the targeted audience is also rather affluent, as seen by the cw website's "Top Picks" for fashion that include $125 jackets, $218 jeans, and $250 clutches ("CWTV Store"). Bearing this demographic in mind, we might wonder why these women are so invested in two non-middle-class men. When viewing *Supernatural* fandom as a whole, it would appear that the Winchesters are perceived as classless hunters.[2] Despite aural, visual, and ideological cues such as their dress, their violence, and their car, the Winchester family and the hunting culture in which they are entrenched are rarely considered by fans to be white trash. Rather, the reading of hunting culture is more often one in which they are considered to be "working class," an identity that is often romanticized as being "authentic," despite the ways in which hunters are coded as white trash by being liminal bodies that exist in and affect culture but are not acknowledged or included within that culture.

Despite the fact that each of these names were once attached to specific geo-political histories, in contemporary American culture, a "redneck" is the same as a "hillbilly" is the same as an "oakie" is the same as a "hick," and all these monikers can comfortably fit within the umbrella term "white trash." Aaron A. Fox identifies an "unmistakably rural aura, a working class ethos" in his study of music and "talk" in redneck bars. It seems possible that this aura, when enacted in the liminal space of white trash (be it either hunting bars like the roadhouse or redneck bars in Texas as Fox observed), acts as a form of identity construction. While he focuses on the use of music, he also identifies how this ethos is marked by a number of mediated and "commodified cultural orientations" such as violence, clothing, vehicles, and politics (113). Fox, as well as Newitz and Wray, remark upon the way in which white trash aesthetics, clothing, or music have become a product-based identity that can be bought and sold. The authentic working class ethos is one that is "constructed in a discourse of desire, with nostalgia for the old [. . .] constructed in a discourse of loss" (Fox 111), while the purchasable "trash drag" allows for middle-class consumers to view class as a fashion choice, "and real impoverished people can be understood as happily hip or even secretly members of the middle class in trash drag" (Newitz and Wray 180).

This type of attitude, of course, fits well into a post-Reagan America wherein the myth of the American Dream — the pulling one's self up by the bootstraps — allows for the middle class to understand "that the poor want to be poor and could recover if they really tried" (Newitz and Wray 180).

The concept of "trash drag" may help to explain why the same audience that is being targeted with $218 jeans is also so enamored of the Winchester brothers. Surely, one may think, Sam and Dean *choose* to exude this "ethos." However, the Winchester life(style), like their family history, has been constructed out of loss and necessity. Sam and Dean do not wear torn jeans, faded flannel, and heavy boots day in and day out because they want to look hip. Instead, they wear these things because the entirety of their possessions needs to fit in the trunk of their car — a trunk that is already full of weapons, relics, and rock salt. During the season 3 episode "A Very Supernatural Christmas" (3.8), it is not clothing that is the indicator of class and trash status, but rather iconic gift-giving. Despite attempts for the perfect (and presumably last) Christmas between them, Sam and Dean exchange gas station kitsch such "skin mags and shaving cream" for Sam and motor oil and a candy bar for Dean. It is only through what Fox defines as the redneck coping mechanism of bracing "against the material world *as it is* in order to articulate a vision of the moral world *as it could be*, which in the local, working-class idiom means a world in image of life *as it was*" (114) that gives these trinkets meaning. Despite the fact that their Christmas tree is decorated with car air-fresheners and red and white fishing bobbers, Sam and Dean are able to recapture with a sense of nostalgia the connection and solidarity that existed during their youth.

Through the episode's use of flashback, the audience becomes privy to the dual-layered sense of loss that permeates the Winchester brothers. While Sam is characterized as longing for the traditional innocence of childhood, Dean longs for the childhood and family that he once had — the life that the death of his mother has denied him. Dean, like Fox's rednecks, longs for life *as it was*. Sam, though, can be understood as even more disconnected from middle-class society because his coping mechanism can only go so far as what *could be.* When young Dean is confronted with young Sam's near constant barrage of questions concerning their father, Dean inadvertently illustrates the different ways in which the boys view their father and, in him, the different ways that they articulate their loss:

> Dean: First thing you have to know is we have the coolest dad in the world. He's a superhero.
> Sam: He is?
> Dean: Yeah. Monsters are real. Dad fights them. He's fighting them right now.[. . .]
> Sam: But Dad said the monsters under my bed weren't real.
> Dean: That's cause he'd already checked under there. But yeah, they're real. Almost everything is real.
> Sam: Is Santa real?
> Dean: No. ("A Very Supernatural Christmas")

This brief sequence helps to illustrate the ways in which Mark Gerzon believes sons will socially and emotionally gravitate to one parent or another. Dean would be his "father's son," and Sam would be his "mommy's boy" (157). Dean was allowed the luxury of having a father who was able to comfort, play with, and love him. However, Sam had a father that "was unavailable to him" (Gerzon 157). John Winchester did not have Gerzon's 20-mile commute and frequent trips abroad, but just as Gerzon remarked that even "when I was home I was often only half there. I did what I could, but my energy was divided. And [my son] knew it" (157), John was inaccessible to his sons, specifically to Sam. Gerzon believes that this absent father figure would cause children to attach themselves to their mother. However, Sam's mother was not in the picture. She was dead. Her death characterizes Sam's loss in two ways: not only did he lack the specialized parental connection that Gerzon explores, but also Sam lacks a memory of time wherein those connections existed.

Not every hunter has a dead mother, but nearly every hunter that Sam and Dean meet throughout their travels has experienced some sort of loss that has propelled them toward hunting. With their loss of husband and father, Ellen and Jo Harvelle parallel the Winchesters. Even the normally level-headed Bobby Singer began hunting because of the death of his wife. Not only are these characters marked by Fox's *ethos* and the material commodities of white trash, but they prove not to be in any sort of "trash drag," if only because so much of their characterization and their culture is based on loss and the means of coping with that loss, which is so strongly linked to the disenfranchised liminality of white trash.

Internal Horror: The Suburban Gothic

In order to see how the Winchesters as heroes challenge the trope of white trash monsters, we must first explore the history that created and fostered this kind of cultural understanding. Judith Halberstam argues that monstrosity will in some way include a sexual outsider, a racial pariah, a national outcast, or a class outlaw (20) while also showing "clearly the markings of deviant sexualities and gendering but [also] the signs of class and race" (4). This set of broad parameters allows us to see not only how humans can be monsters but also the major points of anxiety for middle-class sensibilities. If we look to the 1970s, we can see that with the release of *Deliverance* (1972) and *The Texas Chainsaw Massacre* (1974) American horror films defined white trash families in no uncertain terms.

Deliverance introduced a cinema-based repertory of popular references and cues that defined white trash villains as savage, bestial, and cruel bodies that should be feared. Onscreen, these individuals were characterized as cruel, but they did not become "monsters" until *The Texas Chainsaw Massacre*. The poor whites of *Texas Chainsaw* are not people. Leatherface (Gunnar Hansen) does not speak, nor does he have a traditional face. There is no apparent way for audience members to identify or sympathize with him. After all, what middle class suburbanite would want to empathize with people who work in a slaughterhouse — "just shoot a bolt in [a cow's] head, and then retract it" — or simply kill cows "with a sledge"? (Hooper) The only way, perhaps, to form a bond between audiences and Leatherface's family would be to embrace their fear followed by outrage concerning the encroaching middle class and the loss of financial autonomy, to embrace Fox's ethos of loss. If the audience were to think that, though, they would be no different than the monsters. Monsters who will, as Jim Goad describes in a tongue-in-cheek manner meant to outline middle-class fear, "rape you and then murder you. Or murder you and then rape you. And then drive around for months with your body stuffed in [their] trunk," because these monsters are "just bred for violence" (98). Since these two films created such a lasting impact on American culture, the lower-class body has been consistently read as a source of horror for middle-class suburban America. At best, these "people" should be pitied, and at worse, they should be feared.

Despite what white trash now signifies in popular imagination, *Supernatural* does not code its white trash as villains. Rather in the mythology of the series, these lower-class bodies are the heroes. Likewise, horror does not originate from the backwoods.[3] Rather, it is the middle and upper classes from which horror is spawned that seem to embody the post-war criticism that suburbs "encouraged insularity, materialism, and narcissism" (Murphy 190). Despite these concerns, though, suburbs have steadily crawled across the nation leaving white picket fences and abandoned soccer balls in their wake.

Bernice Murphy explores suburban-set American media and shows that the zeitgeist of the late 20th century and early 21st century is one that is concerned with the fears and anxieties which arise out of suburban living. She examines cult TV show *Buffy the Vampire Slayer* and notes that Sunnydale "is a place only ever a few moments away from violent disorder, and death and disruption are embedded in the very fabric of the community" (168). This analysis of a suburban-set horror series marketed toward young women seems to overlay neatly with *Supernatural*. However, a key difference separates the two series from one another. The leading characters in *Buffy* are (sub)urbanites in a suburban setting. The leads in *Supernatural* are not. In the season 5 episode "The Song Remains the Same" (5.13), audience members become privy to the kind of class dynamics from which Dean and Sam were born. Young John Winchester (Matt Cohen) is a car mechanic who hopes one day to own his own shop. Sharon Bird explains the ways in which small business ownership plays a key part in the formation of masculinity within rural working class communities "by carving out gendered business niches [. . . that embrace] good husbands, fathers, and community troopers" (67). This cultural background places the Winchesters outside of the suburban understanding of community, which is not the prescribed togetherness that was promised during the 1950s, but rather "a culture of atomized isolation, self restraint, and 'moral minimalism.' Far from seeking small-town connectedness, suburbanites kept themselves to themselves, asking little of their neighbor and expecting little in return" (Murphy 188).

However, after Mary's death, John Winchester does not bestow upon his sons the "business niche" of a small town. He is no longer connected to the privilege of the working class to be included within the conception of American community. He instead retreats from this conventional form of identity construction, leaving both the community and dominant conceptions of work to become a grifter who makes his money through cons and various forms of fraud. He (as will his sons) exists outside of suburbs as well as working class small towns. Instead, he is characterized and defined as a transient drifter. The Winchesters and white trash hunters more generally exist at crossroads; they travel between towns while belonging to none. Their loss, in this case, is a loss of locality and community.

Sam and Dean are exorcised against their will from their working-class roots, propelled through childhood by their boundary-pushing father, and as adults end up staring down the historical role of white trash villain. However, Sam and Dean become heroes within this suburban wasteland. This transformation is not for a lack of monsters but rather the way in which these monsters are created. In suburban gothic, the suburbs are "a placid and privileged locale beneath which terrible secrets and irrational forces lurk, waiting for their chance to erupt violently into the open" (Murphy 166). To highlight the internally born and manifested horrors that fill the plot of *Supernatural* from week to week, we may look at one of the episodes from season 1. As we can see, *Supernatural* wastes no time establishing that it is suburbia in the new American frontier that must be tamed.

In "Skin" (1.6), domestic violence is explored as a middle-class terror that the Winchester brothers must banish. When we consider the insular nature of the suburbs, it is easy for us to see how domestic violence is one of the many suburban terrors that may lead to a "family attempting to cover up a hidden secret from the past" (Murphy 188). In this episode, domestic violence takes the form of skin-walkers, fantastic beings that are able to take the form of others and, therefore, create a literal doppelganger, often choosing the forms of spouses and then torturing and murdering their wives. By the end of the episode, Dean must "die." His physical form has been mimicked by the skin-walker, and "he" threatens the dominant middle-class way of life. Dean-the-skin-walker does so by torturing the upwardly mobile Becky, while theoretically, the "real" Dean does this by fulfilling the role of phobic object. As phobic object, Dean acts as a repository for middle-class anxieties; while he exists, he exists most clearly as an imagined object that articulates the middle-class fears of what exists outside of the suburbs as well as, more frighteningly, would could possibly exist within itself. Considering the fact that white trash bodies are outside of class hierarchy, they exist as an unknown and that unknown is filled with suburban terror.

By placing terror and anxiety on that phobic object, individuals in the middle class not only expel these feelings from themselves but also create an identity that can be defeated and, therefore, cleanse the community of these horrors. Dean must die because within suburban ideology, domestic violence is not an issue with which their community struggles — within American understanding, domestic violence is instead a problem for white trash. Dean's "death" banishes these fears from suburbia while placing them firmly on the shoulders of white trash. This exceptional understanding of domestic bliss is in part related to the fact that

> with respect to income and education, agency data are probably not a very good source of information, because middle- and upper-class couples experiencing intimate terrorism are more likely than working-class couples to have the resources that make it possible for them to avoid dealing with public agencies. (Michael P. Johnson 35)

Because of this feigned ignorance, part and parcel of the suburban gothic in that "both local residents and the authorities fail to act upon the fact that something is obviously very wrong in their neighborhood" (Murphy 176), domestic violence is an issue that must be banished to lower-class bodies, the phobic object. It is for this reason that Dean must die. His "death" allows for a cleansing of suburbia and a resetting of the status quo by expelling the anxiety. Most importantly, however, is the fact that this trauma of domestic violence and the fears that are so closely linked to it are banished through the same liminal body that houses them. When Dean kills the skin-walker, it is wearing his face. In this final conflict, the same body that houses these anxieties is that which eliminates them. At the crux of the relationship between suburbanites and their phobic object of white trash is the fact that the former cannot exist without the latter. It is only through this push-pull relationship of abjection that suburbia (and with it dominant American culture as a whole) can be cleansed — a cleansing that occurs notably through violence that is perpetuated on and by white trash.

It is through violence that the Winchesters are able to prevail over the horrors of suburbia. They may have the means to secure the intellectual basis for this violence, but at the end of the day and in the middle of the night, the Winchesters do not talk a horror away. They destroy it. They salt the bones and burn the body. As white trash, even as heroes, they are not entirely devoid of their savagery, bestiality, or cruelty. Therefore, they are not entirely devoid of their monstrosity.

Horror or Hero?: The Function of "White Trash"

In exploring abjection when one comes "face to face with the Other," Kelly Oliver notes how Julia Kristeva defines it as

> above all a revolt of the person against an external menace from which one wants to keep oneself at a distance, but of which one has the impression that it is not only an external menace but that it may menace us from inside. So it is a desire for separation, for becoming autonomous and also the feeling of an impossibility of doing so. (103–104)

White trash is the abject Other that allows for "good" middle-class whites to define themselves in negation, looking at white trash and saying, "We are not that." Perhaps most importantly, though, is the fact that without the existence of white trash, the middle-class suburbanite could never exist. The desire to "become autonomous" but the "impossibility of doing so" comes from the fact that definition of self only exists when there is the ability to define one's self against another, against the Other.

In suburban gothic, "it is one's fellow suburbanites, family members, and personal decisions which pose the most danger" (Murphy 2). Yet, within the framework of *Supernatural*, the abject Others are the ones who save the day. However, we have also seen how the white trash decedents are maligned and rejected. In "Skin," Dean becomes a figure of middle-class anxiety, and his death removes that anxiety from the suburbs. Despite the fact that he did not originally bring these fears (such as domestic violence) with him, his body as white trash becomes the receptacle for these social contaminants and, therefore, must be purged. How is it that these white trash hunters can be both feared and lauded for banishing suburban horror? The

Winchesters and their family in arms, all of hunting culture, are in a precarious position. On the one hand, they exist in the progressive state wherein they are white trash heroes rather than white trash villains or monsters. However, on the other hand, it is their historically white trash monstrosity that banishes the actual horrors of suburbia. We then may find ourselves wondering, especially in light of "trash drag" and the commodification of white trash aesthetics, if the Winchesters truly are white trash heroes, or if they are merely the most attractive and alluring kind of monster.

Renegades and Wayward Sons
Supernatural and the '70s
Simon Brown

> Normality is threatened by the Monster.
> *Robin Wood*

On the surface, the life of Sam and Dean Winchester is only tangentially related to the 1970s. The mighty Impala is from the 1960s, their mother is murdered in the 1980s, and the action of the series plays out in the new millennium. It seems therefore that the only thing that relates Sam and Dean to the 1970s is the music that plays on the stereo from Dean's prehistoric cassette tape collection. At its heart, however, *Supernatural* is an all-American horror show set in the now, and significantly the 1970s was a moment of primal assertion for contemporaneously set American horror. Arguably, therefore, the relationship between *Supernatural* and the 1970s goes beyond the tunes to encompass the thematic, the aesthetic, and the historical. In this chapter I will be examining these links to the 1970s, drawing upon the writing of Robin Wood, one of the foremost theorists of 1970s American horror, and focusing upon the significance of family and mother, themselves indelibly linked to the 1970s, to the Winchester boys.

"The American Nightmare"

In his seminal essay "The American Nightmare: Horror in the '70s," Robin Wood argues that in 1970s American horror films "the true subject of the horror genre is the struggle for recognition of all that our civilization represses or oppresses, its re-emergence dramatized, as in our nightmares, as an object of horror, a matter for terror" (75). Writing from the perspective of a Marxist homosexual, for Wood this means the repression of basic sexual and intellectual freedoms due to the prescriptive nature of bourgeois heterosexual society and the dominance of the family. The threat comes from everything that must be repressed in order to idealize the family, and so it is out of the family that the horror emerges.

Wood argues that this shift toward the family as the locus of horror is tied to a geographical shift in horror away from the Europe of the past, found in Dracula and Frankenstein films produced by Universal in the 1930s and Hammer in the 1950s and '60s, toward contemporary America, maintaining that, "since *Psycho* [1960], the Hollywood cinema has implicitly recognized Horror as both American and familial" (87). The 1970s was therefore the period in which, more than just cinematically, horror found its home in present-day America. As Mark Kermode notes, "[e]schewing the costumed high-campery of the traditional Hammer romps, *The Exorcist* presented a credible portrait of the modern urban world ripped apart by an obscene, ancient evil. For the first time in a mainstream movie, audiences witnessed the graphic desecration of everything that was considered wholesome and good about the fading American Dream — the home, the family, the church and, most shockingly, the child" (9).

Thus in *The Exorcist* (1973), as well as in films like *The Last House on the Left* (1972), *The Texas Chainsaw Massacre* (1974), *The Hills Have Eyes* (1977), and *The Omen* (1976), the family unit is beset by repressed forces that represent base instincts of cruelty, selfishness, survival, and lust. Krug in *Last House on the Left* is an unrepentant criminal who tortures two girls because he can, his own cruelty releasing the violence hidden behind the gloss of the family unit. In *The Omen* a single lie, a moment of self interest masquerading as care when Robert Thorn cowardly agrees to adopt a child and not tell his wife her natural child is dead, allows evil to force its way into the family unit. That evil is itself part of a family; the unholy trinity of Catholic mythology, comprising the devil, anti-Christ, and false prophet (which is the mirror image of the Father, Son, and Holy Spirit). The family in *Texas Chainsaw* represents not only the survival instinct writ large, but also the effects of poverty and social deprivation bourgeois society tries hard to ignore. It is no accident that the family members are slaughterhouse workers; the industrialized slaughter of animals for meat being something that the majority of consumers of meat products are aware of but never want to see. In *The Exorcist* the burgeoning sexuality of an adolescent girl becomes a demonic primal howl, destroying a family unit already disrupted by its absent father. The monster can be an escaped convict ripped from the headlines, the anti-Christ, poor white trash, or a demon, but for Wood "these apparently heterogeneous motifs are drawn together more closely by a single unifying master figure: the family" (83).

The breakdown of the individual family unit under intense pressure has been seen in these films also as a metaphor for American society. Wood's basic concept has been read politically as reflecting the traumas that America was undergoing at that time. Vietnam; the assassinations of JFK, Bobby Kennedy, Malcolm X, and Martin Luther King; Watergate; economic recession and the Oil Crisis; the civil rights and feminist movements — all combined to fracture American society, pitching young against old, conservative against liberal, black against white, poor against rich. Wes Craven, speaking in the documentary inspired by Wood's essay, *The American Nightmare* (2000), says that the "the nation was repeatedly traumatized by the events of that time" which left it "at the mercy of this drunken fate." According to Craven, the shooting of Mary at the lake in *The Last House on the Left* was influenced by the images of a Vietcong operative being shot in the head by a South Vietnamese General. George Romero in the same documentary says he made *Night of the Living Dead* (1968) in black and white partly due to the fact that real horror — the reports from Vietnam and across America seen daily on the nightly news — was on TV in black and white. Tobe Hooper claims the image of stranded and isolated kids, which was one of the initial sparks that led to *The Texas Chainsaw Massacre*, came "straight out of the 'no gas' time." The slaughterhouse family at the heart of the film is unemployed, a direct result of the economic crisis and decline in American industry that happened in the early 1970s. Thus the family in these films is not just *a* family but also American society, threatened by the things that slipped through the cracks and were papered over by the post–World War II myth of the American Dream, with its focus upon family, consumerism, and white suburban affluence.

Supernatural and '70s Horror

Despite nods to classic monsters, notably in "Monster Movie" (4.5), it is the horror films of the 1970s that echo throughout *Supernatural*. A self-conscious allusion to *The Exorcist* is made in "The Usual Suspects" (2.7) in the casting of Linda Blair as Detective Ballard. This is made even more explicit by Dean craving pea soup at the end, a reference to the scene where Blair's character Regan vomits green goo onto the priest who is exorcising her. "Playthings" (2.11) draws heavily on Stanley Kubrick's film of Stephen King's *The Shining* (1980), both subtly — with the notion of the two ghostly girls haunting a hotel — and more explicitly with the visual homage to the bartender scene — Dean standing in for Jack Nicholson listening to stories of the old days told by the hotel's faithful old retainer. "The Benders" (1.15), while clearly drawing upon *The X-Files'* legendary "Home" episode (4.3) featuring the Peacock family, is, like "Home," derived from the image of the family in *The Texas Chainsaw Massacre*. Like the farmhouse in Hooper's film, the Bender house is decorated with bones, and the scene of Dean creeping around the house while the father chops up a corpse with a meat cleaver references Hooper's original. Both "Croatoan" (2.9) and "Jus in Bello" (3.12) draw upon John Carpenter's non-horror but nevertheless iconic '70s siege movie *Assault on Precinct 13* (1976), with "Croatoan" having the additional reference point of a musical score that suggests Ennio Morricone's music for Carpenter's *The Thing* (1982). The images of Mary Winchester pinned to the ceiling in "Pilot" (1.1), and Monica being pulled up the bedroom wall by the demon in "Salvation" (1.21) are directly taken from Tobe Hooper's *Poltergeist* (1982), while the monster truck from "Route 666" is a clear echo of various killer vehicle films of the 1970s and 1980s, including *Duel* (1972), *The Car* (1977), and *Christine* (1983). Finally, the father who brutally stabs the feral child in "Family Remains" (4.11) echoes the murderous father in *Last House on the Left*, driven to violence by the assault on his family.

ꭓ It is not just the imagery but also the color palette of *Supernatural* that reflects these '70s films. Horror in the 1970s turned away from the garish gothic reds and bright colors of Hammer Studios' melodramas and Roger Corman's Poe adaptations. *The Exorcist* and *The Omen* have little color, and like them in *Supernatural* tones of black, brown, and dark blue predominate. This is most evident in the earth tones worn by Sam and Dean. Dean is most frequently dressed in a dark T-shirt, dark blue or olive shirt, jeans, and black boots, while Sam, despite wearing a wider range of colored shirts, most often wears a brown jacket that tones down the color of his outfit.

The clothes they wear, reflecting the color palette of the cinema of the 1970s, contribute to a network of signifiers that codify Sam and especially Dean as representatives of that same decade. Key among these is the celebrated 1967 Chevy Impala, which becomes the home for the Winchester boys in place of the one that was taken from them. When their actual home is destroyed by fire when the yellow-eyed demon comes for Sam in 1983, it is on the hood of the Impala that the family gathers to mourn ("Pilot"). Likewise at the very end of the story it is the Impala and memories of the car as home that give Sam the strength to overcome Lucifer's grip on his body and toss himself into the cage ("Swan Song," 5.22).

Tender moments and key discussions take place in or around the Impala. For example, in season 5 when Dean reaccepts Sam as his hunting partner, the deal is sealed by Dean giving Sam the chance to drive ("Fallen Idols," 5.5). The car is more of a home than the sleazy motels and flop houses in which the boys so often find themselves.[1] The temporal scale of the Impala — made in 1967, bought by John in 1973, becoming the family home in 1983 — is clearly linked to the 1970s. Passed down from father to son, it is, as Mary Fetcher points out, "the only constant in [their] lives" (209).

"Back in Black"

This isn't quite true however, since accompanying them wherever they go, along with the collection of weapons in the trunk, are Dean's cassette tapes, which Sam refers to as "the greatest hits of mullet rock" ("Pilot"). This music defines both of them, but particularly Dean, in more ways than one. In "The Kids Are Alright" (3.11), the first clue that suggests to Dean that eight-year-old Ben might be his son is when Ben receives a CD for his birthday and shouts "AC/DC rule!" While there are other clues to shared biology with Dean, this foregrounding of AC/DC is significant as it highlights the important place that this type of music plays in codifying the Winchester boys.

Indeed the association of the brothers, the car, and the music with the life they lead is there from the outset. In the pilot, after the opening sequences (the death of Mary, Dean going to fetch Sam at Stanford), the episode's narrative proper begins with a young man driving on a dark highway. On the soundtrack is the song "Speaking in Tongues" by the Eagles of Death Metal. Immediately rock music and driving are linked together, and setting the convention for the use of such music, the song comes in loud over an establishing shot of the road and the car before quieting over a cut to the interior of the car, revealing the song to be on the radio. While this is a heavy metal song, it was written in 2004 and so is contemporary to the modern world of 2005 in which Sam and Dean are operating. After the unfortunate driver's demise, we get our first glimpse of Sam, Dean, and the Impala. Here the soundtrack is immediately older, 1973's "Ramblin' Man" by the Allman Brothers.[2] While this is far from the hard rock sound which we will come to associate with the Winchesters, here they are not moving but parked at a rural gas station, the music coming from an indeterminate source. This low-key introduction to the boys on the road is evidently designed first to introduce the idea of "born a ramblin' man," which is practically the only audible line, but secondly to establish what seems to be a peaceful and rural scene. As the Allman Brothers disappear from the soundtrack at the gas station, the next sequence is the conversation in which Sam berates Dean for his mullet rock tapes, noting significantly that Dean needs to "update" his collection, suggesting that Dean is behind the times. The following moment sees Dean firing up the Impala's engine to the opening riff of AC/DC's iconic "Back in Black."

"Back in Black" was recorded and released in 1980 and represents AC/DC at their peak as one of the second generation of heavy rock bands, alongside Judas Priest and Motörhead, following on from the first generation of bands such as Led Zeppelin and Black Sabbath. From this point much of the music associated with the boys and their car — referred to by fans as "Metallicar" — comes from this 1970s period and bands like Lynyrd Skynard, Rush, Blue Öyster Cult, UFO, Black Sabbath, Kansas, and Styx.[3]

Alongside the blatant disregard for contemporary views on health — the drinking, the high trans-fat grease-burger diner food — the use of '70s rock in association with the drab-colored clothes and the gas-guzzling, lead-spewing Impala clearly separates Sam and Dean from the contemporary world and associates them with the 1970s, despite Sam's occasional attempts at flourishes of modernity (like the iPod dock he fits in the car in "Lazarus Rising," 4.1).

Of course, Sam's iPod lasts only a few seconds before Dean tosses it away in favor of his own outmoded style. Ostensibly Sam's inability to change things is because this is Dean's world. The car, the music, and the clothes are an established part of Dean when he arrives to collect Sam in the pilot. Sam is the outsider, and it is through Sam that the audience gains access into the world of hunting, with the car and the music representing steps on that pathway to a life less ordinary. But as Dean openly admits, this isn't actually his world at all; it is his father's. He says, "I worshiped him. I dressed like him. I listened to the same music" ("Jump the Shark," 4.19). Like his father, he is a mechanic, and thus is able to take care of the car his father gave him. The aforementioned trappings that surround Sam and Dean are all adopted by Dean to imitate his dad and are therefore inherited from the father, so in order to understand the significance of that '70s coding we have to look at the figures of John and Mary Winchester.

The 1970s and the Highway to Hell
When we first see young John ("In the Beginning," 4.3), he is a different person. He is a Vietnam vet in love with a beautiful woman who loves him back. Despite what he has been through as a corporal in Vietnam, he retains an optimistic spirit. Mary tells Dean that John "still believes in happily ever after." Yet that optimism that we and Dean see in John and Mary goes quickly to seed, for their happiness is built on a lie. Mary lies to John about what is hidden in her family and in the world. She is a hunter and knows what's out there, which quickly explodes into their lives in the form of the yellow-eyed demon. That lie initially has the best of intentions, since she sees John as a way out of the hunter's life, but as Sam tells Dean, "Last I checked it wasn't the road to Heaven that's paved with the best of intentions" ("Dark Side of the Moon," 5.16). The demon kills Mary's parents, and also John, prompting the first of the Winchester family sacrifices for love. At this point the lie becomes part of their ongoing lives, not something left behind. Mary agrees to the demon resurrecting John for the price of making a visit 10 years later. She marries John and settles down to raise a family, repressing

the hunter aspect of her life and the impact it will have on her family. While she doesn't know it yet, even though Dean has warned her of the danger, the visit of the demon will kill her and infect Sam with demon blood, resulting in the destruction of her family home.

Her death sets the remaining family members on the road, leaving behind their home and adopting the nomadic lifestyle of the hunter. The link between the hunter's life and the road is explicit throughout the series. All of the early episodes in season 1 end with a shot of the boys leaving town, on the road in the Impala. In season 2 the hunters gather at the Roadhouse. In "Time Is on My Side" (3.15) hunter Rufus Turner tells Dean, "Even if you manage to scrape out of this one, there's just gonna be something else down the road." The final episode of each season begins with a recap entitled, "The Road So Far." Kripke openly admits his original intention was to call Sam and Dean *Sal* and Dean as an homage to the most famous road narrative couple, Sal Paradise and Dean Moriarty in Jack Kerouac's *On the Road* ("Interview," *Supernatural: The Inside Scoop*). In "The Monster at the End of This Book" (4.18) the comic store clerk, trying to remember the names of the characters in Carver Edlund's *Supernatural* series, comes up with Sal and Dean as one of the options. Like the woman in white in the pilot, Sam and Dean are forced to wander and cannot go home. Not literally, of course — they do go home, notably in "Home" (1.9), but home in this respect is just a house full of bad memories and spirits, not a home in the traditional sense of a place where one belongs. Their home was destroyed when the yellow-eyed demon infected Sam and killed Mary, sending John on his vengeful quest. From the moment we see the family unit huddled outside the burning house on the hood of the Impala, Sam and Dean, like the woman in white, belong on the road.

But this is more than just a literal road consisting of highways criss-crossing America from small town to small town. Mary's good intentions do indeed pave the way to Hell, since the road they are on is also a metaphorical road of destiny that leads them to perdition. John Winchester goes to Hell at the beginning of season 2. So too does

Dean at the end of season 3, while season 5 ends with Sam trapped in a cage in an eternal battle with the spirit of Lucifer living inside him. All three brothers of the Winchester family (we can also include half-brother Adam here) spend their time literally on a "highway to Hell." The road is therefore both spatial but also temporal. It connects the various locations and small towns that the boys visit while doing their job, but at the same time it represents the sequence of events that lead them to their ultimate destiny. While their life on the spatial road begins in 1983 when the family home is destroyed, their path on the temporal road begins on a single day 10 years earlier.

That day is April 30, 1973, which also happens to be the day on which Nixon took responsibility for Watergate and announced that there would be "no whitewash in the White House." Undoubtedly Watergate was one of the final nails in the coffin of the American Dream of the 1950s, alongside Vietnam, the assassinations of John and Bobby Kennedy and Martin Luther King, the shooting of protesting students by the National Guard at Kent State, and the Oil Crisis. This tumultuous period saw America lose both its innocence and its confidence as it turned upon itself in a frenzy of violence and recrimination. As Dewey Grantham points out, "By the early 1970s a deep crisis of the spirit had settled over America, accompanied by a pervasive pessimism" (361). First Vietnam "destroyed a large part of the public's confidence in the country's capacity to deal with foreign and domestic problems and bruised the national spirit," then Watergate "made Americans acutely aware of the fragility of their political institutions" (362). The experience of the Winchesters (I am including Mary here as a soon-to-be Winchester) on that fateful day in 1973 therefore mirrors the general experience of the American people at that time, which was in turn reflected in the horror films of the 1970s. Calm is replaced by violence, confidence by fear, security by uncertainty, truth by lies. These elements do not surface in the lives of the Winchesters until November 2, 1983, the day when the demon comes to call, but from April 1973 to November 1983, the family is on borrowed time, their suburban dream doomed.

Supernatural, Normality, and the White Picket Fence

The 1970s horror film and the social and political upheavals to which it reacted, are carefully woven into both the look and the narrative trajectory of *Supernatural*. In an interview recorded prior to the start of season 1, creator Eric Kripke described the look of *Supernatural* as "decrepit Americana . . . 1950s American optimism rusted and gone to seed" ("Interview," *Supernatural: The Inside Scoop*). Arguably Kripke is overstating the case here. Certainly in season 1 the majority of small towns Sam and Dean visit are relatively pleasant — the majority of homes they go into are comfortable (for example in "Bloody Mary," 1.5; "Skin," 1.6; "Route 666," 1.13) — and the more decrepit locations they visit such as Hell House (1.17) and the creepy farmhouse that is home to the Benders are associated more with pre–World War II Americana than the 1950s.

But although I dispute Kripke's observation from an aesthetic perspective, it is nevertheless very useful in terms of a thematic reading of *Supernatural* when one ties his description to the concept of the white picket fence. Far more than just a literal marker of property boundary, the white picket fence is a symbol of the middle-class suburban home-owner lifestyle that formed the core of the 1950s consumerist American Dream. This metaphor for suburban family life is one that is picked up over and over in *Supernatural*, with the white picket fence symbolizing normality to Sam and Dean, one which they both reject and have been denied. In "Bugs" (1.8) Dean gives Sam his opinion of life in the upmarket suburban development they visit: "The manicured lawns, the 'How was your day, honey'? I'd blow my brains out." Sam tells Dean, "There's nothing wrong with normal," to which Dean responds, "I'd take our family over normal any day." Normal is instantly linked to "suburban" property ownership, which I take here to mean not in the sense of property in city suburbs but rather a type of spacious, detached family home, distinct from the urban apartment or the isolated farmhouse, which is equally visible in the small American towns that the Winchesters for the most part frequent.

This linking of normal with property ownership becomes encoded in the metaphor of the white picket fence. The yellow-eyed demon tells Mary she can be done with hunting forever and have instead the "station wagon, white picket fence, and a couple of kids" ("In the Beginning"). In "Wishful Thinking" (4.8), Dean asks Sam if he would like to make a wish in the enchanted wishing well at Lucky Chin's Chinese Restaurant, offering that Sam could wish to go back to a time before everything happened and have a different life as a lawyer with a white picket fence. In "Jump the Shark," Sam defends his father, saying, "So we didn't have a dog and a white picket fence . . . Dad taught us how to protect ourselves."

At the end of season 5 it is precisely this white picket fence and normality that Dean finally embraces. Indeed, Dean's trajectory in the series is increasingly toward security. Having sneered at the concept of the white picket fence in season 1 and at various points throughout the series, he expresses his exhaustion with the hunt, the desire to give it all up and accept the only alternative apart from death — the white picket fence. Sam's trajectory is in the opposite direction. Having sought out the white picket fence through his escape to college, he gradually rejects the trappings of normality. The penultimate shot of season 5 is taken from the street, looking in through the window at the family scene. Sam is on the outside while Dean finds comfort on the inside with old flame Lisa Braedon and her son Ben. The white picket fence therefore represents comfort, home, and normality. Significantly, however, we do not see an actual white picket fence outside Lisa's house, nor is there one outside the Winchester family home in Lawrence. What is different about Dean's world at the end of season 5 is the presence of a mother figure taking care of him. While the white picket fence is the metaphor used by the Winchester boys to represent normality, it is the presence of a nurturing mother figure that actually represents normality in the world of the Winchesters.

The Nurturing Mother

What happens in November 1983 that sets Sam and Dean apart is not so much the yellow-eyed demon's infusion of demon blood into Sam but the death of the mother, Mary. In discussing the family in *The Texas Chainsaw Massacre*, Wood notes that "the absence of a woman (conceived as a civilizing, humanizing influence) deprives the family of its social sense and social meaning while leaving its strength of primitive loyalties largely untouched" (91). Similar primitive loyalties codify John, Sam, and Dean Winchester as they repeatedly attempt unnatural sacrifices for each other. The absence of the mother does indeed deprive them of their social sense, leaving them as outcasts outside the family home and the white picket fence. The father figure of John represents the opposite of the mother figure — coldness, self-reliance, and transitory spaces. Sam and Dean, once their father takes over, have motel rooms and the road.

Once John dies, Bobby takes on the mantle of the father figure, and while he has a home, it too is missing the nurturing mother. All the women who are invited into Bobby's house are some form of demon, angel, or ghost, be it Ruby, Anna, the witnesses ("Are You There, God? It's Me, Dean Winchester," 4.2), or indeed Bobby's departed wife who appears as either a vengeful dream spirit ("Dream a Little Dream of Me," 3.10) or an unnatural revenant ("Dead Men Don't Wear Plaid," 5.15). Bobby's place, which is often invaded, is hardly a place of comfort for the Winchesters, nor is it a permanent residence. Like the roadhouse and the motels it is a hunter's space and therefore a transient space.

In *Supernatural* it is the absence of the mother that both precipitates and represents Sam and Dean's sense of being apart from normality. Sam and Dean's mother is seen in the family home as a loving and protective presence — after her death ("Home"). When Sam and Dean take an enforced road trip through Heaven, reliving their happiest memories, Sam's is a time when he escaped from John and Dean and lived on his own in Flagstaff, whereas Dean's heavenly idyll is in the family home, being made sandwiches and pie by his mother ("Dark Side of the Moon," 5.16). Similarly, when the djinn transports Dean to a world in which his mother doesn't die ("What Is and What Should Never Be," 2.20) and shows him the home life he could have had, stability and happiness is based around the figure of the mother. The father is absent, having died some time before, and though his absence is felt, the presence of the nurturing mother overcomes that loss. She makes him a sandwich that looks moderately healthy (it has lettuce in it), and Dean eats it with gusto declaring it to be the best sandwich ever, echoing his earlier comment about greasy diner food and wanting to eat something he hadn't had to microwave in a mini-mart ("Simon Said," 2.5). Despite his earlier dismissal of the well-manicured lawn, Dean even finds a true moment of peace in the episode when he mows the grass outside the family home.

But this moment of serenity is short-lived as Sam arrives and Dean realizes that to accept this happiness he must sacrifice his relationship with his brother. This prefigures the end of season 5, when Dean finds emotional comfort with a woman within the boundary established by the white picket fence, but at the expense of the alternative family relationship he shares with Sam. Sam and Dean are defined throughout the series by their brotherhood, despite being drawn to alternatives (the nurturing mother in the case of Dean, the absence of family in the case of Sam), so while the nurturing mother and white picket fence may represented normality — a normality that is increasingly attractive to Dean — it equally becomes a destructive force exerting pressure upon the alternative family unit that is the reason for every action he takes.

The figure of the nurturing woman for Sam and especially Dean may therefore be linked to the white picket fence, to home, and to stability, but they are an illusion. The home Dean finds at the end of season 5 is one to which he has retreated in sorrow, and the nurturing woman not the result of true love but a desperate attempt to find something to hold onto in the absence of his alternative family. After all, while Mary may represent the nurturing mother in the minds of the Winchesters, it is she who precipitates their downfall. Just as the horrors of Vietnam exposed the lie at the heart of the suburban family dream, the horrors which Sam and Dean face every day expose the lie at the heart of the very origins of the Winchester family.

Sam and Dean are aware they are different. Dean describes them as "the poster boys for the unnatural order," while Sam tells him, "I'm infected with demon blood. You've been to Hell. Look, I know you want to think of yourself as Joe the Plumber, Dean, but you're not" ("Death Takes a Holiday," 4.15). But while they associate their difference with Hell and demons, it is in fact the lie at the heart of the illusion of family that sets Dean and Sam apart from normality. Even the bond of brotherhood that identifies them is an illusion; they are chosen by God to be the vessels of Michael and Lucifer, destined to turn on one another. This illusion of family pushes them into an unnatural world — unnatural because it is replete with demons, monsters, and wendigos, but also unnatural because it is based on a desire to be the family they never had any chance of being, to live a life they never had any chance of living. Like the films of the 1970s, the horror in *Supernatural* comes from that which is repressed by the Winchester family. All that is repressed to keep the façade of a normal family throughout the 1970s, the destiny that is already in play, is unleashed in John when Mary dies, driving himself and the boys down a road to literal damnation. Any chance of a normal life comes to an end for the Winchesters in 1973, and so the codification of John, Dean, and Sam as 1970s men links them not only to the last moment of free will and happiness the family was allowed, but also very concretely to the family-led American Nightmare described by Robin Wood.

Part 3

"Jerk . . . bitch"

Representations of Gender and Sexuality

The Road to Lordsburg
Rural Masculinity in *Supernatural*
Lorrie Palmer

> Because, you know, basically we're shooting a Western
> . . . a modern-day Western with monsters.
> *Eric Kripke (*Supernatural *creator)*[1]

In the 1939 John Ford Western *Stagecoach*, the Ringo Kid (John Wayne) pursues the men who murdered his family. His journey takes him across a hostile, open landscape, and when he finds the Plummer brothers in the frontier town of Lordsburg, he loads his gun with the three bullets he has left, one for each of them. The origin tale embedded in *Supernatural* echoes this trajectory as the Winchester brothers go on the road in pursuit of the yellow-eyed demon that killed their mother and, along the way, find a mystical Colt revolver, with a small (and finite) number of bullets, that is the only thing capable of killing it. In "Salvation" (1.21), the younger Winchester brother, Sam, fires the gun at yellow-eyed Azazel in the nursery of a baby girl named Rosie before the demon can carry out his plans for the child, leaving them with only three bullets. Sam's intended target dissolves into black smoke before it can be killed by the Colt, but it has further diminished their supply of ammunition.

The legend of the Colt is recounted to his sons by John Winchester, who tells them Samuel Colt made a unique gun in 1835. "He made it for a hunter, a man like us, only on horseback. The story goes, he made 13 bullets" ("Dead Man's Blood," 1.20). When John goes missing after tracking Azazel across the dangerous rural terrain that characterizes the series, his two sons pick up the mantle of demon hunting as they search for their father and, eventually, join him to destroy the demon. Carrying them on their quest is the vehicle that John left with Dean, his coal-black 1967 Chevy Impala.

The Colt and the Impala forge a narrative and visual continuity between *Supernatural* and two distinctive, yet interconnected, film genres: the Western and the road movie. The transformation of this dual cinematic lineage into long-running serial television has enabled the show's creator, Eric Kripke, to build a formidable mythology of angels and demons and of the hunters for whom these entities are both allies and enemies in a shifting, evolving arc. The deliberate evocation of these two key generic influences (in addition to the show's more obvious horror imagery) is discernible in, for example, the auditory cues that introduce the series DVDs. The metallic crack of rifles being cocked, the sudden boom of gunshots, and the rumbling growl of the Impala's revving engine are prominent in the sound mix of the teaser clips featured on the main menus. Kripke further contextualizes the show's masculinist framework by marking his male protagonists (who hail from Lawrence, Kansas) as distinctly Midwestern, rural, and working-class through environment, costuming, and back story. The muted brown/gray color palette of the series reflects an exterior aesthetic of mud, wood, nighttime skies, and winter grasses. The rugged settings and the violence required for the Winchesters to stay alive in the battle between good and evil (and their frequently blurred boundaries) situate them within a particular mode of masculinity.

In *Gunfighter Nation*, cultural historian Richard Slotkin discusses the myth of the American frontier and the ways in which the "hunter-hero" traverses the wilderness outside the corrupt commercial centers and embodies a "regression to the primitive" (34). As beings that exist outside the vision of those whom Sam and Dean call "civilians," the demonic Others that threaten humankind within the context of the show are simultaneously the primitives the Winchesters must battle and the living reflections of dark powers that lie within themselves, powers the brothers will often be required to access. In order to be the Western gunslingers they have to be (and that the iconography of the show suggests), they must walk in two worlds. Multiple regressions from their initially idealistic quest, geared toward "helping people, hunting things" ("Pilot," 1.1), appear throughout the series. Azazel crept into Sam's nursery when he was six months old in order to deposit his demon blood into the boy's mouth, a scene he exhibits in mystical playback for the adult Sam ("All Hell Breaks Loose, Part 1," 2.21). Sam is later revealed to be addicted to demon blood, "essentially becoming a vampire" (Chan), because of the powerful abilities it enhances in him. Likewise, Dean confesses to Sam that he tortured souls during his four months in Hell,[2] becoming an expert at inflicting pain and eventually growing to enjoy it. He picks up the blade again to torture Alastair at the behest of the angels ("On the Head of a Pin," 4.16).

Slotkin characterizes the archetypal Western figure as "The Man Who Knows Indians" (Lichtenfeld 10), whose "experiences, sympathies, and even allegiances fall on both sides" of the frontier between "savagery and civilization" (Slotkin 14). One of the most notable examples of this dark frontiersman is the character of Ethan Edwards (John Wayne) in *The Searchers* (1956), who pursues bloody vengeance, tinged with psycho-sexual fears of miscegenation, against Native American Chief Scar (Henry Brandon), his double in the narrative. Both men are adept at reading the cultural and symbolic signs of the other. Their hunter–hunted (as well as hero–villain) relationship is deeply intersected by common characteristics and is repeatedly complicated by Ethan's moral ambiguity. Sam and Dean tread equally uncertain terrain, often mirroring their dangerous prey, notably through the trope of blood (whether through human–demon hybridity, physical violence, or in connection with the appetites of vampires and demons).

The most vivid intersections of blood and physicality are linked in *Supernatural* to the brothers' anxieties over the potentially open, borderless territory between themselves and the Others they pursue. "In My Time of Dying" (2.1) finds Dean refusing to go with the reaper Tessa, who tells him he can choose to stay but that he will wander alone and invisible, maybe even becoming violent, until he is driven mad: "How do you think angry spirits are born?" She advises him that he will be just like the creatures he hunts. Dean later receives a similar warning from Ruby, as she reveals that all demons start out as people like him whose humanity Hell has burned away ("Malleus Maleficarum," 3.9). In "Metamorphosis" (4.4), Dean watches unseen as Sam psychically exorcises a demon from its human host, with Ruby standing nearby, and later confronts his brother with two consecutive right-crosses to the jaw, demanding, "Do you know how far off the reservation you've gone? How far from normal, from human?" Sam insists that he is saving people with these demon-enhanced abilities and promises not to let it go too far, but is stunned into silence when Dean delivers the bruising *coup de grâce*: "If I didn't know you, I would want to hunt you."

The dialogue spoken by Jensen Ackles (Dean) in this scene evokes the Western through its delineation of consigned boundaries, specifically the forced containment inflicted on indigenous Americans during westward expansion in the latter half of the 19th century. Further, it hints at the uncontainable. The racial overtones implicit in this reference point are reflected in *Supernatural* through its symbiotic relationships between humans and demons. In the final scene of "The Kids Are Alright" (3.2), Ruby exposes herself as a demon to Sam for the first time. When her eyes turn black, he scrambles for a weapon, to which she retorts, "Don't be such a racist," and in "Malleus Maleficarum," she complains to Dean, "You Winchesters can be pretty bigoted." When bodies are permeable, boundaries are revealed to be as fluid as blood itself.

Both Sam and Dean, like Ethan Edwards, have deep fears about their own sense of embodied borders and who they might be without them. Recurrent loss of control haunts the Winchester brothers in that "neither Sam nor Dean has an exclusive claim on his own body — or his own fate" (Chan), not the least because the Archangels Michael and Lucifer wish to conduct their epic shootout by inhabiting the brothers' bodies ("Sympathy for the Devil," 5.1). Shari Roberts cites Jane Tompkins' work on the Western, noting that this genre is about "men's fear of losing their mastery, and hence their identity" (47). Sam is afraid of the side of his nature that was set in motion by Azazel's scheme to raise an army of human-demon psychics to help him open the Devil's Gate ("All Hell Breaks Loose, Part 1") while simultaneously being inexorably attracted to it, giving over his body to sexual appetites aroused and the insatiable thirst for demon blood Ruby awakens in him. Sam needs something positive to come from the power that his internal darkness brings him, so he channels it into saving lives. Without this, he fears he is nothing but "a whole new level of freak" ("Metamorphosis").

Likewise Dean, for all his swagger, endures another kind of fear. After John's whispered warning to him about Sam's dangerous, hidden self ("In My Time of Dying"), Dean has more to worry about than Sam's stated intention to return to Stanford University once they achieve their goals on the road. He is instructed by John to watch his brother for signs of demonic possession and be prepared to treat him like any other monster by killing him. As Catherine Tosenberger's examination of the narrative traditions in *Supernatural* points out, Dean's admonishment is echoed in "the folklore that circulates in the hunting community about Sam's power" which "forcibly aligns the Winchesters with the folkloric entities they hunt, in opposition to the hunters." Issues of identity and loss of it are central to the series. Like his father, Dean has no identity beyond that of hunter, both of them lacking the more mainstream options that come naturally to Sam. Dean is inculcated in the military chain-of-command structure by John Winchester, a former U.S. Marine. Clear-cut parameters and borders, of hunting strategies and a mission against a foe that is unambiguously Other, give both men an identity and a sense of self. John's former role as husband and father is subsumed by his relentless momentum as a hunter, a searcher.

The journey that results, first for John Winchester and later for Sam and Dean, is represented by the road that takes them deep into the rural wilderness, the dominant thematic setting for the series. Even *Supernatural*'s title graphics foreground this connection — the show's recurring recap feature often reads "The Road So Far" as it cuts together a montage of relevant previous scenes. Shari Roberts describes the generic transformation of the Western frontier into that of the road movie, "characterized by an absence of civilization, law, and domesticity, marked instead by primitivism" (52), providing a link between the particular frontier masculinity sketched out by Slotkin and the Winchesters' quest. Ethan Edwards' journey in *The Searchers* is catalyzed by the murder and sexual violence inflicted by a Comanche tribe upon his brother's family and by their kidnapping of his young niece, Debbie (Natalie Wood). This enactment of the captivity narrative is emblematic of the Western and merges with "the road hero, whose journey is often motivated by death" (Roberts 55).

Women (either real or symbolic) frequently serve as a conduit between masculine combatants in a zone outside traditional law and order. "As the Western condensed further into what we now refer to as the genre of the road film," Roberts observes, it became "frontier masculinity" (45) that linked the two genres together. This masculine space is one devoid of both effective institutional justice and domesticity. It is to "male fantasies of control and natural justice" (Roberts 54) that the plotlines of *Supernatural* gravitate. When Mary Winchester and Sam's girlfriend Jess are killed, the Winchester men enter a purely undomesticated, masculine, rural space — of dark forests and plains, isolated homesteads, and rustic back roads — to avenge their deaths. Bobby Singer, another hunter who joins forces with the brothers after John serves up his own soul to Azazel to save Dean ("In My Time of Dying"), also lost the woman in his life (his wife, Karen) to demonic possession ("Dead Men Don't Wear Plaid," 5.15). He now lives a marginalized existence, surrounded by the detritus of civilization, a junkyard of abandoned vehicles that literalizes the show's narrative concerns with the road.

While female antagonists abound,[3] it is in keeping with this determinedly masculine space that there are very few storylines that feature women as allies to the Winchesters. (For more on *Supernatural* women, see Calvert's essay in this book, pp. 90–104.) In "Abandon All Hope . . ." (5.10), as she cradles her fatally wounded daughter, Jo, Ellen Harvelle detonates a hardware store rigged with explosives in order to kill a pack of hellhounds, buying time for Sam and Dean to get away. The psychic Pamela Barnes is first blinded and then killed ("Lazarus Rising," 4.1; "Death Takes a Holiday," 4.15) in the course of helping the Winchesters, while the British hunter Tamara appears in only one episode ("The Magnificent Seven," 3.1) and is never seen again.

The absence or violent elimination of the ("good") feminine is reflective of the lost domesticity that traditionally informed the narratives of early American television series such as *Bonanza* (an all-male family in the Old West) and *The Fugitive* (Dr. Kimble's journey to find the one-armed man who murdered his wife). *Supernatural* goes where these early series could not in terms of physicality and consequences. Further, in 1960, a men-on-the-road series called *Route 66* emerged into a television landscape dominated by domestic family sitcoms (*The Andy Griffith Show, The Lucy Show, Leave It to Beaver, Bewitched*). It featured two young men, one educated and thoughtful, one streetwise and tough, who drive a Chevy Corvette along the fabled route through the American heartland, helping people along the way. Mark Alvey describes the "chivalric tradition" of the show's duo, with their life on the road serving a "paladin function" (153). The Winchesters' journey is likewise marked by an excessively literal "have gun will travel" sensibility — and the graphic blood-letting that results.

In the *Route 66* pilot episode, "Black November," Tod Stiles (Martin Milner), whose deceased father left him the Corvette, travels with his childhood friend, Buz Murdock (George Maharis), across a barren, rural setting that leads them to a broken steering column on a muddy back road. They must persuade a ferryman to carry them across a forbidding river to a town called Garth that seems literally possessed by a man called Garth, whose past is fetid with buried secrets, a haunted grave, and violent obsession. The borders of the town are closed to outsiders, setting up a confrontation with those deemed Other by the fearful locals. Instead, Tod and Buz motivate a chain of events that results in the exorcism of the town's psychological demons.

Such motifs would not be out of place in *Supernatural*. After all, an episode entitled "Route 666" aired during Season 1 (1.13), which is later referenced in "The Real Ghostbusters" (5.9) when coffee mugs with the real-life highway logo changed to read "Route 666" are on sale at the first-ever *Supernatural* conference; and a wall of Route 66 postcards appears in a Flagstaff motel room ("Dark Side of the Moon," 5.16). In addition, the original title proposed for *Route 66* was *The Searchers*. These interconnections tie the masculinity of the rural landscape to the vehicle that propels the protagonists through and within it.

The Winchesters' Impala, according to Melissa N. Bruce, serves a linking function between the genres of melodrama and horror and, further, provides the setting for many of the brothers' most revealing conversations. The presence of the car, she notes, makes those moments of vulnerability and raw emotion acceptably masculine. Bruce points out that the Impala is simultaneously a "muscle car" and an "arsenal" with its weapons cache in the trunk and, crucially, that it serves as Sam and Dean's "domestic space," thus associating it and them with the "traditionally feminine." I would suggest, on the other hand, that the car actually unmoors them from real domesticity (and from the feminine) through the alternative genre traditions of the Western and the road movie, both of which depict largely homosocial environments populated by male characters. The series' endless (and imaginatively un-pretty) motel rooms creates a visual reminder of the absence of any kind of "normal" family life for the Winchesters. (See Jowett's essay, pp. 33–46) The kitchen, usually a site of communal bonding, home-cooked meals, and sense-memory, is portrayed in *Supernatural* as an empty space. The black kitchen walls in "Death Takes a Holiday" overlook a single coffee maker where Dean pours himself a cup (as he does in an Iowa motel in "Salvation," 1.21); likewise, another hunter, Travis, pours coffee as he confers with the brothers in "Metamorphosis," surrounded by mounted antler heads, stuffed fish, and a mural of an outdoor wildlife scene. A similar mural adorns the motel room of "A Very Supernatural Christmas" (3.8), in which the Winchesters have what they believe will be their last Christmas together before the hellhounds come for Dean. The camera frames the wilderness painting (a rural barn, dark trees, winter wheat) with Sam and Dean, then pulls back through the window to reveal a light snow falling on the hood of the Impala, creating a symbolic integration between the background and foreground of this unbroken shot. Like the Impala, these settings defer real domesticity in favor of unsettledness, mobility, and the predominant absence of women.

This gendered framework simultaneously evokes the Western and the road movie. It also fuels the scholar (and fan) writing about *Supernatural*. Monica Flegel and Jenny Roth, in "Annihilating Love and Heterosexuality Without Women," examine slash fiction and how it reflects the "dangers inherent in the intense love Sam and Dean share." In "Mystery Spot" (3.11), the Trickster reminds Sam, "Dean's your weakness. Bad guys know it, too," and, similarly, Flegel and Roth cite "No Rest for the Wicked" (3.16) in which Dean "says to Sam, 'You're my weak spot. And I'm yours'" and go on to point out the instability of such an "annihilating relationship."

Women in traditional gender roles are rare in *Supernatural* in order to situate domesticity as alien — further emphasized by numerous episodes in which new suburban developments prove deadly ("Bugs," 1.8; "The Kids Are Alright"), or the family itself is a mere illusion ("What Is and What Should Never Be," 2.20). Eric Kripke acknowledged that the show does seem to have a habit of killing off its women and understands "why people keep reading a homosexual vibe when it's all just men on the show" ("Commentary for 'What Is and What

Should Never Be,' 2.20"). Self-reflexivity, in terms of gay subtext, is often playfully overt.

In the *Groundhog Day* episode, "Mystery Spot," the brothers stay in a motel room resplendent with a pink flamingo motif, and Dean teases his brother, "Oh, Sammy, I get all tingly when you take control like that." Dean also remarks, in another episode ("Wishful Thinking," 4.8), that he would rather forego "couples therapy" when Sam presses him to share his nightmares/memories of Hell. In "The Real Ghostbusters," Sam and Dean wince when it is announced that the conference will include a talk on "the homoerotic subtext of *Supernatural*," clearly referencing awareness on the part of the series' writers of both the onscreen chemistry between Ackles and Padalecki as well as the real-world production of "Wincest" fan fiction (first paralleled diegetically in "The Monster at the End of This Book," 4.18). Tellingly, Barnes and Damian, the Sam-and-Dean wannabes who assist the real Winchesters at the *Supernatural* conference, identify themselves as a couple at the end of the episode ("The Real Ghostbusters").

The Howard Hawks Western, *Red River* (1948), features a much-discussed scene that clearly plays with subtextual homoeroticism. Matt Garth (Montgomery Clift, a closeted gay actor) and Cherry Valance (John Ireland) each whips out his pistol for the mutual admiration of the other ("That's a good-looking gun. Can I see it?") and then proceed to fire together at a tin can to see how long they can keep it up in the air. As Stephen Hunter writes, "Ideas — particularly forbidden ones among heterosexuals, like male beauty and grace, male love, male bonding, and really tight blue jeans — creep in and haunt the edges of the most mundane and straightforward macho tales about horseback he-men. Gay subtexts in westerns have been nothing special and everything ordinary for decades." It has been *journeys away* that have structured the narratives of the Western and the road movie. Freud noted that dissatisfaction with home and family often motivates the traveler, and, as Robert Lang adds, the road movie allows a queer subject to function "along lines of desire, not moving toward marriage and the containment of sexuality" (345) but "leaving the spaces of home and family" (344).

Supernatural renders the traditional family home as dangerous — thematically established in the first episode — and replaces its domesticity with a muscular Chevy Impala moving through a rural landscape that is anything but pastoral. The masculinity enacted by Sam and Dean Winchester, by virtue of the narrative's location within a monstrous American heartland, encompasses difference in its identity politics. The brothers, as part of the demon/hunter/angel trifecta that pulses beneath the sightline of most of the "civilians" in the *Supernatural*verse, live a secret life. The few people who know what they really do are often appalled by the loneliness and danger of such an existence. Despite their transgressive appeal, the outlaws of Westerns and road movies provoke the same response. The show's rural setting, fused to the intra- and extra-diegetic undercurrents of homoeroticism between Sam and Dean, is an emblematic reflection of the Western and road genres' motif of journeys into an open wilderness.

In contrast, numerous literary and pop culture narratives have situated monsters (and those who hunt them) within cities, the symbolic location frequently representing cultural fears of modernity and technology, while small towns and countryside settings were reserved as idyllic sites of rebirth. The literary critic Northrop Frye attributes "perspective and renewal" to what he calls the "green world" (Cavell 49). In the contemporaneous, 19th century events of *Dr. Jekyll and Mr. Hyde* and the gruesome, real-life Jack the Ripper murders, as well as the atomic age metaphor of Godzilla rampaging across Tokyo and in dystopian imagery from Gotham City to *Blade Runner*, the metropolis has been the central site for dark mayhem. The severing of this urban tradition marks the Winchesters' story as unique. In addition to its frontier lineage and the homosociality that goes with it, the masculine rural setting in *Supernatural* represents a noticeable iconographic departure from other television incarnations.

The urban milieu of the demon-hunting team in the Joss Whedon series *Angel*, for example, presents a nighttime city skyline jagged with lights and glass and steel. Its male characters (Angel, Wesley Wyndam-Pryce, and Charles Gunn) are depicted as notably metropolitan in attitude and costuming and in their skilled navigation through Los Angeles (including its hidden subterranean recesses). Instead of the worn flannel shirts, tattered jackets, greasy caps, work boots, and rough denim of *Supernatural*, the men of *Angel* sport tailored suits, expensive black leather, and urban street attire. *Angel* is, likewise, a hybrid, mixing the superhero genre with film noir, both of which have traditionally relied on the city to analogize their heroes, from Batman to Sam Spade. In *More Than Night*, James Naremore describes the "modernist ideology involving male subjectivity and urban darkness" (171) as part of the "cityscapes" and "skyline" aesthetic that situates them within the noir genre. Further, in "Los Angelus: The City of Angel," Benjamin Jacob synthesizes this approach with serial television through his exploration of the vampire "Angel as the noir detective hero" who moves through a "Los Angeles [that is] steeped in literal and metaphorical darkness" (80). Alongside this hunter who can only come out at night, "the city as a place of threat and alienation" aligns with Angel's ontological monstrosity so that his "lifespan corresponds to that of the modern metropolis" (83).

On the other hand, *Supernatural*'s vampire mythology begins in "Dead Man's Blood" (1.20) in a rural setting that emphasizes the threat of the wilderness as a lawless frontier where, significantly, we first hear the legend of the Colt from John Winchester. A band of vampires, led by the outlaw Luther, battles all three Winchesters for possession of the gun. Western tropes abound in this episode as multiple scenes unfold in the interconnected generic settings of a rural country barn, the dark woods, and a deserted blacktop road with the cars and trucks of the opposing forces facing each other. Luther hangs the holstered Colt from his bedpost; he shows up for a parley in the middle of the road wearing it strapped, gunfighter-style, around his right thigh; the Winchesters shoot an arrow through the chest of one of the vampires; and a female vamp is filmed from a low camera that shows only her cowboy boots. The series, through juxtapositions like these, foregrounds the Western and the road movie as formal influences on its mise-en-scène as well as its narrative strategies.

By walking in two worlds, by being the Men Who Know Demons (both external and internal), Sam and Dean inhabit the rough and shifting border between civilization and the wilderness. In season 5 of *Supernatural*, they learn of a way to imprison Lucifer by gathering together the rings of the Four Horsemen of the Apocalypse ("Hammer of the Gods," 5.19) after which they go on the road, back to their prairie roots in Kansas ("Swan Song," 5.22). Once there, it is the Impala that keeps the brothers connected amidst the ensuing struggle between Lucifer and Michael, stopping Sam (as Lucifer's vessel) from killing Dean when he sees the toy soldier he left in its backseat ashtray. This small, fleeting image conjures manhood as a rite of passage in battle, an appropriate one within the world of *Supernatural*. The "regression to the primitive" (Slotkin 34) enacted in the mythic spaces of the Western hero's journey endows him with the precise ammunition he needs to prevail, whether it is three bullets in a town called Lordsburg or a split-second of memory at the end of a long road in Stull Cemetery. The Winchesters (Sam, Dean, and their doomed father, John), as well as their later father-figure, Bobby, enact a ragged, unrefined masculinity that plays out its frontier justice on the rural middle ground between the demons of Hell and the angels of the Lord.

Angels, Demons, and Damsels in Distress
The Representation
of Women in *Supernatural*
Bronwen Calvert

The emphasis in *Supernatural* would seem to be, as Lorrie Palmer shows in the previous essay, firmly centered on the masculine world of the Winchester brothers and their demon-hunting adventures, yet this world is frequently and regularly interrupted by a female presence. Over the first five seasons, the series included a vast range of female characters, from mothers and mother-figures, through many damsels in distress, to a range of dangerous supernatural females. Female characters have been used to motivate and drive the plot of this show from its pilot, where the parallel deaths of Mary Winchester and Sam's fiancée Jessica propel both brothers into the demon-hunting life.

The series' creator and its writers are aware of the difficulties of introducing female characters ("A Closer Look"; Kripke Commentary), but when female characters do appear, critics and fans are quick to analyze their problematic representation. A further difficulty is that many fans appear invested in the story arcs primarily as they affect the characters of Sam and Dean, seem less interested in peripheral characters, and indeed may reject potential recurring female characters. Several of these women have been written out of the narrative following poor fan reaction (Kripke, theinsider.com).[1] At first glance it seems that *Supernatural*'s depiction of female characters simply underlines the troubled masculinity of the series as a whole, where the focus remains upon the masculine world of the demon hunter, and the possibility of any "happy ending" — often imagined as an idealized heterosexual pairing — must be constantly deferred or denied so that the brothers' quest, and thus the series, can continue. However, examination of some key female characters reveals complexities at work in the narrative. There are possibilities for a more sympathetic reading of female presence when it is tied to the ongoing character development of the two brothers.

Supernatural presents some narrative difficulties in terms of its combination of genres — what Catherine Johnson calls "generic hybridity"(146; see also Parks 122–123). Aspects of horror, action, and the road movie combine to create a shifting and changeable narrative, with some problematic elements for secondary characters. Since the road movie "functions [. . .] narratively, in terms of an open-ended, rambling plot structure; thematically, in terms of frustrated, often desperate characters lighting out for something better" (Laderman 2), it works very well to underpin a series narrative. However, the focus is on characters on the move, which, as writer Ben Edlund recognizes, limits the numbers: "Since they're on a road trip there are very few regular characters. . . . " ("A Closer Look: *Supernatural*: 'Bad Day at Black Rock' with writer Ben Edlund"). The horror element of the show requires individuals in peril,[2] with many random bodies to act as fodder for monsters. Here we do find female characters, but these are more usually presented as "damsels in distress" in need of rescue, and this is how Sam and Dean frequently react to them. The fantasy narrative does allow more opportunities for strong female characters. There are certainly many recent examples in fantasy television of "positive and powerful" women (Heinecken 26); for example, *Buffy the Vampire Slayer*, *Dark Angel*, *Firefly*, and *Alias*. However, "[t]he female hero takes up space" (Heinecken 21), and in *this* narrative a strong female character is often perceived as taking up *too much* space. Mary Borsellino is right to say that when it comes to *Supernatural,* "There are strong female characters in a number of the [first season] episodes [. . .] but they are never the ones to solve the mystery, kill the monster, or help the helpless" (108), but this has more to do with the fact that *Supernatural* already has its heroes. Sam and Dean are the focus of the narrative, and so, logically, they have to do the saving, solving, and helping. In short, this series is never about its occasional female characters; it is about its two leads. In general then, *Supernatural*'s genre hybridity works to make the introduction of *any* secondary character difficult, and the genres within its mix are also problematic for female characters. However, I do not believe that means female characters are necessarily relegated to "damsel in distress" or villain. Instead, the complex representation of women in *Supernatural* is bound up with the series' representation of Sam and Dean, their struggles with ideas of masculinity, and the ethical and moral questions they negotiate.

Angels in the House, Damsels in Distress

The presentations of both Mary Winchester and Sam's fiancée, Jessica, ("Pilot," 1.1) owe much to the notion of the "Angel in the House," a Victorian figuration of the perfect wife and mother[3] that identifies both characters with domestic activities and the home. Dean's memories focus on Mary's "angelic" mothering: she made him "tomato-rice soup" when he was ill, sang "Hey, Jude" as a lullaby, and told him "angels were watching over [him]" ("The Song Remains the Same," 5.13).[4] Similarly, Jessica's character is an uncomplicated, nice, and supportive girlfriend who encourages Sam ("I'm proud of you — you're gonna get that full ride [a scholarship to law school]") and leaves home-made chocolate-chip cookies out for him. Both women are also situated *in* domestic space (although this may also demonstrate that the brothers idealize "the normal"): Dean's memories of Mary and the short section at the opening of the pilot episode show Mary in the Winchester house putting baby Sam to bed; Jessica's brief appearances are inside the apartment she shares with Sam, and she is not permitted to go with Sam when Dean arrives to fetch him ("Pilot"). The narrative plays on the figure of the angel-woman[5] in the pilot episode as first Mary's death, and then Jessica's, is shown to be the motivating forces behind the Winchester brothers' hunting careers. Since the two women are murdered by the same demon, the two deaths are visualized in near-identical bookends at the start and finish of the episode. Both women are seen shot from below (taking the viewpoint of husband and fiancé), pinned to a bedroom ceiling at an awkward angle, with a bloody gash across their stomachs. As John (in the first scene) and Sam (in the last) look up in horror, the ceiling above them bursts into flames that consume first the women's bodies and then the building around them. Some particular aspects of these scenes are worth noting in detail. The attacks take place at night, so it is not surprising that both women are in nightwear; however, both are wearing white nightgowns (even though earlier in the episode Jessica is not wearing a nightdress to bed but shorts and a Smurfs t-shirt). The image of the blonde woman in white plays on the association of white (and of paleness and blondeness) with purity and goodness, and this fits with the presentation of these two women earlier in the episode. In contrast to the pure white of their clothing, their bodies are rendered bloody and horrific; indeed, their blood dripping from the ceiling alerts John and Sam. Since Azazel, the "yellow-eyed demon" who attacks them, has the power to cause a conflagration severe enough to engulf entire houses or apartment buildings, the gash across their stomachs appears as an excessive wound. It is nevertheless an image connecting the female body with blood, pain, and (since the wound is across the stomach) childbirth. In short, these deaths seem coded female. (We see the same imagery repeated in "Salvation," 1.21, though this time, Sam and Dean succeed in saving the mother, and her "death" turns out to be one of Sam's visions.)

Mary's and Jessica's deaths lead the brothers, and thus viewers of the series, to a succession of mysterious events that frequently feature "damsels in distress" who need rescue. Such characters feature especially strongly in Season 1: for example, Andrea in "Dead in the Water"

(1.3), Charlie in "Bloody Mary" (1.5), Lori Sorenson in "Hook Man" (1.7), and Emily in "Scarecrow" (1.11). For the most part, the viewer encounters quite straightforward depictions of this character trope, the youthful, often blonde, woman in peril. As they are threatened by supernatural events, a strong connection is established with the classic horror narrative, in which young, attractive characters are often victims; character names like "Charlie" and "Lori" suggest Carol Clover's "Final Girl," the survivor of the horror film with the masculine name (260; Borsellino 112). The damsel in distress is a trope that has been deliberately challenged in other recent television drama, especially *Buffy the Vampire Slayer* (with Buffy as the blonde "damsel" who does kill the monster, see Crosby 161), and *Supernatural*'s return to it underlines this series' context and underlying mythology. In this show, what is important is the brothers' involvement with "damsels" and their ability to help and rescue them. In the early stages of season 1, this is frequently contrasted with their inability to rescue either Mary or Jessica.

The "damsel" trope is itself challenged as the series progresses. This can be seen in two episodes, "Faith" (1.12) and "Roadkill" (2.16). In each episode, the brothers encounter a young blonde woman while hunting a demon.[6] In each case, their ability to help these damsels is compromised. In "Faith" the damsel figure Layla is dying from a brain tumor and hoping to be cured by faith healer Roy Le Grange, whose cures are made possible by the enforced participation of a reaper (a being that guides dead souls). The brothers cannot save Layla from dying, nor can they allow Roy to heal her because to do so will mean that an innocent person will have to die. I note that Layla and Dean are placed in opposition: at the start of the episode, Dean is healed, while Layla remains terminally ill; Layla's potential healing is always compromised because Dean becomes the reaper's prey, and the narrative demands that he survive.

In "Roadkill," the damsel figure Molly is similarly positioned. The brothers work together with Molly to solve the mystery of Jonah Greeley, whose ghost haunts a stretch of highway where Molly has crashed her car. What is withheld from the viewer until the closing moments of the episode is the fact that they also know that Molly is a ghost, and that she died in the first crash that also killed Greeley. Again, conventional rescue is impossible: they cannot bring Molly back to life; instead, they work to bring Molly to a realization of her own death and existence as a ghost and enable her to "move on." The ending of this episode is uncertain, and neither brother can say whether they have done good in persuading Molly; they are not even sure she is in "a better place." In both "Faith" and "Roadkill" the "damsel" figures create uncertainty and doubt for the brothers. Sam and Dean question aspects of their work "saving people, hunting things," especially whether their actions are always "good" and helpful to people.

The recurring figure of the damsel in distress also begins to both blur the line between good and evil and reveal important aspects of the brothers' moral and ethical development. In the season 2 episodes "Bloodlust" (2.3) and "Heart" (2.17), the damsel figures are also classic horror-movie "monsters," a vampire and a werewolf respectively. "Good" vampires and werewolves are a recurring trope in recent popular fiction; we find both good vampire and good werewolf characters in the *Twilight* series, in *Buffy* and *Angel*, and in *Being Human*. However, vampires and werewolves in *Supernatural* are more frequently represented as monsters that must be killed. "Bloodlust" and "Heart" complicate this, as they raise questions about the nature of evil and the ethics of "hunting" (i.e., killing), while they present other kinds of "monstrous" behavior.

In "Bloodlust" the opposition of good and evil is disturbed in two ways. First, the brothers encounter another hunter, Gordon Walker, whose aims and methods they come to question. Second, while the "monsters" in this episode are vampires, this particular group has made a vow not to feed on humans. The disruption of good and evil is established at the opening of the episode, though this is not apparent on a first viewing. The teaser shows a frightened girl running through a dark, wooded area in moonlight. Her panicky looks and breathing are emphasized and her terrified face highlighted in close-up, while her pursuer is only seen from the knees down. At the culmination of the teaser, the pursuer catches up with the girl, produces a scythe, and (distanced, in long-shot) cuts off her head. This grisly and graphically horror-oriented opening is in marked contrast to other horror-inflected episodes in which far more is left to the viewer's imagination and killings occur off-screen (for example, "Hook Man" or "Scarecrow").

Although the frightened girl turns out to be a vampire and the pursuer a hunter just like Sam and Dean, nevertheless, this teaser does help to establish viewer sympathy with the girl, and the rest of this episode builds on that sympathetic foundation. The crux of the episode is whether the brothers will side with the vampire Lenore and her group (the monsters), or with Gordon (the hunters). As in the teaser, the identification of "good" and "evil" characters is complicated throughout: Gordon is apparently an ally and a good hunter, but when Sam mentions his name to Ellen Harvelle she warns him to stay away from Gordon; Sam is captured by Lenore's group of vampires but returned "without a scratch."[7] The crisis of the episode finds Gordon torturing Lenore, who is repositioned as a damsel in distress, helpless and unable to save herself. The torture scene certainly makes uncomfortable viewing; however, there appears to be more to it than the overtones of race and gender that Julia M. Wright detects (para 26).This whole episode highlights differences between the brothers, and similarities between Dean and Gordon. At first Dean matches Gordon's attitude and happily exchanges hunting tales, while Sam hangs back. In the torture room the differences between the brothers are emphasized. Sam, who believes and supports Lenore, maintains his caring persona when he does not fight, but carries Lenore outside. Dean, in contrast, fights physically and verbally with Gordon. And while Dean (violently) rejects Gordon as a "sadistic bastard," he also recognizes the same tendency in himself, saying that when he killed one of the vampires with a power saw "I didn't think — I even enjoyed it." In addition, the shift in Dean's attitude has as much to do with his complex relationship with his brother as it does to his rejection of the torture of a (white) woman, as Wright suggests. Sam, with his demonic attributes, is surely included among the "supernatural" beings that Dean insists they must kill. Indeed, Dean's father has given him the command to kill Sam if he cannot save him from Azazel ("In My Time of Dying," 2.1).

Sam's problematic position in relation to the supernatural resurfaces in "Heart," where once again the brothers attempt to help a damsel in distress. This episode has a complex narrative structure containing several twists. For half of it, the brothers are trying to find and kill a werewolf that threatens a woman, Madison. Midway through the episode, they discover that Madison is a werewolf, and she becomes the object of the hunt. This episode is strongly overlaid with themes of female objectification and threat, "hunting" and "prey": Dean is excited to be hunting a "badass" werewolf; the werewolf suspect is Madison's violent ex-boyfriend Kurt who is "stalking" her; she has been the victim of a mugging; the brothers decide she is in enough danger that one of them should become her bodyguard. However, she is "prey" in another sense: both brothers see her as "the hot chick," and so do her boss and Kurt. Yet Madison is not simply a damsel in distress or a monster in this episode. She is presented from the outset as quick and resourceful, and Sam notes that she is intelligent, with "lots of great books" in her apartment. When Madison tells the story of her mugging (actually a werewolf attack), she portrays it as a turning point that allowed her to "take control" of her life, break up with Kurt, and start anew. She does something similar at the end of the episode, turning the very idea of "being saved" on its head when she asks Sam to kill her: "I don't want to hurt anyone else [. . .] I need you to help me. . . . I'm a monster." This episode makes a direct identification between Sam and supernatural "monsters" in general. Sam himself accuses Dean of being selective in his definition of "monsters": "So *me* you won't kill but *her* you're just gonna blow away?" The focus shifts so that by the climax of the episode we are not watching Madison's death, but the brothers' tearful reaction to it and to the implications of Sam's demonic potential.

Demonic Women

The questions raised in conjunction with human and supernatural damsels in distress can also be applied to the demonic adversaries Meg and Ruby (seasons 1, 5, and 6 and seasons 3 and 4, respectively). The brothers' dealings with demon characters throughout the series are infused with unease and a sense of the uncanny, possibly more so because these demons are not conventionally "monstrous" in appearance, but persuasively imitate gendered human beings. We can see this in the Crossroads Demon who appears in female and male bodies (female in "Crossroad Blues," 2.8, and "All Hell Breaks Loose: Part 2," 2.22; male in "I Know What You Did Last Summer," 4.9, and "The Devil You Know" 5.20). Azazel appears in different male bodies ("In My Time of Dying"; "In the Beginning," 4.3; "Lucifer Rising," 4.22). Meg and Ruby appear as young, attractive women with different bodies over time, and the only outward sign of their demon selves is their occasionally black eyes. The sense that these demons can pass as humans (something that is more difficult for characters like Lenore and Madison) adds to the sense of the uncanny. It also makes for a stronger link with Sam: he is also part-demon, but appears human; his eyes occasionally turn black; and he has special powers and strengths specifically related to his demon aspect.

The brothers' reactions to Meg and Ruby, and especially those characters' shifts from villains to damsels and back again, make for complex and often confusing characters.[8] While Meg is positioned as a villain for much of season 1, her "damsel" aspect becomes more pronounced in "Devil's Trap" (1.22). Her exorcism and death present differences in the way each brother reacts and behaves. Both brothers participate in the exorcism ritual, but each brother takes on a significantly different role; Sam reads out the ritual in Latin, while Dean physically confronts demon-Meg and abuses her verbally while Meg's body is tied to a chair and imprisoned within a devil's trap. The exorcism makes for a grim and disturbing death scene (see Borsellino 108, 117) as the brothers and Bobby use the ritual to torture demon-Meg for information. Differences are played up: neither Bobby nor Sam wants to continue to the end of the ritual, but Dean uses the idea of the damsel in distress, the "innocent girl" that was Meg to persuade the others to continue until the demon has left the body. As with Molly or Madison, the success of their actions does not alter the fact that they have not "rescued" the human Meg, and they cannot prevent her from dying, something her spirit taunts them for in "Are You There, God? It's Me, Dean Winchester" (4.2).

The demon Ruby has an extended presence throughout seasons 3 and 4 and, like Meg, is played by different actors. Ruby's character is presented in such a way as to deceive both characters and viewers.[9] Ruby appears willing to adapt in order to work with the brothers; for instance, she vacates a live body, apparently because Sam orders her to, and possesses a dead "Jane Doe" instead. Throughout seasons 3 and 4, she seems to offer help by warning both brothers of demonic activity that has an impact on them. She also appears to put herself in peril to aid them; for instance, in "Heaven and Hell" (4.10) she is horribly tortured by the demon Alastair because she is following Sam's plan. Ruby is depicted as persuasive and confident, and she displays a combination of both sincerity and evil when her betrayal is revealed ("Lucifer Rising"). While her involvement with Sam and subsequent betrayal reveals the separation between the brothers, both brothers are certainly united at the end of "Lucifer Rising" when they both participate in killing Ruby (which also clears the decks before season 5 begins). Sam is more actively involved than in Meg's death; he holds Ruby while Dean stabs her with the magical knife; there is a strong focus on Ruby's gasps and death throes before her body is flung to the floor, discarded by the brothers as they turn to face the next season's adversary.[10]

Action Heroines?

In contrast to the juxtaposition of Sam with female supernatural beings or "monsters" throughout the series, Dean is paralleled with human women who nevertheless share elements of his character. This can be seen in particular with Jo in season 2 and Bela in season 3. Bela is an amoral foil to Dean in several season 3 episodes; Jacob Clifton calls her "Dean's double" (126), and like Dean she has bargained with her soul and is hunted by hellhounds. Bela is represented in a way that emphasizes her character's independence and amorality. She is shown as clever, crafty, and devious, often using and deceiving the brothers to achieve her own ends; indeed, for fans "Bela's initial prowess as a hunter, matching or overwhelming Dean's own, seemed like betrayal" (Clifton 139). Her opposition to Dean, specifically, often gives rise to exchanges of banter and quick repartee that are reminiscent of classic screwball comedies, and episodes with Bela often introduce comic elements to the plot. For example, in "Bad Day at Black Rock" (3.3) Bela creates disaster for Sam by stealing a magically lucky rabbit's foot; moments of slapstick comedy follow as Sam's luck turns bad. This episode continues its comic overtones with a sequence of twists, in which first Dean and then Bela get the better of one another. Elements of comedy persist in "Red Sky at Morning" (3.6), in which an extended sequence references film noir but with comically reversed gender roles. In this episode, Bela, Sam, and Dean must dress to infiltrate a black-tie event, something Sam takes in his stride but Dean finds acutely uncomfortable. Bela taunts Dean about his reluctance to appear in formal dress with "What are you, a woman?" When Dean does appear he is shot as a femme fatale, descending a staircase: his feet and legs and then his torso and sultry glance are the focus of the camera's look, intercut with images of Bela sighing in appreciation. When she suggests they round off the evening with "angry sex," Dean appears discomfited, yet interested, and takes a full six or seven seconds to retort, "Don't objectify me," underlining, if it were ever in doubt, the shifted gender roles in the scene.[11]

Roles shift back again by the end of season 3, and importantly Dean is once more in control of the situation. He deduces that Bela is hiding from a demon with whom she has made a deal ("Time Is on My Side," 3.15). The moment of revelation is rendered distant, and therefore less cathartic, as the characters do not confront each other face to face, but over the telephone. It is noteworthy that Bela makes no attempt to justify her actions, and while the viewer has two short flashback scenes that efficiently establish Bela's past with a sexually abusive father and so give a believable reason for her actions, neither of the brothers learns about her history. Bela does finish season 3 with a duplication of Dean's own fate in the season finale, but there is a sense that she is really doomed because she has been scheming and duplicitous instead of straightforward and honest: "If you had just come to us sooner and asked for help we probably could have . . . saved you." Read in conjunction with season 4, Bela acts as a cautionary tale to both brothers to be honest with each other and work together, something they spectacularly fail to do.

The character of Jo Harvelle also works as a foil to Dean. The characters have a similar history, share reminiscences about their fathers, and pursue the hunting life. Although Jo was introduced as a potential love interest for Dean (and this can be seen in their banter when they meet in "Everybody Loves a Clown," 2.2) Eric Kripke confirms that the character did not work as conceived: "she was always more of the little sister than what her character was created to be, a love interest" (insider.com).[12] While it is evident that changes were made to her character development in response to negative fan reaction (Kripke, insider.com; Borsellino 115–116), there are still aspects of Jo's character that partially fulfill the role of action heroine. Jo is represented as competent and resourceful. She is able to hold Dean at gunpoint and can punch him in the face hard enough to hurt him ("Everybody Loves a Clown"). In "No Exit" (2.6), Jo joins the brothers to hunt a serial-killer demon. She shows intelligence and determination and proves tenacious enough to overcome her fear and lure the demon into a trap. Although in this episode Jo accuses Dean of misogyny — "You think women can't do the job" — it is clear that his problem is with "amateurs." His opinion of Jo's knife both exposes and overturns this viewpoint. Dean calls the knife a "little pig-stick" and offers to give her a "proper" (the sense is "bigger") one. However, phallic overtones notwithstanding, this knife has meaning and history for Jo; it belonged to her father and has his initials on it and is therefore both a "proper" man's knife and a working knife, and Jo uses it successfully to defend herself.

If we put the Winchesters and the Harvelles into a family context the characters' relationships make more sense. Jo as "sister" to Sam and Dean is understandable:[13] indeed, the question of her parentage hovers in the background once the brothers have met Ellen and learned that "John was like family once" ("Everybody Loves a Clown"). Ellen takes a maternal stance toward the brothers, calls them "boys," and offers them first a place to stay at the Roadhouse and then advice and information in the same way that Bobby does. (Furthermore, Ellen in season 2 reads as a contrast to Mary Winchester, but by season 4 the similarities between these two characters are evident.) Jo's negotiation of independence with Ellen bears similarities to the brothers' with John.

In season 1, Sam and Dean hunt as a team, make their own decisions, and decipher clues together; once John returns, they must strategize and fight on his terms. John's death does give the brothers the opportunity to develop according to their own codes, whether for good or bad. Arguably because of Ellen's overbearing influence, Jo's character never achieves this independent development, and so the deaths of Ellen and Jo at the midpoint of season 5 ("Abandon All Hope . . . ," 5.10) are potentially problematic. These deaths could be read negatively, as a rejection of the action heroine, or more positively, as a vindication of family and sacrifice. While Jo might be seen as moving from action heroine (rushing to defend Dean against invisible hellhounds) to damsel in distress (fatally injured and unable to save herself), she does manage a measure of control and agency as she insists on activating a bomb to kill the hellhounds. Ellen's heroism can likewise be seen as either undercutting Jo's independence (Jo does not live long enough to set off the bomb) or as a validation of the self-sacrificing mother like Mary. However, their collective self-sacrifice is consistent with the way all the Winchesters are constantly ready to (and do) sacrifice their own lives, and in this context it is possible to read Ellen's and Jo's deaths as good, noble, and heroic.

The family dynamic of the Winchesters and the Harvelles foreshadows the storyline of "In the Beginning," which reverses the whole "mythology" of the Winchester family. It is not John, but Mary and her family, the Campbells, who are the hunters. In many ways the introduction of Mary the hunter solves many problems that female characters pose for the series writers. Mary has been a part of the mythology from the pilot episode, so fans do not have to get used to a "new" character. Mary Campbell as hunter creates an action heroine that is safe for both characters and fans, since there is no chance that either brother will ever have a romantic relationship with her (though, characteristically, Dean is allowed to say, "Mom is a babe. . . . I'm so going to Hell, again"). In terms of casting and costume, Amy Gumenick as Mary bears a strong resemblance to Alona Tal as Jo with blonde, curly hair, wearing simple shirts and jeans. Even Mary's attack on Dean in "In the Beginning" is strongly reminiscent of Jo's in "Everybody Loves a Clown," with both presented as capable and intelligent fighters.

Through seasons 4 and 5, the series undeniably dispensed with many major female characters — Ruby, Meg, Jo, Ellen — and the concluding half of season 5 saw a reconfiguration of the Winchester substitute family as all-male with Castiel and father-figure Bobby alongside the brothers. The end of the season 5 finale, with Dean returning to his ex-girlfriend Lisa, was widely criticized for implausibility. But this scene does make narrative sense. It neatly bookends the pilot with its idealization of the domestic, and underlines both brothers' wish for "a normal life." In this, they are following their mother; indeed, the greatest temptation offered by Azazel was that Mary could have "the white picket fence, the station wagon," and all the trappings of suburbia ("In the Beginning"). As with the other female characters discussed here, Lisa can be read most clearly in relation to Dean's character development, and since the "normal" life does not persist long into season 6, this domestic scene is only a momentary pause on the continuing "road trip" of the series' narrative. What is clear is that the brothers remain the focus of the series, and any female character, whether angel, vampire, demon, or would-be action heroine, will always have to exist on their terms.

"Go be gay for that poor, dead intern"
Conversion Fantasies and Gay Anxieties in *Supernatural*
Darren Elliott-Smith

Academic writing about *Supernatural*'s appeal to queer spectators has largely dwelled on the cult series' Gothic milieu and mise-en-scène. Further still, its knowing treatment of the homoerotic relationship between its two attractive male leads, the demon-hunting Winchester brothers Sam and Dean, clearly offers up their fraternal love for queer appropriation and fantasy. It remains to be seen whether such fantasies operate to subvert the show's (clearly problematic) presentation of heteronormative (heterosexual, monogamous, procreative) ideology. Most critical analysis of *Supernatural*'s "queerness"[1] seems to focus upon Sam and Dean in particular and the scenes in which their traditional heterosexual masculinity is questioned, queered, and marginalized. A more informed understanding of the show's appeal for gay male spectators might be served by studying the show's representation of explicit gay male characters, specifically gay intern Corbett in "Ghostfacers" (3.13) and gay *Supernatural* superfans Damien and Barnes from "The Real Ghostbusters" (5.9). I will argue that the show's overriding appeal for gay men lies in a disidentification[2] with the show's hypermasculine protagonists, revealing a simultaneous desire *to be with* (to bed) and eventually *to be like* Sam or Dean. This collapse of desire and identification, rather than allowing for a subversive queering of the show's presentation of brotherly love and straight masculinity, reveals instead the gay masculine anxieties in contemporary Western society. Horror narratives that have queer appeal such as *Supernatural* revisit, recollect, and replay cultural notions of trauma pertinent for the gay male subculture, chief among them the association of a submissive femininity with gay men within a dominant culture that expects heterosexuality of its subjects.

Much of the critical analysis of *Supernatural's* queerness revolves around the homoerotic fantasies inspired by the show, specifically the fan-scribed "slash fiction"[3] that reconfigures the implicit homoerotic tensions between Sam and Dean as explicit gay sex between the brothers and between various peripheral male characters, including the angel Castiel. Catherine Tosenberger considers the show's queer (and incestuous) erotic and paratextual afterlife in "Wincest" slash fan fiction, which fantasizes a consensual homosexual relationship between the brothers. Her claim is that its transgressive elements do not build *sub*versive, *per*verse, or oppositional texts that foster a "resistance to a heterosexual, nonincestuous show" ("The epic love story of Sam and Dean" 0.1). Instead, she suggests, the romanticized, paratextual Wincest slash fiction offers Sam and Dean a redemptive happiness that they are perpetually denied by the show's writers both in a diegetic sense (via Chuck Shurley, the show's writer/prophet who publishes novels based on the boys' adventures) and in a non-diegetic sense (via Eric Kripke, Sera Gamble, and the show's returning writers). Tosenberger concurs with Sara Gwenllian-Jones' reading of "The Sex Lives of Cult TV Characters" and understands the queer inscription of Sam and Dean, not as an attack on the show's seemingly obvious celebration of straight machismo, but as "an actualization of [the show's] latent textual elements" (Gwenllian-Jones 82). Both critics agree that slash fictions merely tap into and foreground the cult television show's implicit queerness:

Cult television series are already "queer" in their constructions of fantastic virtual realities that must problematise
heterosexuality . . . It is the cult television series itself that
implicitly "resists" the conventions of heterosexuality; the
slash fiction stories written by some of its fans render
explicit this implicit function and, more importantly, are
a reflection of cult television's immersive and interactive
logics. (Gwenllian-Jones 89–90)

Tosenberger helpfully highlights instances of queerness inherent in
Supernatural's continuing story arcs across the seasons that work to
comically foreground the show's central relationship as one that is
open to gay and queer interpretation.

The "epic love story of Sam and Dean" (as characterized by the
show's executive story editor Sera Gamble [Borsellino]) is in fact
frequently referenced within the show itself. Such instances include
moments where Sam and Dean are mistaken for a gay male couple (see
for instance "Bugs," 1.8; "Something Wicked," 1.18; and "Playthings,"
2.11). These instances often provoke a mildly homophobic panic
— usually in Dean (arguably the more masculine of the brothers).
Homoeroticism is also developed as a consequence of the narrative
prevention of both brothers' heterosexual love lives (Dean's relationships with women are perpetually doomed, and Sam's female partners
are frequently murdered).[4] Perhaps most obviously the siblings' excessively dependent love for one another is also comically misinterpreted
as bordering on the homoerotic. Tosenberger summarizes:

They don't have anyone but each other (and their father) to
love, and since their father's death, they love none but each
other. . . . While this love is not necessarily romantic, our
culture codes romantic love as similarly excessive, so the
show makes it very easy to read Sam and Dean's excessive
love as romantic. (2.2)

Tosenberger's analysis of Wincest slash suggests that it provides a cathartic vent for the sexual turmoil of Sam and Dean (and indeed for the show's fans). The brothers' destruction of the show's monsters (which can be read as projected metaphors of their own repressed homosexual and/or incestuous desires) remains unsatisfactory, and true catharsis is achieved in these unbridled erotic fictions that allow Sam and Dean to find fleeting moments of happiness with one another.

Not only do analyses of queer readings of *Supernatural* focus too tightly upon the characters of Sam and Dean, but I would argue that the study of the seemingly queer fantastical appropriations of Wincest fiction alone is not sufficient to understand the show's specifically homosexual appeal. If, as Gwenllian-Jones' suggests,[5] the majority of slash fiction authors are well-educated, straight women, we must look elsewhere for a male, gay perspective. Further still, I would argue that such female-authored slash fiction only fosters increased perturbation for the gay male subject, who is continually feminized in dominant culture, sharing the same love object as the straight female and therefore considered *unmanly*.

Gay male spectators of the show negotiate a sense of gay masculinity via multiple identifications with the hypermasculine Winchesters (taking pleasure in their attractive physicality, their closeness, and the show's tongue-in-cheek references to their homoerotic relationship), with their female love interests (specifically Ruby), and with the show's many queer-coded peripheral characters who simultaneously deflate Sam and Dean's own performed hypermasculinity while poking fun at clichéd gay male characteristics. In order to understand the pleasures and identification practices offered to the gay male spectator of *Supernatural*, we must return to the show's own treatment of queerness and homosexuality. Focusing on gay male characters from two episodes — "Ghostfacers" and "The Real Ghostbusters" — I hope to show that the gay male subject's (dis)identification with hypermasculinity (here in the form of Sam and Dean) demands a collapse of desire and identification that gives rise to conversion fantasies (bedding and converting the straight male to homosexuality). It also gives rise to masculine masquerade and role-play (in wishing to become hyper-masculine) in order to disavow any anxieties in being shamefully associated with a "feminine" passivity and penetrability.

Despite the show's tongue-in-cheek portrayal of Dean's clichéd homophobic responses to misinterpretations of his and Sam's brotherly love, the show's inclusion of comic, yet sympathetic, gay male characters such as the novice intern Alan Corbett ("Ghostfacers") offsets accusations of homophobia. The representation of Corbett's unrequited gay love has garnered much praise in gay critical circles, awarding the episode a GLAAD (Gay and Lesbian Alliance Against Defamation) nomination in 2009 for Outstanding Individual Episode. Corbett's homosexual feelings for Ed, one of the Ghostfacers' lead investigators, is an unusual acknowledgment of the show's legion of gay male fans who themselves nurse unrequited crushes upon its leads. On behalf of these fans Corbett also manifests a fantasy to seduce the straight male with whom he erotically disidentifies.

"Ghostfacers"

"Ghostfacers" stands out formally, aesthetically, and narratively from other episodes within the season because it is presented as a show in its own right, without the usual *Supernatural* opening titles and with its own contrived advertisement-break placer logos. True to form for a reality TV–style ghost-hunting show, most of the episode is filmed by the team themselves through handheld cameras, night vision goggles, and cameras that are set up at fixed points throughout a haunted building. In essence, "Ghostfacers" queers the cohesion of season 3 of *Supernatural*, with little or no references to the season's plot arc. The gang represents an amalgamation of amateurish, geeky fans on the margins of the dominant culture, all of whom retain a self-referential knowledge of Sam and Dean as übermasculine hunters. Taking the form of a pilot for a new show, lead presenters Ed and Harry introduce the episode's central case study, the Morton House, said to be the most haunted house in America, which reaches its paranormal peak every February 29. The Ghostfacers' team is made up of Ed and Harry (re-appearing as recurring characters from "Hell House," 1.17, much to the chagrin of Sam and Dean), Ed's adopted sister Maggie, their cameraman Spruce and their new intern Alan Corbett (who clearly appears to have a crush on the seemingly heterosexual Ed).

The Ghostfacers enter the police-cordoned house and begin setting up their equipment for their amateur ghost hunting. The team, now split into two groups, are accosted by Sam and Dean, posing as police officers, but Ed recognizes the Winchesters and reveals their true identities to the others. Meanwhile, Harry, Spruce, and Maggie witness a ghost who appears to shoot himself in front of them. Sam and Dean confirm that the inflicted spirit is acting out a "death echo," whereby a ghost relives its own death again and again. Venturing on his own, Corbett attempts to prove his worth to the Ghostfacers by exploring the upstairs rooms of the house, only to be kidnapped by Freeman Daggett (the house's former owner), another, more vengeful, spirit. The house becomes the team's prison as its windows slam shut and doors lock by themselves, just before another death echo appears, this time of a man who is hit by a train. When Sam and Dean attempt to interrupt the ghost's echo by waking it up, they find that their attempts will only work if they form a connection with the victim. While attempting to search for Corbett, Sam and Dean discover that Daggett, once a hospital janitor who stole bodies from the hospital morgue for company, died in 1964. The presence of the unburied bodies in the house explains the recurrences of death echoes. Corbett wakes up tied to a chair at a long dinner table somewhere in the basement of the house, with Sam tied to a chair opposite, having also been kidnapped by Daggett. Around the table sit various other dead bodies. Daggett approaches Corbett from behind and stabs him through the throat, killing him.

While Sam and Dean are assaulted by Daggett, the remaining Ghostfacers witness a spectral vision of Corbett in a death echo. Realizing that they need to end their friend's repeated suffering, Harry understands that the only person with a connection to Corbett is Ed. He confesses to his friend that Corbett had feelings for him and pleads for Ed to "[g]o be gay for that poor, dead intern." Ed does so and connects with the spirit of Corbett, telling him that he loves him and pleading for his help. Corbett promptly snaps out of his death echo and prevents Daggett's assault on the Winchesters.

The formal structure of the "Ghostfacers" episode references the sub-genre of the paranormal reality TV show and, naturally, Sam and Dean's iconic place within a subculture of paranormal enthusiasts. Corbett can be read as a cipher for the gay male fan of *Supernatural* who desires to *be* accepted into a discourse of traditional macho masculinity by demonstrating it himself (as Corbett strives to prove himself as brave and independent by *going it alone*). However Corbett also erotically *desires* masculinity (here in the form of the geeky, but more mature Ed).

With the character of Corbett, the show initially connects with its long-running treatment of implied homosexuality and the resulting homosexual panic in its seemingly straight male protagonists, as Ed is totally unaware of Corbett's affections. Here homosexual desire becomes both a key narrative element but also remains a comic device. The representation of Corbett's homosexuality is decidedly passive. The youngest of the Ghostfacers, Corbett is a pale, thin, and softly spoken young man, marginalized as an intern and reduced to carrying equipment. He is clearly depicted as a supporting character. However, in death, Corbett is seemingly empowered *because* of this passivity rather than in spite of it, when the team relies on his spectral powers to save them from Daggett. As a gay male Corbett is symbolically represented as penetrat*ed* rather than penetrat*ing*. This finds its symbolic conclusion in his death, stabbed by Daggett. Within the camp gothic excesses of *Supernatural*'s milieu, the homosexual remains the preferred Other, but an Other nonetheless, and as such gay love possesses a supernatural potency that Harry comically suggests "can reach beyond the veil of death." This implies something unnatural, an inherent morbidity and a spectrality in homosexuality that is configured as transient perhaps due to an assumption of its non-procreative associations, being unable to 'naturally' reproduce. The episode seems to suggest that as a gay man Corbett is more able to make that transition, already straddling the border between masculinity and femininity and therefore able to transcend that between life and death.

 If the gay male spectator, like Corbett, covets the ideal of hypermasculinity, what are the implications of his appropriation of a hypermasculine form that, in its purest sense, is symbolized in heterosexual masculinity? Leo Bersani considers the effects of the media representation of gay men in light of the AIDS crisis that links homosexuality with death, decay, and infection. Questioning Jeffrey Weeks' argument that gay macho style "gnaws at the roots of a male heterosexual identity" (Weeks 191), Bersani argues if this is true, it is not because of the parodic distance that they take from that identity, but rather because from within "their nearly mad identification with it, they never cease to feel the appeal of its being violated" (Bersani, "Is the Rectum a Grave?" 15).

Bersani posits that sexual penetration is traumatic, even "self shattering" for the gay man placed in the supine feminine position: "to be penetrated is to abdicate power" ("Is the Rectum a Grave?" 24). Further still he claims that anal sex provides a means through which the subject can lose one's self, disrupting "the ego's coherence and . . . its boundaries" (*Homos* 101). Moreover, the pain and pleasure imputed to gay penetration has the potential to shatter macho phallic pride where the façade of masculinity can also be exposed, "if the rectum is a grave in which the masculine ideal . . . of proud subjectivity is buried, then it should be celebrated for its very potential for death. . . ." (Bersani "Is the Rectum a Grave?" 29–30). Following this logic, Corbett's passivity, symbolized by his subjugated position in the Ghostfacers' pecking order, his unrequited (and seemingly feminized) gay love for Ed, and his eventual death, nonetheless gives him the spectral power to kill the phallic male, here ironically symbolized in Daggett (who is eventually exposed as a marginalized mama's boy desperate for his own effeminate, if monstrous, tea party). Corbett's position on the margins of masculinity provides the means for him to "cross over" from life to death and back again. Through the repeated suffering of his own traumatic killing, he becomes re-masculinized. By suffering for his friends over and over and by accepting his death via penetration, Corbett becomes *more of a man*.

Just as Corbett wishes to be *with* Ed, romantically, he also aspires *to be* Ed by emulating his role as one of Ghostfacers' lead investigators. Similarly Ed is encouraged to perform *himself* in order to shatter Corbett's death echo, by offering him the false promise of his reciprocated love. Throughout the series, *Supernatural* thrills in parodying and critiquing masculinity in all forms: straight, gay, and queer. I would argue that it is in those moments of homoeroticized or queered masculinity that the fragility of the hypermasculine ideal is highlighted. In "After School Special" (4.13) Dean masquerades as a PE coach at his and Sam's old school, where he is clearly visualized homoerotically in tight red gym shorts and white polo shirt, tube socks and red sweat bands while brutishly admonishing an all-boy gym class. "Criss Angel Is a Douchebag" (4.12) sees Dean being tricked into visiting a gay S&M club by two aging magicians (Charlie and Jay, whose relationship is suggestively queer) resulting in another resurgence of Dean's homosexual panic.

The question that remains for gay male spectators of the show's comic yet homoerotic parodying of masculinity is whether they "run the risk of idealizing and feeling inferior to certain representations of masculinity on the basis of which they are in fact judged and condemned?" (Bersani, "Is the Rectum a Grave?" 14). Is homosexuality treated as comic relief? If, as Bersani suggests, "Parody is an erotic turn-off and all gay men know this" (14), what pleasures do gay male spectators gain from an erotic worship of parodies of hypermasculine forms? The show's fairly innocuous sexual display essentially achieves only a flaccid eroticism, one that is not designed to arouse, but merely to provide "eye candy," though it nevertheless works to objectify masculinity as an erotic object of spectacle. Is it critiquing heterosexist machismo or simply appropriating such ideals for gay masculinity, effectively negating any subversive potential?

"The Real Ghostbusters"

The queer appropriation of Sam and Dean's characters is taken one stage further in "The Real Ghostbusters" in which the self-reflexivity of the series becomes more complex. When the show's slash fiction writer Becky misleads Sam and Dean into attending a *Supernatural* convention celebrating the writings of Carver Edlund (Chuck Shurley), they become aware that the venue is haunted by ex-owner Leticia Gore and the three spirits of the young boys who killed her son. The gathered delegates include Demian and Barnes, two male fans who masquerade for the duration of the convention as a copycat Sam and Dean. Demian (as Dean) attempts to make Dean understand the reason behind their impersonation,

> In real life he sells stereos. I fix photocopiers. Our lives suck. But Sam and Dean, to wake up every morning and save the world. To have a brother who would die for you. Well, who wouldn't want that?

Convincing Dean of the purpose of their fight, the four hunters eventually team up to burn and salt the bones of Leticia and the monstrous children. Before Dean leaves Demian and Barnes, the pair reveals that they met each other online in a *Supernatural* chatroom, and that they are "more than just friends." As the pair lovingly hold hands, Demian continues, "We're partners." Barnes, the taller of the two men, leans over and rests his head on his lover's shoulders in a comical pose, at which Dean looks assuredly uncomfortable and comments, "Oh . . . well, howdy 'pardners'" before retreating. With Barnes' camp response, "Howdy!" Demian coquettishly leans his own head into his partner's and the comical display of their height difference intensifies the visual ridicule of these nerdy, roleplay-addicted computer geeks.

In the masquerade theory discussed by Joan Riviere and Mary Anne Doane, the feminine masquerade is posited as an *exaggeration* of gender, performed as a defense against heterosexual male reprisals toward women should they display traits of empowered masculinity in certain social contexts. The masquerading female subject achieves a distance from her own image by ironically performing an excessive femininity. Similarly, both the macho hypermasculinity as performed by Sam and Dean and its camp parody by Demian and Barnes work to disavow femininity one way or another. The clichéd comic revelation of Demian and Barnes' homosexuality on the one hand refreshingly seems to offer a non-stereotyped representation of feminine gay male subjectivity, but on the other undercuts their heroic masculine performance as being just that. Once the *mask* of masculinity (in performing Sam and Dean) is dropped, homosexuality is once more associated with passive, feminine traits. While this may offer a critique of all masculinity as performance and reveal the gay man's potential to be heroic, in the case of Demian and Barnes, heroism can only be achieved via the masquerade. In both Demian and Barnes' straight-acting performance, and Corbett's shamefully concealed affections for Ed and his eventual empowerment through the repeated masochistic suffering of the death echo, gay male passivity and its associations with feminine masochism are disavowed by means of a covering up of any shameful desires that may be construed as feminine.

Corbett's shattered masculinity in "Ghostfacers" and the parodic lampooning of masculinity in "The Real Ghostbusters" both operate to highlight the fragility of masculine ideals, which speaks particularly to the gay male subject who must negotiate his own masculinity within a culture that assumes heterosexuality, and frequently associates gay masculinity with the feminine. Though this conflation with seemingly shameful femininity gives rise to anxieties surrounding concepts of 'manliness,' I would argue that *Supernatural*'s representation of gay masculinity instead offers a critique of the limited culturally gendered positions available for gay male subjects. In heteronormative culture the ambiguous appeal of a gay masculinity paralleled with femininity provides both an anxiety and a transgressive access to a subversive and unnatural potency, yet it also highlights the gay men's possession of an essential masculinity to a mere *performance* of it through *role play*.[6]

Part 4

The Gospel According to Chuck

Narrative and Storytelling in *Supernatural*

"That's so gay"
Drag, Camp, and the Power of Storytelling in *Supernatural*
James Francis, Jr.

Sam: So what are we today, Dean, um, rock stars? Are we
  army rangers?
Dean: Reality TV scouts looking for people with special skills.
  Well hey, it's not that far off, right?
"Provenance," 1.19

Television series with a niche market often start pilot episodes and opening seasons with a gimmick: *Nip/Tuck* (2003–2010) depicts gory, invasive plastic surgery procedures; *Queer as Folk* (2000–2005) visualizes explicit sex between men; *Six Feet Under* (2001–2005) showcases a random death at the beginning of each narrative; and *Psych* (2006) typically provides a flashback to two of its ensemble cast members as children who are always in trouble. *Supernatural* (2005–) began its programming by showcasing the otherworldly, but the subject matter does more than simply capture the viewer's attention.

In the pilot episode, Sam's girlfriend is set ablaze on the ceiling by the demon Azazel. Her death invokes images from *Poltergeist* (1982),

A Nightmare on Elm Street (1984), *Firestarter* (1984), and other visual works dealing with the supernatural. The pilot — and the season's subsequent installments — has an episodic feel à la *The X-Files*, in which viewers witness the Winchester boys taking on demons, shape-shifters, and other evils. Unlike Scully and Mulder, Sam and Dean are somewhat different in every episode; they change outfits and identities as much as characters in a Russian spy thriller. The costuming was simply a foundational arrangement or plot device for the show — it allowed the brothers to impersonate figures of authority in order to help them interrogate witnesses and further investigate cases. Although it served as a means to an end, it helped catapult the series into its season 6 fevered and complex storyline, and it is important throughout the entire series. Like its television predecessors and peer shows mentioned earlier, *Supernatural* employed surface devices like costuming as a way to pull its audience deeper into the content of the series.

The abundance of costuming in the first season turns Sam and Dean into drag performers; however, drag in *Supernatural* is different from stereotypical or denotative meanings. Drag performances usually conjure up images of men dressed as women singing powerhouse songs by celebrated divas or belting out popular dance hits in clubs. The men in drag are also typically assumed to be gay. But anyone can put on a costume; drag occurs when a *performance* is enacted. Sam and Dean do more than wear costumes; they perform the identities that the costumes portray or symbolize. The continual depiction of costumed performances throughout the series make it a vehicle for drag. And, drag in *Supernatural* incorporates costuming, naming, and the action of performance.

★ *Supernatural* has featured neither Sam nor Dean in costume for a party nor dressed as a woman singing . . . yet. Sam outright refuses costuming when Jessica asks, "And where's your costume?" He replies, "You know how I feel about Halloween" ("Pilot," 1.1). But Sam — in an effort to live a normal life — has been in drag for years, playing the role of a college student bound for law school. The perfect life he planned for himself is a false costume he must remove in order to live the life for which he was destined — the life of a hunter. The series, however, has often cloaked the brothers' identities by use of different names, job titles, badges, outfits, back stories, professions, and voices or dialogue. Their varied disguises allow them to investigate crime scenes, question witnesses, and, on some occasions, flirt with beautiful women. Drag, in the traditional sense of a man being able to perform as a woman, allows him access to territories (restrooms, dressing rooms, clothing stores), outfitting (dresses, high heels, makeup), and mannerisms (vocal pitch, walking style) that are allocated to women. The Winchester boys are not police officials, coroners, FBI agents, or rangers, but "in drag" they are admitted into areas and permitted to talk to people they would otherwise have no chance of contacting as ordinary guys, just as drag performers onstage are admitted into an arena of performance they wouldn't typically access as their everyday selves.

In season 1, Dean takes on the role of almost 30 other identities, and Sam lags behind with a little over 20. Some of the costuming lasts throughout a full episode, and other times the drag performances are extremely temporary. In "Pilot" Dean checks into a motel with a credit card under the name of Hector Aframian, tells the police his name is Ted Nugent, pretends to be a U.S. marshal to other police, and also assumes the role of an uncle. Sam, on the other hand, mentions he is a reporter and is introduced as an uncle, as well — viewers can only assume he tackles fewer identities because this is his first time out with his hunter brother. There is not much physical costuming required in this episode, but the characters perform drag via names, titles, and badges. Names continue to pop up throughout the season — Dr. James Hetfield ("Phantom Traveler," 1.4), Nigel Tufnel ("Asylum," 1.10), Father Simmons and Father Frehley ("Nightmare," 1.14) — and somehow Dean never fails to let his knowledge of rock 'n' roll disappoint viewers. (Hetfield is the lead singer for Metallica, Tufnel is the lead guitarist for Spinal Tap, and Simmons and Frehley are from KISS.)

Although the names — especially from Dean — are usually pop culture references to big names in music, the professions are often the same: reporters, college students, or law officials including police, rangers, and marshals. There are random exceptions such as Sam and Dean being mistaken for lovers ("Bugs," 1.8), which certainly fueled fan fiction, but the brothers typically adhere to a strict formula of identities that helps them conduct investigations. Sam and Dean are also not the only characters to appear costumed — John Winchester has fake IDs, Bobby Singer has multiple phone line identities ("Dead Men Don't Wear Plaid," 5.15), and Bela names herself after the actor who played the title role in *Dracula* (1931) — but they are the driving force behind drag performances throughout the series.

Season 1 sets up *Supernatural* as a story about estranged brothers, a missing father, supernatural forces, revenge, death, and other dark subject matter; however, the presence of costuming lightens the mood and tone of the series. It is also during season 1 that Sam realizes he has to welcome costuming and drag into his life — Dean has already been doing it by the time the brothers reunite. Catherine Tosenberger comments on this transformation when she writes,

> Jessica's murder marks the end of Sam's attempt at a normal life — and moreover, shows how illusory that normality was. . . . The narrative trajectory of the entire first season is designed not only to force Sam to abandon his quest for normality, but also to come back to the world of the 'freaks' to which he truly belongs — freaks like Dean, who fully embraces both the life and the label. (3.4)

Once Sam accepts a life of costume and drag — he takes Dean to Mort's For Style to purchase suits to complement the fake IDs Dean created to help them pose as Homeland Security officers in "Phantom Traveler" — the brothers solidify themselves into a team hellbent on finding their father and fighting evil.

Costuming and drag performances pervade all seasons of

Supernatural. As mentioned earlier, the characters often take on differ-ent names to go along with the costuming. Naming is a part of drag; in drag communities or circles, there is a specific manner in which to derive a drag name for a performer or for someone who simply wants to know what his or her name would be as a drag queen. The mainstream way is to take the name of one's first pet and combine that with the name of the street s/he grew up on as the surname. In the series, our two heroes name themselves specifically in homage to rock music pioneers, actors, film directors, and more. The naming is not as calculated as devising stage names for drag queens, but the series has its own strategy that connects it to recognizable people in pop culture. Both processes, however, originate from a place of nostalgia. Drag queen names connect performers to past homesteads and child-hood pets. Along those lines, Dean accesses memories that link him to music his father enjoyed and played for him when he was younger. Naming — for drag queens and our *Supernatural* characters — takes on personal meaning to reflect people, places, and things to celebrate.

We see Dean and Sam hunt a werewolf as Detectives Landis and Dante in "Heart" (2.17), a reference to film directors John Landis and Joe Dante who created werewolf films — *An American Werewolf in London* (1981) and *The Howling* (1981), respectively; in "Bedtime Stories" (3.5), Dean is Robert Plant and Sam is Jimmy Page; the broth-ers become FBI agents Murdock and Stiles in "Sex and Violence" (4.14) in order to pay homage to the TV show *Route 66* (1960–1964); and in "Fallen Idols" (5.5), Dean assumes the name John Bonham from Led Zeppelin and Sam takes on Stewart Copeland from The Police. It is all extremely tongue-in-cheek, but this so-called gimmick of costuming lends itself to deeper readings of the series and turns the drag perfor-mances into camp.

There is no one definition of camp. The term has been associated with B-movies, drag queens, over-the-top acting, and much more. It is simultaneously designated as high-brow and low-brow depend-ing on the context of its use. One element that often ties the differ-ent representations together is self-awareness. B-movie filmmakers acknowledge bad special effects, drag queens know they are not women, and actors deliver their lines with affected performances. The aspect of self-reflexibility in camp is what matters most in connection to *Supernatural*. Although this component of camp sometimes functions to add comedy to serious subject matter, it can also work to bring intelligence, wit, and sophistication to TV entertainment usually deemed silly by critics and audiences. *Supernatural* is not camp because it uses the names of rock 'n' roll legends, film directors, and actors to costume Sam and Dean. It is also not camp because of the way the brothers act when they perform their temporary identities. The series embodies a camp sensibility because of the characters' awareness of performance. On more than a few occasions the viewer gets to see the brothers struggle with their performances because they realize how difficult it is to pretend to be someone else. In more traditional drag situations, there is usually a "tell" or reveal that lets audience members know the woman standing before them is really a man: the hands or feet are too large, the legs (calf muscles) are overdeveloped, stubble appears on the face, the voice is deep, or an Adam's apple is present. Sam and Dean are no different because there is always something amiss with the identities they try to embody — they are too young for a certain profession (clergy), Dean's physical appearance does not match a name's ethnicity (Hector Aframian), and Sam's badge will not grant him hospital access unless he flashes it too fast for the nurse to read the title "Bikini Inspector" ("Something Wicked," 1.18).

Camp unfolds in the tells of the characters. It would be different if the Winchesters were really FBI agents going undercover in each episode. The organization would provide them with state-of-the-art and top-notch disguises — suits, a government-issued car, untraceable phones, weapons, and badges they could let other people see to check validity instead of flashing them quickly. The flash-a-badge method and presence of tells are tested in "Yellow Fever" (4.6). Dean is infected with ghost sickness, which causes anxiousness, fear, and eventual death. On the way to interview a victim's brother, Dean questions the idea of costuming. He tells Sam, "This isn't gonna work. I mean c'mon, these badges are fake. What if we get busted? We could go to jail." Sam reassures Dean but his fears increase when the victim's brother asks to "see some ID" and then proceeds to take hold of their badges for a closer inspection. Dean tells the man, "Those are real — obviously. I mean who would pretend to be an FBI agent, huh? That's just nutty." Camp is present in the character tells, but in this situation Dean verbalizes what are usually gestures and awkward glances. His words represent an awareness of audience response to many of the situations the brothers tackle in their case investigations.

Sam and Dean have to act on the fly for most of their investigations, and even when they receive help from Bobby, Jo, Ellen, or Dad, the costuming is still very much DIY. It is this connection between the supernatural forces they strive to overcome matched with the reality of limited resources that breaks the barrier of the show's serious content to partner it with camp. This type of camp exists within the *Supernatural* universe, but it branches outside the narrative to highlight people in pop culture — real and fictitious.

The names chosen for the Winchester identities are in no way random. The television, film, music, and nonfiction references help create an intertextual world that connects the series to other pop culture art forms beyond its fourth wall. It is here that camp brings an intelligence and wit to the series; viewers are entertained by the show, but simultaneously educated about the world in which they live. Allusions are made to *Star Wars*, ZZ Top, and the Son of Sam to name a few. These names and titles cloak the brothers for investigations, but provide the series with a great breadth of knowledge to impart to viewers, albeit always in a comical manner. In "Free to Be You and Me" (5.3), Dean labels himself and Castiel as Alonzo Mosley and Eddie Moscone respectively — two characters from *Midnight Run* (1988). He can usually make false-identity introductions in dire situations without blinking an eye, but the viewer at home will always have a chuckle or two at the absurdity of the reference. In this respect, camp becomes a secret connection between characters on the screen and the viewing audience that can identify the costume. The series also becomes connected to any other show, film, music, or work of fiction/ nonfiction that makes the same allusion. Instead of characters turning to the camera to wink at or talk to the audience, *Supernatural* uses popular names as part of its drag performances to indirectly communicate with viewers. The conversation, however, between characters and viewers is not always one that helps bring the audience closer to the action on the screen.

Carole-Anne Tyler explains this (dis)connection as she comments on the cause-and-effect relationship that camp and drag performance can exhibit: "its distancing effects" (380). When Sam and Dean take on false identities, the viewer is really seeing Padalecki and Ackles play dress-up, and that character play distances the audience from the believability of the show's fictitious narrative. We are reminded that the visual story unfolding is all about costume and performance, and this distancing brings intentional laughter to a dramatic series.

When Sam and Dean talk, the distance created by costuming falls away and communication becomes specific to the narrative world of the show. Speech enables their costumes to become drag performances — their dialogue encamps the series on a verbal level. In "Bedtime Stories" (3.5), Sam explains *Cinderella* to Dean, and the conversation causes Dean to question, "Dude, could you *be* more gay?" The audience (and Dean) knows Sam is not homosexual — it is an expression, akin to "That's so gay!" Dean verbalizes the camp nature of the series by pointing out that the conversation about *Cinderella* between two macho brothers can be seen to be at odds with their hypermasculinzed personas. Camp pits masculinity against a fairytale and the two complement each other in the show. In the same episode, Dean also says, "I'm gonna go stop the big bad wolf, which is the weirdest thing I've ever said" — his words continue the discourse of camp by showing his awareness of how ludicrous it seems to seriously contemplate tracking down a cautionary-tale character in real life. The story of *Cinderella*, in addition, operates on a supernatural level and has a camp nature of its own that concerns drag outfitting, metamorphosis, playing a character outside the normal self, and finding personal identity through a journey. Other stories from that episode — *Snow White, Hansel and Gretel,* and *Little Red Riding Hood* — foster the same camp components.

Story-allusion and dialogue become a focus again in "Shadow" (1.16). When Sam and Dean are dressed as security alarm servicemen, an old school play pops into the dialogue:

> Dean: You know, I gotta say Dad made it just fine without these stupid costumes. I feel like a high school drama dork. What was that play that you did? What was it? *Our Town.* Yeah, you were good. It was cute.
>
> Sam: Look, you wanna pull this off or not?
>
> Dean: I'm just saying these outfits cost hard-earned money, okay?
>
> Sam: Whose?
>
> Dean: Ours. You think credit card fraud is easy?

This discussion is not detailed like the *Cinderella* scene, but mentioning the stage play gives a nod to performance and an understanding of character play and identity transformation. Dean also acknowledges that costuming costs them money, but using fraudulent credit cards keeps them in business — the boys seem to wonder how their dad did all of his jobs without costumes, but the viewer understands that this is a newer, younger generation of costuming and drag that requires a bit more finesse of cloak and dagger. The same is true in the way the brothers talk to each other about popcentric matters.

Winchester dialogue is infused with pop culture references, and although the quips are typically meant to amuse audiences, they often point to a larger issue of camp intertexuality. When Dean says, "I full-on Swayze'd that mother" ("In My Time of Dying," 2.1), we are immediately reminded of Patrick Swayze's memorable performance in *Ghost* (1990). The moment of pop culture recognition comes and goes as quickly as the line is delivered and the episode's storyline continues. But when Dean asks, "Hey Sam, who do you think is a hotter psychic — Patricia Arquette, Jennifer Love Hewitt, or you?" ("Asylum," 1.10), the reference goes beyond a moment of recognition — it is intertextual and ties the series and viewer into a larger discussion of shows that share subject matter with *Supernatural*. In one line of dialogue, the series becomes connected to *Medium* and *The Ghost Whisperer* — television shows with lead characters who have psychic abilities. The line connects the shows and subject matter, and it also links the networks — CBS and NBC — in a way that removes the suspended disbelief of fiction to remind viewers they are watching a constructed set of elements. This is the power of writing. It is one of those components that demonstrates the show's command of authority in television.

The strength of *Supernatural*'s writing makes it a television series that goes beyond its diegetic borders. Its self-awareness and reflexive nature with other shows makes it camp, but not in a detrimental manner — audiences respond more to the show because it incorporates previous television enterprises and peer series like *Buffy the Vampire Slayer*, *The X-Files*, and *Angel*. The actors — Jensen Ackles and Jared Padelecki — also bring with them devoted fans from *Dawson's Creek*, *Gilmore Girls*, and *Smallville*. In *The Essential Cult TV Reader*, Alison Peirse says the "unique selling point [of *Supernatural*] is Sam and Dean: Ackles and Padalecki are demon-busting visions of loveliness who also possess a Whedonesque penchant for razor-sharp dialogue and pop culture references" (263). Their multi-layered constructions of drag performances, costuming, camp, and storytelling make *Supernatural* a successful series for the CW network. False names, badges, and professions; physical outfitting; performative actions in costume; viewer response; and intertextuality all play big roles in making *Supernatural* the show it is today. These elements work within the show and outside of its fictitious structure, but there is one more layer that pushes the series to a higher level of drag, camp, and storytelling — it is a blend of metafiction and literary self-awareness.

In "Wishful Thinking" (4.8), Sam mentions somewhat off-the-cuff that he is writing a book called *Supernatural* as one of his false back stories, but this literary disguise comes back a few episodes later in season 4. Chuck Shurley, introduced in "The Monster at the End of This Book" (4.18), really is the author of the *Supernatural* book series that he writes under the pen name Carver Edlund. Chuck writes the stories about Sam and Dean that we watch each week as audience members. As his storyline unravels, Castiel informs him that he is a prophet and is protected by an Archangel. But at the end of season 5, a strange thing occurs — Chuck is revealed to be God. Not everyone subscribes to this embedded character explanation, but it is the most logical or probable because the big picture is about the eternal fight between angels, demons, and humans caught in the middle of it all.

Robert Benedict as Chuck Shurley as Carver Edlund as prophet as God is the ultimate costumed character in the series, but there is no tell or giveaway to his drag performance until he disappears at the end of season 5 and the audience is left to be in awe, confused, or disappointed. *Supernatural* uses this character to illustrate the power of storytelling — basically that writers are gods in television — and to show that costuming is not always as overt as that of Sam and Dean. Surprises are possible even in a series that comments upon itself and connects to other pop culture work in television, music, film, and literature. Chuck is the Average Joe, but he ties real-life actor Benedict to the metaphysical, spiritual, and religious embodiment of God.

The characters of *Supernatural* are regular people playing parts to survive. Sam and Dean are challenged to be vessels for Lucifer and Michael, but their bodies are conduits for character play throughout the series: via scripted role play in "Changing Channels" (5.8) the brothers are made to take part in game show and television narratives as people other than themselves in order to appease the Trickster's whims; as comic-book creations in "The Real Ghostbusters" (5.9) Sam and Dean discover alternate versions of themselves in comic-book form that fans adore in the same manner we know fans celebrate the characters of the series; and in the big book of life in "The Monster at the End of This Book" our protagonists realize they are literary protagonists in a series of books being written by Carver Edlund. In each of these situations that cross media — television, comic book, and serial novel — the brothers' bodies are never fully their own because they have to act out or acknowledge other versions of themselves in order to understand their surroundings and maneuver through tough life situations. In this manner, sometimes the drag performances are not so much about access to a restricted area or information; they can represent ways to escape situations, blend in, or understand the self better. These smaller roles they are forced to perform coordinate with the big picture concerning the otherworldly bodies of Lucifer and Michael. Basically, "Sam and Dean's destinies are defined by the interests that claim their bodies" (Chan 5.1). They have personal problems to overcome as regular guys who had difficult childhoods, parental issues, sibling rivalry, and now they are required to save the world. And the same can be said about the actors — Padalecki and Ackles — who bring their own experiences in life to the roles to make us believe they are brothers on a never-ending quest to save the world from evil. This is identity subversion at its best, and it all plays out with a little help from costuming, drag, and storytelling in the series and outside its scripted realm.

The title of the series also helps identify its content and characters. A *super*natural existence evokes hyper-realism — Sam and Dean are natural, regular guys with hyper-characterized personae/aliases. In stage performances, drag queens are *super*natural women — from makeup knowledge to body grooming to demeanor and action. It is only natural that Sam and Dean are *Supernatural* characters. The brothers are not superheroes, although Sam's psychic powers, Dean's knowledge of the occult, and both of their escapes and returns from death are extraordinary. They are basically young men who find themselves in terribly scary times, and in order to conquer evil they sometimes resort to a little costumed performance. Rest assured, the brothers are not drag kings — that designation is reserved for drag-gender reversal in which women dress as men — but they are certainly kings of drag on the cw.

Supernatural is a show of performance, from Sam and Dean's constant outfit changes, badges, and character embodiments to the machismo of the black rumbling '67 Impala, strained affection between brothers, competition for women, and demon bashing to the telling of folklore, ghost stories, and local legends, and, of course, sketchy witness accounts of things going bump in the night. Unparalleled by any other series on television at this time (though *The Vampire Diaries* does try hard), *Supernatural* captures a quirky blend of camp; it takes supernatural subject matter seriously to the point of ridiculousness, turns dire situations into comedic brilliance, showcases its main character brothers as true drag performers with the slightest outfit change (jacket, shoes, hat, etc.), name designation, or claim to an assumed government identity, and revels in the telling of a good story from local legend to international moral tale in an effort to deliver quality television to audiences.

"There's a ton of lore on unicorns too"
Postmodernist Micro-Narratives and *Supernatural*
David Simmons

It is common fan knowledge that much of Eric Kripke's impetus behind wanting to create *Supernatural* was based upon his desire to do a series that explored popular myths and legends, with an eye to his belief that "every town has a really great, terrifying ghost story" (Kripke qtd in Reed). Indeed, comments made by the show's writers online suggest a concerted wish, not only to utilize the cult repute of such narratives, but also to do justice to what they consider to be misused or distorted instances of these stories; in the process, working toward a greater sense of fidelity to the original source material, as Kripke suggests:

> The show has to be "Google worthy" and the mandate to all the writers is that the stories have to be as authentic as possible when it comes to the urban legends and myths that are presented. It's only when they are backed into the ugliest of story corners do they resort to fabricating something to resolve the issue (Reed).

Diverging from Catherine Tosenberger's belief that *Supernatural* differs from "the myth arc–heavy *Buffy the Vampire Slayer* and *The X-Files*," which she argues are "far more focused upon their respective invented mythological narratives than they are on 'real-world' folklore" ("Kinda like the folklore of its day" 1.2) this essay will examine what I see as the show's gradual transition from an emphasis on micro-narratives (often in the form of standalone episodes focused on a single urban legend) toward a grand or meta-narrative of an ongoing seasonal narrative arc of "religious" Armageddon (albeit one indebted to other popular representations). I will finish by exploring fan reaction to this development and what this might mean in terms of the possibilities for storytelling that are available to those working in contemporary U.S. mainstream television.

In *The Postmodern Condition: A Report on Knowledge* (1978) the philosopher Jean-François Lyotard proposes that the contemporary era will see a move away from the all-encompassing narratives of modernism: "Simplifying to the extreme, I define postmodern as incredulity toward meta-narratives. This incredulity is undoubtedly a product of progress . . . but that progress in turn presupposes it" (15). Lyotard believes that supposedly universal narratives such as religion or historical progress will be replaced with "petits récits," or more "localized" narratives. Such "local" narratives are what structure and inform *Supernatural*, with the two central characters frequently referring to and utilizing "urban myths" — supernatural narratives that are regarded as being within the realm of the superstitious (with no scientific merit) — in a manner that intentionally gives rise to postmodern questions of historiography and the subjectivity of knowledge. As Brenda Marshall proposes in *Teaching the Postmodern: Fiction and Theory* (1992), "Postmodernism is about histories not told. . . . Histories forgotten, hidden, invisible, considered unimportant, changed, eradicated" (4). The confidence that Sam and Dean place in the veracity of urban myths to aid them in solving the troubles they encounter suggests a conscious turning away from Enlightenment concepts of the rational in an attempt to cope with the difficulties posed by a supernatural U.S. landscape. Indeed, the problems that the two brothers come across are typically excluded from the grand narratives of scientific thinking, existing, instead, in more localized stories passed around through unofficial channels and oral communication.

The Winchester Brothers' primary means of researching such narratives is often decidedly localized in a geographical sense, requiring them to familiarize themselves not only with an area's population but with its history and traditions; as Tosenberger notes, "protagonists Sam and Dean Winchester are themselves presented as careful folklore researchers — each episode depicts the boys combing through libraries, archives, public records offices, and the Internet, investigating the folklore record" ("Kinda like the folklore" 1.1). London E. Brickley also examines the sources of information that the Winchesters engage with. She doesn't explicitly use the term micro-narratives, choosing instead to refer to the stories that Sam and Dean research as "sources that may not be accepted in a mainstream or academic setting" (272). Brickley's exploration of the "*negative* forms of fiction" (270) that the show deals with in the first three seasons concludes with the assertion that *Supernatural* is "about legitimizing the marginal source" (271).

The show's emphasis on the importance of local narratives is evident in two season 1 episodes: "Wendigo" (1.2) and "Dead in the Water" (1.3). At the start of "Wendigo" we join Sam and Dean as they drive toward a small town by the name of Blackwater Ridge that is located in the Colorado woods. Though following a set of co-ordinates that they believe will take them to their dad, upon looking at a map of the area Sam remarks, "There's nothing there, it's just woods." However, given the format of the show, we are led to believe the opposite is likely to be true and that there will in fact be something lurking in the woods. Thus, from the outset, the episode encourages us to reject the validity of official knowledge.

Upon arriving in the town, Sam and Dean meet the local park ranger who tells them of a group of boys who recently went missing in the woods. After speaking to Haley Collins, the sister of one of the boys, who tells them that all their official channels of communication ("cell, email, stupid little videos") seem to have been closed down, Sam and Dean do some investigating of their own utilizing local newspaper clippings and the recordings of her brother that Haley has given them. Discovering that every 23 years the town seems to experience a spate of supposed bear attacks, Sam and Dean also note that one of the recordings they have shows a mysterious black shadow running past Tommy Collins' tent. Intrigued by the possibility of something supernatural taking place, the brothers decide to go to see Shaw, the only survivor of the previous attacks. Over the course of the first quarter of the episode, Sam and Dean can be seen to reject "official" narratives (the map, the park ranger's account) concerning the events at Blackwater Ridge and instead turn toward stories that originate from more local and "unofficial" channels. Indeed, the foregrounding of such narratives is perhaps exemplified most clearly in Shaw, a tenacious character (think Sam Quint in *Jaws*) whose initial reluctance to let on that he too disbelieves the accepted, rational version of events gives way to a more subjective and ostensibly irrational explanation:

> Mr. Shaw: Look ranger, I don't know why you're askin' me about this. It's public record; I was a kid. My parents got mauled by a . . .
>
> Sam: Grizzly? That's what attacked them?
>
> Dean: The other people that went missing that year . . . those bear attacks too? What about all the people that went missing this year? Same thing? If we knew what we were dealing with, we might be able to stop it.
>
> Mr. Shaw: I seriously doubt that. Anyways, I don't see what difference it would make. You wouldn't believe me, nobody ever did.
>
> Sam: Mr. Shaw, what did you see?
>
> Mr. Shaw: Nothing. It moved too fast to see, it hid too well. I heard it though, a roar, like . . . no man or animal I ever heard.

Following Shaw's comments, Sam and Dean join with Haley, Ben Collins, and a local hunter, Roy, in the search for Tommy, and through consulting their father's diary discover that a wendigo, a creature from Native American folklore, is responsible for the disappearances. Later in the same episode Dean returns to the diary, stating its importance both as a kind of grimoire (an instructional book on magic) or collection of postmodern micro-narratives — Lyotard's "petits récits" — and as a driving force for the brother's lives: "This is why. This book. This is Dad's single most valuable possession. Everything he knows about every evil thing is in here. And he's passed it on to us. I think he wants us to pick up where he left off. You know, saving people, hunting things. The family business." Dean proceeds to rationalize his hunting lifestyle by suggesting that he does it to help people. "I mean, I figure our family's so screwed to Hell; maybe we can help some others. Makes things a little more bearable." We are meant to understand the brothers' access to the micro-narratives contained in the text as a positive, enabling force while preferring such narratives in the postmodern era can have an empowering effect, Marshall explains, "That does not mean we are paralyzed or helpless; rather, it means that we give up the luxury of absolute Truths, choosing instead to put to work local and provisional truths" (3).

At the end of "Wendigo," Sam and Dean consult the "unofficial" knowledge contained in their father's diary in order to find a way to destroy the creature, relating the information to their fellow travelers in order to instruct them on what to do when they encounter it. As Tosenberger suggests:

> *Supernatural* relies heavily upon existing legend texts, and the majority of every episode involves Sam and Dean investigating the folklore record to determine which ostensive action will be most efficacious in defeating the creature of the week. *Supernatural* dramatizes the "practical" in "practical folkloristics" (1.5).

In "Dead in the Water," the emphasis placed on the importance of local knowledge is sustained. The whole episode revolves around the brothers' attempts to access the narrative of Lake Manitoc, Wisconsin, with Sam and Dean needing to expose a singular family's dark history in order to solve a series of grisly drownings that they read about in a local newspaper. After speaking to the town sheriff, the Winchester brothers do some research of their own, examining online reports on a range of seemingly interrelated topics, including urban legends concerning lake monsters and the drownings themselves. At this point in their investigation the brothers are limited to the information that is available to them; as Sam suggests: "This whole lake monster theory, it just bugs me." Interestingly, such a process of selection and deduction is mirrored in the show's own writers and actors, who are frequently required to familiarize themselves with the many and varied sources of information on the narratives that are referenced in episodes of the series.

While the brothers are able to deduce that the murders are perhaps being caused by a vengeful water spirit by asking the townsfolk, it is significant that Sam and Dean's primary means of uncovering the event that has created the spirit is found through the help they receive from the traumatized son of one of the previous victims. Lucas, a young child who has been shocked into becoming mute by the terrible nature of the death he witnessed, forms an interesting device through which the show can foreground the crucial role that familiarity with localized micro-narratives has to play in enabling the Winchesters to solve the supernatural problems they encounter. Though initially unable to articulate the details that lead to his father's demise, Lucas, with Dean's encouragement, eventually shares some of the knowledge he has locked away in his head, stressing the importance of communicating such localized narratives to others. Through a series of Lucas's drawings that act as primitive maps for Dean and Sam to follow, the brothers are led to the supernatural origin of the water spirit.

"Dead in the Water" suggests that it is only through Lucas remembering and communicating to Sam and Dean the details of the localized narrative — of which he has become a part — that they are able to solve the riddle of who is responsible for the drownings that are taking place in the town. Sam and Dean's unearthing of several clues that all relate to the local nature of the water spirit and his victims facilitates important breakthroughs without which the case may have remained unsolved.

The show's prizing of localized unofficial forms of knowledge above that offered by more official and supposedly rational channels is most clearly manifested in "Asylum" (1.10). As the episode opens we join two police officers entering an abandoned asylum in Rockford, Illinois, as they wonder aloud why the asylum has been the site of so many break-ins.

> Walter: What is it, anyway?
> Danny: I forgot you're not local. You don't know the legend.
> Walter: Legend?
> Danny: Every town's got its stories, right? Ours is Roosevelt Asylum. They say it's haunted with the ghosts of the patients. Spend the night — the spirits will drive you insane.

Duly, after leaving the asylum, Walter returns home and shoots himself and his wife. Sam and Dean arrive in Rockford following another set of co-ordinates sent to them by their father which seem to match up with a collection of clippings in their father's diary about a spate of deaths in the local asylum. They encounter Danny Gunderson and find out his version of events, which places the blame on the asylum itself.

In order to find out more about the asylum, Sam poses as a patient for the local psychiatrist James Ellicott, whose deceased father they know used to be chief of staff. Sam poses as a "local history buff" (a nod to the show's reliance on localized stories) in order to try to reveal more of the micro-narrative of the hospital. While Ellicott seems at first to hide the narrative of the hospital from Sam, eventually he reveals the secret history of the asylum, at which point, with a knowledge of the local narrative of the building, they are able to proceed in their quest to solve the case.

Sam works out that the ghosts in the asylum aren't trying to hurt people but are in fact trying to communicate the history of the experiments that happened in room 137; in effect, a local micro-narrative that has been suppressed by those who ran the hospital. Dean finds Sanford Ellicott's old casebook detailing the horrific experiments he used to perform on his unwilling patients and disposes of Ellicott's body to banish the spirit.

More so than the other episodes under discussion here, "Asylum" seems to overtly endorse the importance of micro-narratives. In a version of what Carol J. Clover refers to as "the conflict between White Science and Black Magic" (98) Sam and Dean are pitted against the forces of "rational" enlightenment science, represented by the ghost of Sanford Ellicott, and must utilize their understanding of the irrational field of the supernatural alongside an acquired set of local knowledge concerning the area's history in order to defeat him.

Though the first season episode "Scarecrow" (1.11) is often seen as the point at which the show's creators began to introduce a more overarching mythology to the show, primarily because of the inclusion of Meg Masters, by the final third of season 2 the show's creators seem to be consciously laying the groundwork for the narrative that will be instrumental in seasons 3 to 5. While functioning as a stand-alone episode, "Houses of the Holy" (2.13) introduces us to the concept that angels may really exist, a fact that has a large part to play in later seasons of the show. Furthermore the aptly titled "Tall Tales" (2.15) marks an interesting shift in the show's attitudes toward its own use of micro-narratives. Throughout that episode, the clichéd urban legend–related stories Sam and Dean are told about by various members of a university campus are revealed to be the work of a trickster who (we find out in season 5) turns out to be the Archangel Gabriel in disguise. Finally, season 2's "All Hell Breaks Loose, Part 1" (2.21) and "Part 2" (2.22) see an escalation of the brothers' battle against the demons to stop an impending Apocalypse that will come to define the overarching mythology of the remainder of the show to date.

Comments made by Kripke suggest that those behind the show consciously shifted their intentions from individual episodes centered on the kind of horror inflected micro-narratives outlined, to constructing a cohesive master narrative or 'mythology' centered on the character's relationships with one another.

> When we started out, we were going to make a horror movie every week. It was about the monsters, and it was about Hook Man and Bloody Mary and the urban legends and the boys honestly, in the beginning, Sam and Dean were an engine to get us in and out of different horror movies every week. [Now] for me, the story is about, 'Can the strength of family overcome destiny and fate, and can family save the world?' (Ryan, "It's the Fun")

In taking this new direction, *Supernatural* stands as an interesting example of a text that has moved to purposefully disinherit the supposed artistic freedoms of postmodernity and instead return to a modernist dependence on a totalizing grand narrative. In the case of *Supernatural*, the show seems to have adopted a particularly humanist stance in its later seasons, with the mythology of the show — Sam and Dean fight angels and demons (and each other) in an attempt to stave off the impending Apocalypse — constituting a kind of grand narrative but also belying a belief in the relevance of larger meta-narratives. As Kripke suggests: "If I had a worldview, and I don't know if I do, but if I did, it's one that's intensely humanistic. [That worldview] is that the only thing that matters is family and personal connection, and that's the only thing that gives life meaning" (Ryan, "It's the Fun").

Kripke's comments reflect the ideological struggle taking place within the show's overarching mythology in which the humanism of Sam and Dean, the love and compassion they share for each other and those around them, will eventually triumph over the extremist views of the angels and demons they fight and in the process bring about a better world: "[I]t's basically about two red-blooded, human brothers giving them all the middle finger and saying, basically, 'Screw you; it's our planet. If you want to have a war, pick another one'" (Ryan, "It's the Fun").

While a sense that the lives of the two brothers have been prede-termined by larger forces permeates the Apocalypse storyline, much of the narrative of seasons 4 and 5 suggests that Sam and Dean are engaged in an active and conscious struggle to fight against their pre-ordained destiny. In the process they can be seen as effectively working to subvert the grand narrative that has been set out for them, as though it is the all-encompassing nature of this story (and their supposed lack of control over it) that proves to be the biggest bugbear for them, as Sam humorously suggests in the last episode of season 5: "Remember when we used to just fight wendigos?" ("Swan Song," 5.22)

It is interesting to note that the shift to an overarching meta-narrative also allows for a greater sense of serialization in *Supernatural*, with the humanistic element of the show providing a recurrent point of focus from one episode to the next that was otherwise missing in some of the very first episodes of the show.

In his essay on the serial narrative and popular Showtime series *Dexter*, David Lavery examines the differing storytelling formats open to the contemporary television show. Lavery proposes that two main avenues exist: "The Traditional/Episodic, in which each episode stands alone, adding little or nothing to the cumulative memory of the show over seasons/years. In sharp contrast, serial narratives [tell] open-ended, linear stories" (46). One must note here Lavery's implicit support for the serialized format; he suggests that *Dexter* must work out how to embrace such an organizational methodology if it is to be truly successful in the long term. Lavery's belief that many of the more successful shows tell their narratives in a serialized fashion that allows for greater character development and narrative depth is a common critical stance in writing about contemporary or quality television. Jane Feuer, writing on the concept of quality television, suggests that "First of all, it is serialized" (149), while Roberta Pearson notes that "Since the early 1980s, increasingly high production values and increasingly dense serial narratives have boosted television several rungs up the cultural hierarchy" (248).

While later seasons of *Supernatural* have undoubtedly embraced a more serialized format, the structure of the show remains perhaps closer to what Robin Nelson terms "the flexi-narrative," or "a hybrid mix of serial and series forms" (qtd in Lavery 46). That is to say that while *Supernatural* has shifted toward an overarching mythology or grand narrative, it still intersperses Sam and Dean's fight to stop Lucifer and save the world from the Apocalypse with occasional stand-alone episodes that tackle a more traditional "monster of the week" (see season 5's "Fallen Idols," 5.5, or "Changing Channels," 5.8). The show's adherence to this flexi-narrative format, which differentiates it from many other heavily arc-driven series, allows for "breaks" in which an uninitiated audience member can enter and begin watching the series without needing to have familiarized themselves with its (often complex) ongoing mythology. Such a dual structuring of *Supernatural*'s later seasons may suggest a degree of hesitancy on the part of the show's creative team to fully alienate potential new viewers, a move that proved an annoying distraction to some long-time viewers who wanted the show to focus on the Apocalypse story arc alone.

Indeed, such an approach may be wise. For, in spite of the fairly widespread critical proclivity for serialized narratives apparent in some of the material on quality TV, there is evidence to suggest that some members of the show's audience did not embrace *Supernatural*'s concerted move toward a more continuous (or flexi-narrative) form of storytelling to the same extent that many scholarly critics did.

Discussing the possibility of budgetary cuts brought about by the ongoing concerns of Warner Brothers, one fan of the show, Charlotte Dampier, writes on an internet message board: "I am pleased that the budget will be cut. Season 1 was the best [season] in my opinion, because it had that 'classic, urban myth' type feel to it. Plus, it included a lot of emotional family issues which the boys were struggling with" (Dampier). Overlooking the fact that progressive seasons of the show would appear to have increased the focus on the brothers' handling of issues related to their familial ties, this fan noticeably highlights the show's gradual elision of urban myth–based content at the expense of a wider overarching mythology. Her preference for the kind of episodic micro-narratives common in earlier seasons speaks to a desire for noncontinuous, structural repetition that would seem to stand in opposition to the critics' wish for complex and ongoing serial narratives.

Dampier's opinions are expanded on by "Seth" in the quote below:

> What happened to horror and urban legends? Kripke used to talk about how writing a show focusing on those two things was his absolute dream from the time he first came to Hollywood. Now he's writing a show about morals and turning Dean and Sam from lone, bada$$ hunters into the boyscouts of the hunting world where everyone they meet is even worse than they are. Taking his originally unique premise and making it like half a dozen other TV series in recent memory (Seth).

The partial rejection of the show's move toward serialized narrative seems to be attributable to two factors: firstly, the show's diminishing engagement with the often overtly horror-inflected urban legends, of the kind found in early episodes such as "Bloody Mary" (1.5) and "Hook Man" (1.7), and secondly, its substitution of these episodic installments with serialized ones containing more socially and familial-based concerns. This move has proven to be off-putting to a sector of the audience whose primary interest in the show appears to have been tied to its successful emulation of the often visceral nature and concentrated suspense of more conventional horror narratives. The show's perceived shift away from its "'classic, urban myth' type feel," its supposed "watering down" of horror content, and its move toward a more serialized and ostensibly "soapy" format appears to lie behind Seth's (and many fans') heated rejection of *Supernatural*'s later seasons. Indeed, fan aversion to the show's later direction is self-reflexively commented upon in the season 4 episode "The Monster at the End of This Book" (4.18) when Dean reads a disgruntled fan's comments that "the demon story line is trite, clichéd, and overall craptastic."

In his study of the cultural presence of the horror genre, Matt Hills discusses scholarly work on horror on television, noting the lack of recent material that addresses the subject: "one could still be forgiven for assuming that 'Horror TV' does not meaningfully exist as a category" (*The Pleasure of Horror* 112). Hills comes to the conclusion that "Horror as a generic ascription is rendered structurally absent in these discourses, or *academically exnominated*" (112; italics in original). It is not too much of a stretch to see *Supernatural*'s move toward serialization as a bid for greater critical legitimacy, moving it away from a reliance on and emulation of horror movie narratives and toward an (arguably no less) original engagement with a more biblically inflected storyline.

Seth also questions the originality of the show following the changes that have taken place over its later seasons. While such fan discussions have a tendency to overlook the inherently derivative nature of many of *Supernatural*'s earlier episodes (which frequently and consciously repackage the narratives of popular horror films for television), there is a kernel of truth in the belief that in refocusing the show on Sam and Dean's moral battle to stop the impending Apocalypse, *Supernatural* has become derivative of other shows with serialized ongoing narratives. Despite its attempts at a flexi-narrative format, the show does seem to have become noticeably more akin to other significant genre series such as *The X-Files* (1993–2002) and *Lost* (2004–2010) in its reliance on an increasingly convoluted mythology that may be impenetrable to new viewers. Indeed, while an episode such as the season 5 opener "Sympathy for the Devil" (5.1) may be indicative of both the strength and depth of the show's overarching narrative, the episode's reliance on characters (Lilith, Meg, and Bobby) and plot points (the relationship between the brothers and Castiel, the 66 seals) introduced and explained in previous seasons might prove indecipherable to a newcomer to the show who is unfamiliar with the mythology that preceded this particular episode.

Lavery notes in his aforementioned essay on *Dexter* that the "narrative eschatology of a television series is a matter of great complexity" (47). While *Supernatural*'s concerted move away from the engagement with the micro-narratives offered by its earlier monster-of-the-week format to a mythology or grand narrative of the brothers' battle to stop the impending Apocalypse has proved successful in terms of ratings, the ending of the Apocalypse storyline at the close of season 5 alongside the appointment of Sera Gamble as showrunner in place of the departing Kripke, suggest a new direction for the show. Jared Padalecki recently commented that season 6 is "kind of like monsters on steroids, things have picked up a notch . . . we're fighting the 'big baddies,' so it's a whole other cup of tea, where we are going back and honoring our roots of the show" (qtd in Rundle 8–9). The series' creative team might now be attempting to combine the two previously disparate strands of *Supernatural*'s narrative in order to ensure that the show maintains its large and "vocal, sometimes demanding, sometimes difficult" fan base into the future (Felschow).

Breaking the Mirror
Metafictional Strategies
in *Supernatural*
Alberto N. García

> Like those guys, from the book. What are they called?
> Uh . . . *Supernatural!* Two guys use fake IDs with rock
> aliases, hunt down ghosts, demons, and vampires.
> What are their names? Uh . . .
> *"The Monster at the End of This Book" (4.18)*

When the seller of the "Golden Comic" bookshop describes the protagonists of the novels written by Carver Edlund, viewers share the surprise of Sam and Dean, the protagonists of *Supernatural*, the TV show. With the characters' realization that their own lives are being reflected in the books, the illusionist mirror created by this fantasy series of horror and adventure is shattered.

Illusionism, argues Robert Stam, "pretends to be something more than mere artistic production; it presents its characters as real people, its sequence of words or images as real time, and its representations as substantiated fact" (1). But what happens in the "The Monster at the End of This Book" is not an isolated occurrence. Because one of the most unique narrative strategies of *Supernatural* is the way it creates a break with the mirror that characterizes traditional fiction and turns it in upon itself, underscoring its own fictitiousness. This rupture occurs, in varying degrees, throughout the entire series and proves essential in the Winchesters' battle against the army of darkness.

Patricia Waugh defines metafiction as "a term given to fictional writing which self-consciously and systematically draws attention to its status as an artifact in order to pose questions about the relationship between fiction and reality" (2). Stam, Burgoyne, and Flitterman-Lewis, meanwhile, use the term "reflexivity" to refer to "the process by which texts foreground their own production, their authorship, their intertextual influences, their textual processes, or their reception" (200).

These definitions identify the main characteristic of metafiction: its attempt to lay bare the conventions of realism and the artifice produced by fiction. Accordingly, in *Supernatural*'s metafictional fragments, the "demarcations between text and context, story and interpretation, and writing and reading can become blurred or reversed" (Martin 174), introducing into the heart of the TV series realities coming from outside the work itself.

Although it is a widespread phenomenon in the audiovisual universe, metafiction cannot be defined as a genre unto itself like detective fiction, horror, or comedy. It is, rather, a transverse category that runs across a work. As a result, this essay will discuss comic episodes ("Tall Tales," 2.15), drama ("Swan Song," 5.22), reality television ("Ghostfacers," 3.13), and even retro pastiche ("Monster Movie," 4.5), all examples of different genres that are, at the same time, metafictional. I will analyze how the elements that define illusionism are cast into doubt or directly challenged in *Supernatural* because metafiction is born from pushing the boundaries of the classic artistic tension between illusion and reflexivity (Stam 1). It is an attempt to unveil the mechanisms that shape such an illusion, negating the idea of transparency and realism that has traditionally been granted to fiction.

With this theoretical background, this essay attempts to sketch a map of the reflexive strategies that the creators of the series gradually employ: the juxtaposition of fictional and real worlds, the recurrent intertextuality, the satire of the television medium, the self-consciousness of the story, and the breaking down of the fourth wall.

"How are we in Heaven?"

Firstly, *Supernatural*'s narrative exhibits a conventional format, where characters live in a fictional world and act out fictional plotlines. However, there are some episodes that call into question their boundaries by contrasting the fantasy world and that of the "real world" (the fictional world of the story). These are episodes where the writers slowly break the illusionism little by little, but not totally. The characters move within the plotline from the "real world" to the "fantasy world," but they never address the camera or step out of character. Thus the viewer is simply an outside observer looking into this two world diegetic[1] story.

These alternate realities — a convention of the fantasy genre — occur for the first time in "What Is and What Should Never Be" (2.20), where Dean is attacked by a djinn, a kind of genie from Arabian mythology, that knocks people out and makes them dream peacefully. Dean enters a fantasy world without demons where his mother is alive and his relationship with Sam is cold and distant. While this alternate reality is in many ways preferable, he comes to realize that it is not real and he needs to wake up. This narrative strategy causes a stinging melancholy for a life that might have been but is not. Something similar happens in "It's a Terrible Life" (4.17) in which the brothers live dull and boring lives in an alternate reality. This time, a number of hinge elements present in both universes — such as the Ghostfacers' website or the Winchesters' recurring dreams of hunting things — cause them to become aware of existing in a parallel world. An even more hallucinatory dream takes place in "When the Levee Breaks" (4.21), in which Sam is confined in order to overcome his addiction to demon blood and, in full withdrawal, imagines being tortured by Alastair, visited by a young Sammy, and supported by his mother.

There is still a final, diegetic leap into an alternate reality in "Dark Side of the Moon" (5.16) when the Winchesters are killed and relive happy memories in a heavenly journey through their pasts. "How are we in Heaven?" Sam asks Dean, surprised by the new geographical surroundings. This juxtaposition of "fictional" and "real worlds" does not want to make the viewer aware that he or she is watching a TV show, but rather to reinforce to the viewer that the character has come from "reality" and has moved to a "fictional reality." This is just the first degree of playing with the illusion.

In this cartography, I will leave aside the temporal leaps presented in episodes such as "After School Special" (4.13) or "In the Beginning" (4.3) because they don't weaken the illusion very much, since time-travel is a part of the fantasy genre. However, the narrative structures of *Supernatural* employ one formula that tarnishes the illusionistic mirror: storytellers who become entangled in the story. Thus, the episodes that play with perspective and temporality cause the viewer to suspend their belief in the illusion to focus on the constructed nature typical of every narrative.[2] "Tall Tales" chronicles the playful spells of the Trickster; in this episode, narrative form and content combine to offer a story that plays with the point of view of every character. The illusion is constantly broken when the delegated narrators (Sam and Dean) stop the action to discuss the events they are relating and shape them to make plain the subjective nature of a memory that ridicules the other brother. For example, when Sam portrays his brother as a glutton, stuffing his mouth full of snacks, Dean interrupts Sam's narration complaining: "C'mon! I ate one . . . maybe two!" while Sam answers: "Just let me tell it, okay?" In fact, one of the favorite mechanisms of the self-conscious narrators rest precisely in the way they "call explicit attention to the shifting relations between the twin time schemes of story and discourse" (Stam 140), so that the humor of the episode consists in an element of metatextual distancing within the story itself and its different versions.

"Roadkill" (2.16) acts in a similar way, although it does not have a narrator: the story conceals vital information from the viewers to maintain the suspense and surprise. At the beginning of the episode, Sam and Dean meet Molly, a woman who has just suffered a car accident and is running away from a bloodied and eviscerated man. By the end, the events of the episode are retold and a vital piece of data is added: Sam and Dean knew that Molly was a ghost who would not accept her death and, consequently, they decide to play along with her game to unveil her true identity.

"Like my man Jack in *The Shining*"

"Roadkill" is also one example of the strong intertextuality that forms part of *Supernatural*, which plays an important role in its popularity. As Peirse affirms, "*Supernatural*'s success can be partially attributed to its popular culture references, exploration of urban legends, and incorporation of horror film tropes" (264).

Intertextuality breaks down the illusion when the show makes allusions that cause viewers to recall references outside the show itself. In its attempt to question the relationship between reality and fiction, intertextual references emphasize the idea of language as a constructor of reality. Consequently, these audiovisual texts offer several meanings for a single signifier, a "semantic superimposition" that operates on two levels: "that of the narrative, where it continues to signify like any other utterance, and that of the reflection, where it intervenes as an element of metasignification" (Dallenbach 44). For one level to live off the other, more competence is required of the audience, who, by hearing a particular word or phrase, immediately recalls other pop culture allusions relating to it. In the case of *Supernatural*, external references are endless: from the now-classic presentations of Sam and Dean with the names of rock stars[3] to re-interpretations of movie titles, *Supernatural* is a *horror vacui* of cultural events from music, television, and popular cinema.

Standalone episodes predominate over the first season — brief adventures that draw a map of evil teeming with witches, spirits, vampires, zombies, and other monster-of-the-week cases — an ideal approach for embedding re-readings and tributes to the genre. Thus, "Dead in the Water" (1.3) includes shots reminiscent of *Jaws* (1975), "Bloody Mary" (1.5) uses the visual imagery of *Ringu* (1998),[4] "Asylum" (1.10) has a similar premise to *House on Haunted Hill* (1999) and makes several explicit references to the films of Jack Nicholson, "Scarecrow" (1.11) takes elements of *The Blair Witch Project* (1999), and "The Benders" (1.15) alludes to *The Texas Chainsaw Massacre* (1974), *The Hills Have Eyes* (1977), and *The X-Files* episode "Home" (4.2).

The second season, marked by the internal evolution of Sam and the fight against the yellow-eyed devil, boasts more continuity. The visual references are still present in "Children Shouldn't Play with Dead Things" (2.4), which recalls Romero's zombie films; "Croatoan" (2.9) is constructed with figures from infection movies like *28 Days Later* (2002); and "Playthings" (2.11) borrows the barman from *The Shining* (1980) and *The Others'* (2001) dead children.

Among the allusions of the third season, highlights include the titular comic book by Frank Miller, which emerges from the plot and the viscous moral tone of "Sin City" (3.4); "Bedtime Stories" (3.5) recycles numerous fairy tales; "Mystery Spot" (3.11) honors *Groundhog Day* (1993); "Jus in Bello" (3.12) remakes *Assault on Precinct 13* (1976); and the villain of "Time Is on My Side" (3.15) seems to be a Highlander-inspired version of Buffalo Bill from *The Silence of the Lambs* (1991).

The fourth season, the most baroque of the series, is also rich in semantic relationships that demand the viewer's familiarity with multiple references in order to be completely and correctly interpreted. "In the Beginning" (4.3) could not be understood without knowing *Back to the Future* (1985); "Wishful Thinking" (4.8) represents ironically the shower scene from *Psycho* (1960); "Family Remains" (4.11) contains plot elements of *The Evil Dead* (1981); and "It's a Terrible Life" (4.17) turns the classic *It's a Wonderful Life* (1946) on its head.

In the fifth season, although the intertextual fecundity decreases slightly, "The Curious Case of Dean Winchester" (5.7) recalls the plot of a film of similar name (*The Curious Case of Benjamin Button* [2008]); "Changing Channels" (5.8) reuses the premise of *Stay Tuned*

(1992) and an episode of *Doctor Who* ("Bad Wolf," 1.12); and "Sam, Interrupted" (5.11) takes its psychiatric idea from *Girl, Interrupted* (1999). Beyond this list, which is not intended to be exhaustive, there are episodes that feature a story where the world of fiction itself becomes the driving force of the plot.

"I hate procedural cop shows"

Faced with the narrative exhaustion announced by John Barth, the medium of television has now turned back in on itself in search of originality for its narratives, with deliberately illusionistic stories whose plots are about the fictional universe in some of its different manifestations: the shooting of a film, a pastiche of classic horror films, and television satire.

"Hollywood Babylon" (2.18) shows us the world behind the screen. The Winchester brothers observe the filming of *Hell Hazers II: The Reckoning* in order to solve the mystery of a series of paranormal deaths. The opening scene of the episode adopts the thematic conventions and style of a typical horror film to show the dark picture and the cliché of a young woman alone in the forest. But abruptly, the voice of the director yells, "Cut!" and the spectator realizes the images are from the filming of a terror movie. The viewer is first drawn in by the illusion — a process Coleridge called "the willing suspension of disbelief" (Cuddon 413) — and then jolted back to reality when the mechanisms upon which the fiction is built are revealed. In general, the entire episode is a scathing "making-of" applied to the horror genre, because the viewer sees how visual tricks involving color or makeup are constructed, how corny the director is, the main actress's difficulties in producing a believable scream, naïve studio executives who ask how ghosts can hear the chanting, and scriptwriters who borrow their material from "real life" just to have it ruined onscreen.

Semantic overload also occurs through parody, as in "Monster Movie." At times like this, metafiction can be regarded as parody when it becomes "a 'mirror' to fiction, in the ironic form of the imitation of art in art, as well as by more direct references" to authors, movies, and viewers (Rose 65). The episode recycles classic elements and characters from the genre, with explicit references to the classic myths of Dracula, Frankenstein, the Mummy, and werewolves. Furthermore, it is a special episode in which the visual continuity of the series is broken from the black and white opening credits that call for a nostalgic reading by the viewer, aware that Kripke is subverting the referents and adapting them to the playful environment of *Supernatural*. Consequently, "Monster Movie" is a kitsch[5] product, a work of terror from the '30s, but without the terror — all the monsters the shapeshifter recreates are "grand and elegant" while, at the same time, quite antiheroic and not frightening at all: Dracula, for example, rides a scooter, and uses a coupon to pay for the pizza he ordered (without garlic, of course).

"Changing Channels," in which Sam and Dean, victims of one of the Trickster's spells, are literally trapped inside TV Land, is an exercise of style that satirizes other TV shows by emulating the grammar of sitcoms, police procedurals such as the *CSI* franchise, medical dramas like *Grey's Anatomy*, and even TV ads. As a result *Supernatural* becomes a parodic mosaic of quotations. Dean, dressed as *CSI: Miami*'s Horatio Caine, complains: "I hate procedural cop shows. There are like three hundred of them on television. They are all the freakin' same." This episode is a highly meta-fictional artifact, ranging from playful references to *Knight Rider* to denouncing humiliating game shows from Asia. But this CW series also knows how to laugh at itself, as my discussion of the self-consciousness of "Ghostfacers" and the use of amusing cameo appearances will make clear in the next section.

"I could really go for pea soup"
Cameos are a common practice in television fiction and many actors have played occasional roles on TV series. But these cases do not cease to be actors playing a role and, although the confusion of seeing a familiar face in a familiar universe not associated with that actor can

be somewhat disruptive to the illusion, cameos maintain the pact between the author and the viewer inherent in any work of fiction.

There are three especially significant appearances that, in varying degrees, serve to shatter *Supernatural*'s fictional mirror by employing the simulacrum of the self; that is, an actor who plays with his own identity, both real and fictional. In "The Usual Suspects" (2.7), Linda Blair plays a cop who helps the Winchesters. At the end of the episode, after saying goodbye, Dean says she looks familiar and that "for some reason" he "could really go for pea soup." It is an obvious allusion to Blair's role in *The Exorcist*, which used pea soup to simulate the thick, green vomit her possessed character hurled at Father Karras. In the aforementioned "Roadkill," Tricia Helfer's role resembles the one she played in *Battlestar Galactica*, a story also built on the ambiguity of identity, where some humans do not know they are Cylons. In this way, Molly is related intertextually with *Battlestar*'s Number Six, for she is a ghost who does not know she is dead. In both cameos, *Supernatural* writers could feel confident that the audience would "get" these references, considering the show attracts both horror and fantasy genre fans.

More complex is Paris Hilton's ironic cameo in "Fallen Idols" (5.5). In keeping with such HBO series as *Entourage* (2004–), *Curb Your Enthusiasm* (2000–), and *Extras* (2005–2007), which playfully break the fictional illusion by introducing into the heart of the diegesis a star who has fun with the sham of playing themselves, Hilton plays herself in a plot in which historical individuals and celebrities attack people, but ends up losing her head. The three examples cited (Blair, Helfer, Hilton) parody projected film or public images, crossing the borders between not only reality and fiction, but the person, the character, and the cameo.

"Fallen Idols" in particular shows the extent of the series' self-referential winks to the audience. Dean claims to have seen *House of Wax* (2005), a film in which Hilton works alongside Padalecki, the actor who plays Sam. Thus, this simulation of the self is extended with little jokes about the past of the show's actors themselves. Similarly, in "Hollywood Babylon," Sam gets nervous when it is announced that they will visit the set of *Gilmore Girls* (2000–2007) and perhaps see some of its stars; as fans of the show know, Padalecki was an actor in that series. In this episode, there is another inside joke that demands metatextual understanding of the fan. Sam asks Dean: "Does this feel like swimming weather to you? It's practically Canadian," referring to the filming of the series in Vancouver. There are even jokes involving the producers and writers: in that same episode, Tara Bentchley declares, "Oh, God, what a terrible script!" in reference to *Boogeyman* (2005), a film written by Kripke just prior to his work on *Supernatural*. In the same way, the director of the false *Hell Hazers II* is McG, one of the executive producers of the series, while, in the episode where Chuck appears for the first time, the Winchesters are having a lunch at a diner called, not coincidentally, "Kripke's Hollow."

"The Dean and Sam you've been writing about"

By self-referencing, the series goes one more step toward breaking the fictional mirror, further blurring the relationship between text and context for the audience. These metafictional devices turn the show in upon itself and make visible what was previously invisible to the viewer (Dallenbach 15): the author and the production process (Chuck's appearance and farewell), the viewer and the reception (the jokes about "sick" slash fandom), or the conventions of the genre ("The Real Ghostbusters" plays on how the fans are aware of the terror movie code).

Although there are other small self-referential winks,[6] the point of no return is the Pirandellian "The Monster at the End of This Book," in which the protagonists arrive at Chuck's house, revealing themselves to "the prophet" who authors the "Winchester gospels" to be "the Dean and Sam" he has "been writing about." Despite the baroque quality of the episode, the text always stays within the diegesis and does not break the fourth wall. The structure presents an initial narrative instance, the overall story presented as the series *Supernatural*, which gives rise to a second instance, the story of Chuck's novels . . . which in turn reveals the mechanisms of creation in the first instance. There's even a moment where two bodies collide. Chuck reads in his notes:

> Sam and Dean approached the run-down, ramshackle house with trepidation. Did they really want to learn the secrets that lay beyond that door? Sam and Dean traded soulful looks. Then, with determination, Dean pushed the doorbell with forceful determination.

And that's exactly what we see as spectators, with Chuck's voice-over narrating events as they unfold so that the subordinate and the main narratives overlap in a textual paradox that creates a disturbing impression of a work-in-progress as it reveals its structures and mechanisms. The apparent impasse is overcome because Chuck is not a creative author, but a prophet, a passive subject who brings to the role whatever the Creator dictates. So the arc of Chuck's story does not initially affect the story of the Winchesters, but the way it is received does, as illustrated by the parodying and self-allusive episode "The Real Ghostbusters" (5.9).

Although the show's fans had already been satirized (and, as Felschow's study observed, "neutralized") in "The Monster at the End of This Book," "The Real Ghostbusters" is where they now become the center of the message in a fictional *Supernatural* convention. The humor of the episode comes from a self-conscious text (the *Supernatural* novels that parallel the television series) that confronts *Supernatural*'s most loyal fans, making fun of the show itself by revealing its tics and recurrent conventions. In doing so, some stylistic and thematic codes from the series itself are laid bare: for example, all the wannabes speak in grave voices, emulating Sam and Dean. They also realize how easily the protagonists lose their weapons in the climax of every episode, and take the recurrent use of fake IDs with rock star aliases to an absurd extreme. However, Chuck's passive status changes in "Swan Song" (5.22), in which the fourth wall finally collapses.

"The bold new future of reality TV"

The most radical move *Supernatural* has permitted itself has been its direct address to the viewer. In this case, the fourth wall disappears and the exchanges between the audience and the television set are immediate. Interactivity with the audience breaks down the illusion, radically exposing the artificial nature of the TV series. But we must also distinguish two different ways of breaking down the fourth wall. On the one hand, the episodes masked by other forms of televised discourse, which happens structurally when the series counterfeits another format. There are cases, as in *The Office* (BBC, 2001–2003), *The Comeback* (2005), *Parks and Recreation* (2009–), and *Modern Family* (2009–), in which a declarative mechanism — television fiction itself — pretends to be another: a docu-show, a device which, by means of frequent indicators that change the focus from primary to secondary statements, ends up making them coincide "to the extent that they occupy the entire space and time of representation" (Savorelli 173). In these mockumentary moments, the viewer is addressed directly, and we are reminded that a camera is always present.

In *Supernatural* the same thing happens upon emulating a reality TV format in "Ghostfacers." This particular episode of *Supernatural* is instead presented as a television program filmed by Ed and Harry, who introduce the "revolutionary" show as an alternative to the "crippling writers' strike" of 2008, referring here to the actual strike by the Writers' Guild of America.[7] "The unsolicited pilot you are about to watch is the bold new future of reality TV," they claim. The footage is made up of constant blurring of fiction and reality that is consistent with those that occur in reality TV programs: repeated takes of the same shots, questions directed at the film crew, the constant appearance of cameras, slates, and microphones in shots, backstage footage . . . even the characters, including Sam and Dean, speak *spontaneously* to the camera, aware that they are being recorded. Thus the episode employs many of the rhetorical techniques proper to the mockumentary format, reminding us that what we are watching is a fictional television show.

"I'm telling you, they're a raging pain in the ass"
On the other hand, the fourth wall can be broken when the characters, albeit sporadically, directly invoke the audience. Therefore, metafictional culmination comes at two different moments when *Supernatural* breaks the fourth wall without the necessity of having to disguise it as just another mechanism. The first occurs in the hilarious coda to "Yellow Fever" (4.6). The textual authority that drives the story, until now always invisible, announces the complete breakdown of the illusion following the identification of Kripke and Singer as executive producers in the end credits. The music starts as we read the sign "*Supernatural* presents Jensen Ackles." The actor begins a goofy performance to the music of "Eye of the Tiger," climbing out of and onto his Chevy Impala while lip-syncing. The laughter, applause, and voices of the production team can be heard in the background throughout the clip, reminding us that we are watching the real-life actor, and not the character he plays on TV.

The second address to the audience is less playful, almost melancholy. Although Chuck's episodes generally place the text of *Supernatural* at the center of the story, only his monologue in "Swan Song" may be understood as breaking the fourth wall. With the script on his desk, the author explicitly addresses the audience in a metatextual reflection, speaking of his own books and the art of storytelling:

> Endings are hard. Any chapped-ass monkey with a keyboard can poop out a beginning, but endings are impossible. You try to tie up every loose end, but you never can. The fans are always gonna bitch. There's always gonna be holes. And since it's the ending, it's all supposed to add up to something. I'm telling you: they're a raging pain in the ass.

These words are a farewell from *Supernatural*'s author, both in fiction and in reality. In fiction the writer acts like a god. Kripke, the creator of the series, says goodbye from the mouth of Chuck, his alter-ego. Kripke's characters have grown so much and achieved such success that they are now more important than the author and can emancipate themselves. Through Chuck, Kripke affirms that things have gone as far as they can go, as he had announced would be the case as he told *Entertainment Weekly*: "Despite what the network and studio may or may not want, I don't have more than five seasons of story." And he does it by leaving clues as to how *his* series will end: in Lawrence, closing the tragic circle, epically facing Lucifer — their greatest enemy — and with Sam sacrificing himself to save Dean. But then Kripke deliberately and clumsily resurrects his characters (Bobby, Castiel, and finally Sam) in a *deus ex machina* that enables another "God-creator" (Sera Gamble) to continue the series. For this reason too, Chuck/Kripke ends up fading into just another implausible and anti-illusionistic plot twist after typing, "The End."

"Nothing ever really ends, does it?"
Eric Kripke once referred to *Supernatural* as "*Star Wars* in truck-stop America" (qtd in Hannah-Jones 55). From the beginning, Kripke sells the series by invoking its intertextual component, with Sam and Dean as imitations of Han Solo and Luke Skywalker in an earthly, rock version of Lucas's adventure story. But the initial references and jokes continue growing until the astonishing turn of events that leads to Sam and Dean's realization that their lives are being novelized. From that point until Chuck's farewell, *Supernatural*'s metafictional strategy transcends the merely playful, and also serves to delve into classical philosophical preoccupations: Who are we? Where do we come from? Can we escape our destiny if it is already written? Is there life after death; that is to say, does "nothing ever really end," as Chuck concludes in his monologue?

The map I have drawn also makes clear how metafiction has become one of the most important strategies of the series. Using the reflexive resources that cinema and commercial television have already developed, *Supernatural* reflects different aspects of the way in which its own discourse functions: the identity of the author, the

critical problems of the work, the process of production and reception, or the story at the time that it is being made. Supported by intertextuality, self-awareness, or direct appeal to the audience, many of
Supernatural's episodes reveal the fictional illusion and the conventions of artistic realism, audiovisually capturing the tension between
representation and reality and transforming the story itself into one
more stop in the fascinating journey of the Winchester brothers.

Part 5

"What's the lore say?"

Exploring Folklore & Religion

"There's nothing more dangerous than some a-hole who thinks he's on a holy mission" Using and (Dis)-Abusing Religious and Economic Authority on *Supernatural*

Erin Giannini

Writing in May 2009, conservative commentator S.T. Karnick posited that *Supernatural*, particularly in its third and fourth seasons, exhibited a "clearly Christian" perspective. He acknowledges that this may be a strange contention to make about a series involving two brothers who fight demons and are part of a subculture of individuals known as "hunters" who are aware of demonic activity and are committed to eradicating these threats. Yet, the series widened its narrative arc each season, with the fourth and fifth seasons focused on an impending and then in-progress biblical Apocalypse, or "spiritual war" as Karnick terms it. To bolster his claim that *Supernatural* is pro-Christian, he cites both "The Monster at the End of This Book" (4.18), in which Dean prays for help, and "When the Levee Breaks" (4.21), in which Dean states to the angel Castiel, "I give myself over wholly to serve God and you guys" and swears obedience to the angels' plans.

What he does not mention is that the following episode indicates that this obedience was neither a wise choice nor one with which Dean will follow through. Zachariah — one of the Archangels and an architect of the exploitation of the Apocalypse set in motion by the Winchesters — reveals that the angels' plan has always been to let it happen. Rather than a true conversion, Dean's aforementioned statement seems born out of desperation. Nor does he later consider following the full thrust of Zachariah's plan — that Dean serve as a vessel for the Archangel Michael and wage a battle with Lucifer (using Sam as his "meat suit") that will cost billions of lives — until he is in total despair.

While using such a Revelations-based apocalyptic narrative easily lends itself to interpreting *Supernatural* as promoting pro-Christian values,[1] I argue, along with Line Nybro Petersen, that the bricolage of religious and folkloric traditions *Supernatural* incorporates in its narratives disallows tying it explicitly to a single religion. It continues a throughline within a series that, as Erica Engstrom and Joseph M. Valenzano assert (73–74), treats organized religion and individuals organized around religion as, at best, deluded, and, at worst, hypocritical and evil. Further, the interactions between humans and angels trade on the positioning of the Winchesters as itinerant and working-class, with their work interpreted as a metaphor for the current economic and political situation: namely, two wars and a worldwide recession. Julia Wright argues that the Winchesters' downward mobility becomes frightening through the use of the gothic as metaphor for the loss. She points to their vulnerability as itinerant "latchkey" kids (2). I will argue that this is exploited by an angelic hierarchy that is run like a corporation, with a concomitant lack of regard for any collateral damages in pursuit of their profits (goals).

In "Sympathy for the Devil" (5.1), Dean Winchester bluffs that all he needs to kill Lucifer and stop the Apocalypse is a "GED and a give-'em-Hell attitude." While he almost immediately undermines this in a private discussion with his brother, claiming that he only said that to comfort a newly paralyzed Bobby Singer (fellow hunter and father figure to Sam and Dean), such a statement very neatly encapsulates the existence of the Winchester brothers. That this statement is uttered by Dean is also significant. While Sam attended Stanford and scored high enough on the LSATS to gain admission to its law school, the undereducated (in the conventional sense) Dean is the one who, throughout the series, makes the choice of self-sacrifice for family. In the first five seasons of the show, Dean has been shown as a replacement for the brothers' absent and vengeance-filled father, including creating a hotel-room Christmas ("A Very Supernatural Christmas," 3.8) and procuring fireworks to entertain a young Sam ("Dark Side of the Moon," 5.16). Perhaps most importantly, he sacrifices his own life and soul to bring his brother back to life ("All Hell Breaks Loose, Part 2," 2.22), suffering a 40-year sentence in Hell ("Lazarus Rising," 4.1). In contrast, Sam is portrayed in the latter seasons of the series as using his intelligence to rationalize bad choices and disparage Dean's capabilities.[2] Sam is further characterized as being manipulated by forces beyond his control, yet his own ego will not allow him to see it until Lucifer tells him that nearly everyone important to him, from his closest college friend to his prom date, were minions of the demon Azazel manipulating him to be Lucifer's vessel ("Swan Song," 5.22). While it is not the focus of this paper to posit one character as heroic over the other, it is important to make these distinctions between the Winchesters and what their choices say about the series itself and its approach to the issue of class.

While hunters share features with certain militia groups[3] (engaging in unsanctioned armed defense against a perceived threat, operating on the margins of society), the series gives one example of a town in which Hunter culture is mainstreamed. The people of Blue Earth, Minnesota, under the direction of their pastor, David Gideon, and his daughter, Leah, have formed what they call the "Sacrament Lutheran Militia" — the first time in the series the world "militia" is directly used. Hunters, a loose conglomeration of individuals who are often drawn into demon hunting due to the loss of a loved one,[4] are a decentralized group that will occasionally work together, but usually seem to operate alone. Thus, before realizing that there is something amiss in Blue Earth, both Sam and Dean marvel at how much more efficient hunting is when it is done in a large group. "So this is what it's like having back-up," remarks Sam, while Dean quips that he doesn't know whether "to run screaming or buy a condo" ("99 Problems," 5.17). Because Sam and Dean operate with no stable address outside the margins of society, funding their demon-hunting through illegal or semi-legal activities such as credit card fraud and hustling pool, they lack the "back-up" of a settled existence. This comes to the fore in the ways in which the angels attempt to manipulate and control the brothers throughout seasons 4 and 5. In Wright's analysis, *Supernatural* represents a portrayal of an "alienated white underclass." Wright argues that *Supernatural* employs the "gothic" to portray "downward mobility" and the ways in which it endangers children; that is, the depiction of such a downtrodden and difficult upbringing renders "downward class mobility as productive of terror and . . . upward class mobility as always-precarious class-passing rather than achievable economic security" (2). In her view, the loss of their mother and an absentee father bent on vengeance made Sam and Dean at-risk children on an epic scale.

This vulnerability is made manifest in the way Dean talks about being a vessel, referring to the act as "life as an angel condom," "wearing you to the prom," and "riding you." All of Dean's metaphors imply something disposable or frivolous; an individual to be used up and discarded. Indeed, Zachariah implies that Dean has no choice, even as he must consent to being thus used. By contrast, Lucifer is gentle with Sam, appearing first as Jess, his fiancée that was killed by Azazel in the pilot episode, and apologetically telling Sam that there is no point in fighting destiny. As will be addressed below, these differing approaches are significant.

In an essay limited to the first two seasons of *Supernatural*, Wright argues that the memory of a middle-class existence is so painful for Dean that he convinces himself he desires no such thing (7). In her analysis of Dean's djinn-inspired fantasy in "What Is and What Should Never Be" (2.20) she notes that it is his brother who is positioned as firmly middle- to upper-middle class, while Dean works as a mechanic and must have his manners corrected by both brother and mother (11). Seasons 3 through 5, however, offer numerous examples

of Dean's longing for a home and family and Sam as the "precarious" class passer whose life is manipulated by those more powerful
than he. Indeed, as Wright points out in her analysis of "Skin" (1.6),
when Sam and Dean fight a shapeshifter who has taken on the physical appearance of one of Sam's wealthy Stanford friends, Sam admits
to Dean that "deep down, I never really fit in." This is particularly
brought to light less through the Apocalypse itself and more through
its solution: that Dean and Sam must play destined roles as vessels
for the Archangels Michael and Lucifer, respectively. While this is
posited as a choice, both the brothers must, in essence, consent to give
up their bodies to fight a celestial war. The real-world parallels to the
multi-front war in Iraq and Afghanistan seem to operate on a subtextual level, particularly when factoring in the "hunting" culture's own
war against demonic terror, in that the brothers (and hunting culture
as a whole), are in essence fighting an amorphous threat that takes
multiple forms; further, the use of the brothers' bodies by these angels
could represent the ultimate in "stop-loss" policy (that is, the U.S.
military policy that allows a soldier's terms of service to be extended
beyond their volunteer limits (White A01).

An additional parallel exists in Jimmy Novak, a willing human
vessel. Previous to possession, Jimmy was a Christian man who sold
"ad time on AM radio," watched televangelists, and prayed at meal-
times; he is a moderately well-to-do father portrayed as slightly naïve.
In the appropriately named episode "The Rapture" (4.20), an angel-
on-angel battle leads to Castiel being dragged back to Heaven and his
vessel abandoned. The episode switches back and forth between a year
previous and the current time, to trace the original possession and
the consequences of being "emptied" of angelic essence. He accepts
without question what he is instructed to do by Castiel; tests of faith
include sticking his hand in boiling water and believing it won't burn
him. Asking only for his family to be safe, he accepts his role as a
vessel and leaves his family behind.

Yet the "faith" that propels him to accept possession without question does not seem to sustain him after Castiel has left and he is Jimmy

Novak again. When his daughter asks him if he'd like to say grace before dinner, Jimmy refuses. When his family is attacked by demons, he is furious, insisting that he has been betrayed by Heaven, Castiel in particular. His faith and acceptance can do nothing to keep his family safe; he must either die or leave his family to become a permanent vessel. Had he not accepted in the first place, his family would not have been endangered. Jimmy's exposure to this celestial war leaves him a marked man on numerous levels; not only is he exposed to the demonic/celestial world, but he is pursued by demons who think he may have knowledge of Heaven's plans that can be extracted from him.[5]

This episode succinctly sets up the choice Dean and Sam must make in season 5: whether to accept becoming vessels and killing one another. In each scenario, "family" (which represents Eric Kripke's avowed "religion") must be abandoned. Such choices cannot help but be coded as negative, or, at best, pyrrhic, within *Supernatural*'s universe. Further, the relative class positioning of the Novaks versus the Winchesters, as well as the "Heavenly" hierarchy of angels, recreates some elements of the current socioeconomic situation in the United States. It is not only the Winchesters' itinerant status and militia-like culture that feels the effects of a world in recession; it cuts across economic and even spiritual lines.

It is explicitly referenced as such in "Point of No Return" (5.18), in which a disgruntled Zachariah enters a bar and orders a drink. The conversation he has with Stuart, an assuming patron, is easily taken as completely normal (with a few exceptions). Stuart immediately recognizes the look of someone who's been pink-slipped (i.e., reprimanded for having made a corporate error), and asks Zachariah what his crime was. Zachariah explains that he couldn't close "the deal of the millennium."

> Zachariah: That's all they care about upstairs, ain't it? Results, results, results. They don't know. They're not down on the ground, in the mud, nose to nose with all you pig-filthy humans, am I right?

Stuart: Absolute— filthy what?

Zachariah: I mean, what ever happened to personal loyalty? How long have I worked for these guys? Five millennia? Six?

Stuart: Seems like it, don't it?

Zachariah: Goddamned straight, it does.

From the self-described angel with "six wings and four faces, one of which is a lion," from whom other angels would avert their eyes ("Dark Side of the Moon"), Zachariah has been degraded to the equivalent of a formerly powerful, disgraced executive. It is significant that when Zachariah offers Dean an alternative existence, it's as director of Sales and Marketing at Sandover Bridge and Iron ("It's a Terrible Life," 4.17). As Zachariah tells Dean at the end of the episode, it was a real place and a real haunting, but both he and Sam were put into the situation without their memories, to prove a point that hunting is "in your blood." Both Dean and, significantly, Sam, express discomfort with a middle-class lifestyle. Such unhappiness adds a particular and troubling resonance to Zachariah's insistence that the life they lead is inherent in who they are. While he puts it in terms of destiny and the excitement of a life on the road helping others, it also touches on Wright's analysis of "class-passing" in *Supernatural*: they cannot move beyond their non-status as homeless hunters (8) because of an innate difference between themselves and "normal" people. It is not just knowledge of an underworld that leads them to become hunters, but that they cannot transcend their class no matter what choices they make.

As an "executive" angel, Zachariah is contemptuous of those beneath him, including other angels, but especially Sam and Dean. While Jimmy Novak is asked to perform a few tests of faith by Castiel and Sam is sweet-talked by Lucifer, Zachariah's approach and characterization from his first appearance to his demise in "Point of No Return" shows varying degrees of disgust at humans in general. To get Dean to agree to serve as Michael's vessel, he first offers to heal Bobby (paralyzed after a demon attack), but, upon refusal, removes

Sam's lungs and gives Dean stomach cancer. He sends Dean five years into the future where Dean is forced to watch his own death at the hands of Sam ("The End," 5.4). While the diegesis is open to interpretation (is it actual time travel or an alternate universe created by Zachariah?), it is a rare episode that takes place in an urban environment. While *Supernatural*'s stories normally take place in small towns and back roads, the episode's use of a mid-sized urban environment is significant in that Dean "lands" in a broken-down industrial center — where alleyways overflow with garbage, a feral child lurks, and factories have been abandoned. Such devastation, unlike the urban legends and historic "lore" of earlier seasons, does not necessarily need to be wrought by supernatural means; it could conceivably be any abandoned industrial center.

In this future, however, most of the population is infected with the Croatoan virus (which causes murderous rage in the infected). Zachariah claims this is in order to fully apprise Dean of the consequences of his defiance, yet certain aspects of this future seem to push the idea that it is an alternate reality. When Dean is faced with his future self, that self's advice is exactly in line with Zachariah's desire — that 2009 Dean says yes to being a vessel. The confrontation between 2009 Dean and 2014 Sam — now the vessel of Lucifer — takes place in Jackson County, Missouri, which Joseph Smith, in the Book of Mormon, claimed was the location of the Garden of Eden (McKeever). As Lucifer, Sam strokes one of the roses growing in profusion around him (a subtle moment, since roses and apples are of the same genus). While certain elements within "The End" come to fruition — such as Sam becoming Lucifer's vessel in Detroit, the slow decline of Castiel's angelic powers due to his rebellion, Lucifer's plan to release Croatoan into the population — the results of the trip were not precisely what Zachariah intended. Dean's "lesson" results in him reconnecting with his brother to help Sam more effectively fight destiny and Sam's own darkness. The "end" that Zachariah seeks does not occur, yet he is willing to take extraordinary measures to see it come to pass. He later resurrects Sam and Dean's dead brother Adam as a bargaining chip, manipulating Adam with promises that he will be reunited with his mother. Thus Zachariah represents the "petty" ("Dark Side of the Moon") face of a Heaven run like a corporation, forcing unconscionable choices on those who work for him (who represent, in essence, a lower socioeconomic class) in pursuit of his own ends.

As for the brothers, two parallel narrative arcs exist for Sam and Dean that are as diametrically opposed to one another as the two angels for whom the Winchester boys are fated to act as vessels. This is made manifest in "Dark Side of the Moon" when both Sam and Dean are transported to their idea of Heaven. Sam's happiest memories focus on independence from his family and a lack of accountability for his actions; from the first episode of the series, Sam vacillates between having to be dragged into the "hunting" life or embracing a vigilante, black and white view of what needs to be done.[6] His two heavenly moments involve a Christmas dinner with his girlfriend's family and the two weeks he spent on his own in Phoenix as a teenager. In Dean's case, his memories focus on the home and mother he lost and the small ways he tried to give his younger brother a sense of family. In this way, Dean represents what Kripke has claimed the show itself is about: "Can the strength of family overcome destiny and fate, and can family save the world?" (Ryan, "It's the fun"). This is a lesson Sam seems to have difficulty learning; in this same episode, he claims that "I never had the crusts cut off my bread," as the reason for why a sense of independence and following his own path takes precedence over family. Taking this logic to its *Supernatural* conclusion, his inability to work as a part of a family leads to the release of Lucifer from Hell. In Dean's case, it is near-pathological self-sacrifice that leads him to Hell, where he breaks the first of 66 seals that will release Lucifer. His trajectory involves knowing the boundaries between himself and others, what needs to be sacrificed and what doesn't. He thus finally allows his brother to take responsibility for his own mistake rather than attempting to spare Sam from the consequences of Sam's poor judgment.

⚜ While religion in and of itself leaps to the forefront in the apocalyptic storyline of seasons 4 and 5, it does not represent the first time that the show itself directly addresses beliefs and practices; indeed, the series itself is built on a number of religious rituals to ward off evil. Engstrom and Valenzano argue that both the banishing rituals (in Latin) and the use of salt, holy water, rosaries, and other symbols (as well as its mostly positive portrayal of Catholic priests) indicates that *Supernatural* prizes Catholicism over other religions. Their analysis concludes that Catholicism is offered as "good" while other religions, particularly evangelical Protestantism, are portrayed as evil. They contrast episodes such as "Houses of the Holy" (2.13) in which the vengeful spirit of a Catholic priest is portrayed as troubled and trying to rectify wrongs, with "Faith" (1.12) in which the wife of a blind tent-revival preacher named Roy LaGrange traps a reaper in order to provide her husband with supernatural healing ability. The downside is that for every life that the preacher saves, another is taken, usually someone the preacher's wife considers evil or sinful. "By debunking and uncovering the evil behind the so-called faith healing power of Roy, the non-Catholic, evangelical-based religious convictions of his congregation turn out to be false and its true source corrupt . . . associating faith healing with black magic" (80). Further, in the aforementioned "99 Problems," the townspeople have formed a religion-based militia at the behest of the "prophet" Leah Gideon. While the militia at first is dedicated to fighting the demonic threats brought on by the Apocalypse, Leah slowly guides them into eradicating personal threats. She promises that if the townspeople stop sinning (drinking, gambling, having premarital sex), they will be reunited with their loved ones in Heaven. She thus turns Blue Earth into what Sam describes as a "fundamentalist compound." It is eventually revealed that Leah is not a prophet, but rather the Whore of Babylon,[7] leading the town to damn itself. It represents an explicit example of Engstrom and Valenzano's contention that the series condemns evangelicals.

Further, a false prophet named Gideon recalls the bibles of the same name that are generally placed in the same kind of motels that Sam and Dean frequent throughout the show. Gideons International is an evangelical organization whose membership is restricted to men, named after one of the Israelite judges in the Old Testament. "Gideon was a man who was willing to do exactly what God wanted him to do, regardless of his own judgment as to the plans or results. Humility, faith, and obedience were his great elements of character" ("The Gideons"). While that serves as one mission statement for Gideons International, it also serves as an apt description of the pastor at the start of the episode. Much like Jimmy Novak, Gideon's faith is severely shaken, if not destroyed, by his interaction with the supernatural. David Gideon attempted to be faithful and obedient, but could not pass the final test of obedience by killing something that looked like his daughter. More importantly, Leah's injunction to cut off the rest of the world and live without sin as she defines it curtails the freedom of the town to make their own choices. Freedom to make a choice is a thread that runs throughout the Apocalypse arc, despite internal and external pressures, demonic or Heavenly threats. In the final moments of "Swan Song" (5.22), Castiel frames it quite specifically. He asks Dean which is better — peace or freedom. Dean's choice is freedom; he eschews a structure that seeks to conscript and define anyone's actions.

While Engstrom and Valenzano's basic thesis asserts *Supernatural*'s pro-Catholicism, Petersen argues that *Supernatural* is not "faithfully selling" any particular religion, but "draw[s] freely upon an immense pool of religious elements and religious narratives circulating in Western society" (1). Kripke's claim of a humanistic brotherhood as *Supernatural*'s religion (Ryan, "It's the fun") does not preclude both borrowing and repurposing various religions within the realm of the narrative in order to advance this particular belief. Indeed, in "Hammer of the Gods" (5.19), the Archangel Gabriel serves as the mouthpiece for this humanism, saying that in the apocalyptic battle, he neither supports the angels or the demons, gods or devils, but humans, despite their numerous flaws. While the eclectic traditions *Supernatural* draws upon allows a variety of interpretations on the part of the viewer, it is Kripke's own insistence on the importance of family relations that comes across the most strongly within the *Supernatural*

Apocalypse. The epic battle between good and evil (Michael and Lucifer) is, across multiple episodes, recast as a conflict between a responsible older brother and his "fallen" younger sibling who rebelled against their shared father. Indeed, when Adam becomes Michael's vessel, his near-dogmatic insistence on following his "father's" script mirrors Dean's earlier inability to accept that his own father might be less than a "hero."

As the first season focused on Sam and Dean's search for the absent John Winchester, season 5 widens the canvas to search for an equally absent God. In "Dark Side of the Moon," God appears to not even be in Heaven; He leaves a message for the brothers. Joshua, who is the only one in Heaven to communicate directly with God, tells them that God knows what is happening and was responsible for saving the brothers when Lucifer rose and resurrected Castiel (killed by Raphael in "Lucifer Rising," 4.22), which is "more than He's intervened in a long time." Keeping with the series' focus on free will, Joshua informs them that God will not halt the Apocalypse. This policy of non-involvement is in line with Petersen's contention that *Supernatural* and other series "repackage" what Grace Davies calls "believing without belonging" and "reflects this ambivalence by confirming the existence of 'a god' but simultaneously questioning the omnipotence of the Christian 'God'" (Petersen 7).[8]

Instead, *Supernatural* raises the brothers' story to one of "gospel" (their adventures are chronicled as a series of novels by prophet Chuck Shurley) and their car, the Chevrolet Impala, to the role of religious icon. As Chuck writes in "Swan Song" (his final book), while the Winchester brothers had no fixed residence since the destruction of their Lawrence, Kansas, solidly middle-class home when Sam was an infant and Dean was a child, they have not in fact been "homeless." In the final moments of the episode, this "home" of Sam and Dean's appears to play a key role in subverting the destruction of earth; a toy soldier pops up that Sam had wedged into the ashtray as a child, triggering a flood of memories in Sam that lead him to sacrifice himself for the greater good. It is an earthbound ending — the collateral damage of a cosmic war (mostly) avoided by a Chevy, Def Leppard's "Rock of Ages," and brotherly love. If Chuck, the prophet/author, is a stand-in for Eric Kripke, his final words before disappearing sum up the "religion" of *Supernatural* succinctly: "They chose family. And well, isn't that kind of the point?"[9]

"I am an angel of the Lord"
An Inquiry into the Christian Nature of *Supernatural*'s Heavenly Delegates
Jutta Wimmler and Lisa Kienzl

Angels are an integral part of folk religion as well as popular culture, yet when *Supernatural* introduced them into the narrative in the first episode of season 4, many viewers were surprised by their depiction. Their scruffy appearance and callous attitude seem to undercut the image of angels prevalent in American popular culture.[1] We are consequently with Dean when he tells Castiel, "I thought angels were supposed to be *guardians*. Fluffy wings, halos — you know, Michael Landon. Not dicks" ("Are You There, God? It's Me, Dean Winchester," 4.2). Castiel plainly responds: "Read the Bible. Angels are warriors of God." In this essay, we intend to test this statement. We will "read the Bible" and other Christian, Jewish, and Islamic sources and consider what traditions *Supernatural*'s angels are following. By looking at the background and characteristics of the "angelus occidentalis" and fallen angels, and comparing the brotherly relationship of Michael and Lucifer to that of Dean and Sam, we will establish that *Supernatural*'s angels are in many ways based on pre-modern, especially biblical representations of Heavenly delegates, but that this representation is transformed by a "modern" interpretation of the free will motif.

Angels in the Christian and Jewish Tradition

The English term "angel" stems from the Latin "angelus" and the Greek "aggelos" (ἄγγελος), which is a translation of the Hebrew word "malach" (מלאך) for messenger (*Lexikon der christlichen Ikonographie* 626). An angel is thus a supernatural messenger between God and humans. Because the term is simply a description for a being, it is not automatically positive: an angel could also be in the service of evil powers. Angels were created by God and differ from humans by their disembodied appearance. Nevertheless, they were often portrayed as humans in biblical texts (New American Standard Bible Mark 16:5).

For the purposes of this essay we will focus on defining and characterizing angels in monotheistic Abrahamic religions like Judaism and Christianity. This type of angel is referred to as an "angelus occidentalis" (Godwin 7), a supernatural being that differs significantly from angels of monistic worldviews that are prevalent, for example, in Asia. Characteristic for monotheistic religions is the division of the universe into three parts, distinguishing between Heaven, earth, and Hell, and further between angels, humans, and demons (Vorgrimler 152–157). The angels' depiction, their role in the universe, and the angelic hierarchy are based partly on the scriptures; namely, the Tanakh (the Hebrew Bible), the Old and New Testament, and the Qur'an. In addition to these codified scriptures, the non-canonical apocrypha (books typically not included in publications of the traditional Bible) as well as folk tales are important sources for illustrations and depictions of angels in the Western world. However, the representation of the modern angel was also influenced by myths, fables, and miraculous adventures from late antiquity and the Middle Ages.

Angels usually appear in male form in scripture, but Zechariah 5:9 suggests that this might not always be the case: "Then I lifted up my eyes and looked, and there two women were coming out with the wind in their wings; and they had wings like the wings of a stork, and they lifted up the ephah between the earth and the Heavens." These two women are obviously supernatural beings and messengers between Heaven and earth, though an angelic interpretation is controversial, since angels are traditionally depicted as men and their appearance as women provokes a Christian gender discourse. Furthermore, the angels' portrayal is accentuated through their preternatural appearance. They are characterized as terrifying and supernatural (Matthew 28:2–3; Ezekiel 1:9–10). In the Gospels they appear in human form but differ in their behavior, their attributes, and their way of life (Matthew 22:30, Luke 20:34–36). The idea of the angels' wings originated in the historical context of the ancient Middle East, which is why similarities to mythological winged creatures of that time can be found. While seraphim and cherubim are described as flying angels, they differ from today's winged angels. Most angels, in fact, are described without wings in the Bible. In the early Christian art of the first century they also appear as ordinary men. The first Christian images of winged angels surfaced in Rome of the 4th century, and from the 5th century onwards this illustration spread to other regions.

Belief in angels is deeply rooted in all Christian denominations, although not all agree about the particulars. While angels have a place in Catholic and orthodox theology, many Reformed churches are reluctant when it comes to angelology. In addition, Reformed churches are content with a simple distinction between Archangels and angels, while both Catholicism and orthodoxy developed a rather complicated angelic hierarchy. This need for a classification of angels emerged early in the ancient world, but the relevant sources often disagree about the nature of the hierarchy. The strongest influence on subsequent hierarchical divisions came from Dionysius the Areopagite's *The Celestial Hierarchy* from the 4th and 5th centuries CE, and Thomas Aquinas' *Summa Theologica* from the 13th century.[2] They divided angels into nine hierarchies or choirs: seraphim, cherubim, thrones, dominions, virtues, powers, principalities, Archangels, and angels. This angelic hierarchy is very important in Catholicism.

Although angels are also understood as supernatural beings in Judaism, they are strictly distinguished from God's appearance and should not be worshiped in the same way. They deliver instructions only to selected people who are able to recognize God's will. In this manner, the appearance of angels plays an important role in the tradition of the early history of the people of Israel. The angels in Judaism, however, are more differentiated and hierarchically structured than in Christianity (Vorgrimler 102, 109). Still, Jewish and Christian sources agree that there are seven Archangels, although it is not entirely clear who they are. Four names appear regularly in this context — Michael, Gabriel, Raphael, and Uriel — which demonstrates *Supernatural's* affinity to Christian and Jewish angelic hosts.

Supernatural's Angels

The angels of *Supernatural* are described in close accordance with biblical sources and other religious scriptures. First of all, angels in *Supernatural* are referred to as having been created by God, which corresponds with the Bible. They differ significantly from humans concerning their character traits and skills. Angels are generally depicted as men, which again corresponds to the biblical tradition, as does the idea that no one can see an angel's true appearance and would lose their eyesight instantly because of the angels' overwhelming glory. In the beginning of season 4, this is what happens to Pamela when she wants to see Castiel's true appearance ("Lazarus Rising," 4.1). Consequently, in order to show themselves to men, angels have to choose human vessels — the humans, in turn, have to agree to being used in such a manner.

The use of hierarchies in the representation of *Supernatural's* angels is intriguing. As mentioned earlier, we need to distinguish between the Catholic and Protestant angelic hierarchy, both of which influenced *Supernatural*. For example, Zachariah describes his true image: "In Heaven I have six wings and four faces, one of which is a lion" ("Dark Side of the Moon," 5.16). On the one hand, this invokes the image of a seraph, as described in Isaiah 6:2: "Seraphim stood above Him, each having six wings: with two he covered his face, and with two he covered his feet, and with two he flew." On the other hand we are reminded of a cherub: "And each one had four faces.

The first face was the face of a cherub, the second face was the face of a man, the third the face of a lion, and the fourth the face of an eagle" (Ezekiel 10:14). The images of the two highest forms of angels are combined in *Supernatural*, illustrating a Catholic influence on the series. The combination of seraph and cherub is not exclusive to the television show, however: in early religious scriptures, the Archangel Uriel appears as a mixture of the two as well. Still, only Archangels and angels are distinguished hierarchically in *Supernatural*, leaning the show back to the Protestant angelic hierarchy. In *Supernatural*, the capabilities of Archangels and angels differ either according to strength or through the fact that certain skills, such as teleportation, telekinesis, or time manipulation, can only be used by Archangels. In the New Testament, angels are also described as superior to men in intelligence, ability, and effective power and are, as mentioned in Luke 20:36, immortal. The Bible also influenced the perception that angels do not reproduce like humans.

Remarkably, fallen angels like Lucifer hold on to their skills in *Supernatural*, even though they are no longer Heavenly delegates. While the idea of good and evil angels is absent from the writings of the Old Testament, at the time of the New Testament the concept of a fallen army of angels was a popular folk theme that occupied an important place in subsequent Christian beliefs. This theme was later mixed with the idea of the fallen angelic Light-Bringer. Especially in apocalyptic writings, many dynamic concepts about Heaven and Hell were developed in this context (Godwin 11, 91). Uriel, who in the Jewish and Christian traditions is considered an Archangel, is one of Lucifer's fallen angels in *Supernatural*. It is possible that this idea appears because Uriel is also known as the angel of atonement, who will wait for the sinners at the gates of Hell (Godwin 52). Furthermore, in Judeo-Christian tradition Lucifer himself is understood as one of the Archangels. This idea may be a result of Lucifer's connection with the myth of the fallen angelic Dawn-bearer, originally a story of a fallen God in the ancient Middle East (McKay 451, 464).

In Season 4's "Heaven and Hell" (4.10), Anna describes angels as unemotional beings that are "like a marble statue," unable to feel anything. However, despite what she said, many angels, especially Castiel, show many emotions and allow them to affect their actions.

The appearance of angels in *Supernatural* mixes together traditional and well-known angelic figures like the Archangels Gabriel, Raphael, or Michael, and modern or unknown ones such as Anna and Castiel. Despite the generally very biblical characterization of angels in *Supernatural*, the main angelic character Castiel has no biblical background. He is only known in folk culture (Bächtold-Stäubli, Hoffmann-Krayer 17) and rather popular in various esoteric groups such as the Angel of Thursday. But this is where the advantage of this character is to be found. While the representation of the Archangels Gabriel, Michael, or Uriel strongly resembles the traditional biblical angel, his character offers the possibility of a fresh and modern interpretation. Classic themes such as doubt, disobedience, and free will play an important role in this depiction.

Fallen Angels and the Issue of Obedience

In *Supernatural*'s fourth and fifth seasons, the issue of free will vs. destiny takes center stage, a topic that is discussed in many religions, as well as philosophy and modern science (Dilman). The series presents the problem in its complexity and delivers a clear message by the end of season 5 by confronting humans and angels with a variety of choices concerning, above all, the matter of obedience. *Supernatural* concludes that free will is a value worth holding on to, even when facing the Apocalypse. Free will emerges as the only truly "good" virtue in the midst of chaos. How the angels handle their choices thus provides valuable insights into one of the series' central messages.

That angels possess free will is a strongly Christian motif (Piepke 51, 54–55). In both Judaism and Islam, angels have no free will and are unable to sin (Jung 13–22; Schäfer 83–85). In Judaism, Satan is one of God's angels, who tests humans on his behalf. Because angels have no free will, many concluded that the Islamic Iblis (Lucifer), who disobeyed God and thus sinned, could not be an angel, but instead must be a djiin (Awn 24–33; Martin 357–358). However, the motif of Iblis' disobedience followed an established trend within Jewish apocalyptic thought, a movement that was prevalent from the 2nd century BCE to the 1st century CE. The idea of fallen angels originated in this context, although it never asserted itself in Judaism. One of these apocalyptic groups was profoundly influenced by this motif: the Jesus-movement, which later became Christianity (Mach 114–127; Sacchi 211–332).

Supernatural uses one of the most popular stories of Lucifer's fall: God creates Adam and asks the angels to bow before him. Lucifer refuses to bow before anyone but God himself. Lucifer's disobedience and his jealousy cause his fall. The gist of this narrative also exists in Jewish tradition, where the angels initially refuse to bow before Adam because they realize mankind's tendency to sin, but God convinces them that humanity's potential for good is worth the risk.[3] Angels who act of their own accord, independent from God's will, do not exist in mainstream Judaism (Jung 65–66, 97–98; Klener 185, 188). *Supernatural* follows the Christian tradition closely: Lucifer is jealous of man and refuses to bow before him, so he is expelled from Heaven ("The End," 5.4).

Lucifer is not, however, the only disobedient angel in *Supernatural*. Many angels fall into despair after realizing (or suspecting) God's absence. Anna, for example, begins questioning her orders and God's existence itself. She falls to earth ("like, literally"), and because she stripped herself of her angelic powers, she is reborn as a human and forgets her origin ("Heaven and Hell," 4.10). Contrary to Lucifer, Anna is not exiled to Hell, presumably because she is without her powers and thus cannot be found. Anna, it seems, is not punished by God, but by her angelic superiors. At that point, her superiors and other angels are already acting independently since they, too, begin to lose faith. Uriel, Raphael, and Zachariah are all in some way "fallen." They disregard God's wishes and disrespect his creation — humanity — because they believe he has "left the building" ("Lucifer Rising,"

4.22). The series thus confronts us with a broad variety of "fallen" angels who disobey God and often oppose humanity.

There is, however, one positive example of angelic rebellion: that of Castiel. He is originally very obedient and God-fearing but begins to suspect that his orders may not come from God. He rebels against his superiors and joins the Winchesters' "Team Free Will." Castiel's rebellion is not directed against God or caused by a belief in God's absence. He acts on faith: faith in God and faith in His creation, as represented by the Winchesters. When it becomes clear that God is not absent but refuses to get involved ("Dark Side of the Moon"), Castiel is heartbroken, but he never stops fighting. He does what he feels is right — God or no God. While most angels go rogue out of despair, Castiel does so because of faith. Being "fallen," in Castiel's case, is a positive example of exercising free will. The value of obedience is thus not interpreted in the same way as it is in the Bible, specifically the Old Testament, where rebellion equals sinfulness (Forsyth 151). *Supernatural's* God thinks differently about obedience: because Castiel's faith remains strong despite the circumstances, because he rebels against his superiors as a consequence, and most of all because he believes in God's creation and does what is "right" despite being told otherwise, he is resurrected and rewarded ("Swan Song," 5.22). This God does not care for blind obedience, which is why the Archangel Michael will not fare much better than Lucifer, as we will see in the next and final section.

Brothers in Heaven and on Earth

"This isn't about a war," Gabriel explains in "Changing Channels" (5.8). "This is about two brothers that loved each other and betrayed each other. You'd think you'd be able to relate. [. . .] Think about it: Michael — the big brother. Loyal to an absent father. Lucifer — the little brother. Rebellious of Daddy's plan. [. . .] As it is in Heaven, so it must be on earth." The Archangel Gabriel clarifies two important issues in this monologue. First, he states that the apocalyptic story of *Supernatural* is not really about the Apocalypse, but about the relationship of two brothers. Second, Gabriel implies that the Winchesters are chosen as the angels' vessels because their relationship resembles that of Michael and Lucifer. Since the show has always been a family drama, it is hardly surprising that *Supernatural* interprets the apocalyptic fight between Good and Evil along these lines. Gabriel illustrates this point as well. He left Heaven because he did not want to take sides in his brothers' conflict. In the end, however, Gabriel will take a side — that of humanity — and stand against both his brothers. "Dad was right," he tells Lucifer, "They are better than us" ("Hammer of the Gods," 5.19). That humans are better than angels is a central message of the narrative that is also known to the Abrahamic religions (Schäfer 89, 95, 106). The issue is best illustrated by comparing Sam and Dean with Lucifer and Michael.

In Christianity, Lucifer is often perceived as the intimate enemy as opposed to a distant foe — he is part of the family you are supposed to rely on (Pagels 49). For *Supernatural*'s Lucifer feels betrayed and abandoned by his family — Michael and God — who, in turn, consider him a threat. Thus Lucifer becomes a mirror for Sam, who was also considered dangerous by both his father and brother. But Sam also turns out to be the hero Lucifer could never be. While Lucifer gives in to his anger and jealousy, Sam finds the strength in himself to do the right thing. Although Lucifer genuinely does not want to fight Michael and tries to convince him that the final battle is unnecessary, Michael refuses and responds that he has no choice — it is his destiny to kill Lucifer (Rosenberg 94–97). When asked to disobey, Michael tells us: "I'm a good son. And I have my orders" ("Swan Song"). He feels compelled to fulfill his destiny and is convinced of Lucifer's crime. Like Michael, Dean is the good son who never questions his father's orders. But contrary to Michael, he learns to trust his little brother and to believe in him. Dean is a more virtuous version of Michael, and unlike his angelic counterpart, he values human life and the importance of free will.

Because Dean never allows Michael to take him as a vessel, the angels resurrect his half-brother Adam as an alternative. As it turns out, everyone was wrong to assume that Dean would send Lucifer back to Hell. The tragic hero of this story is Sam, the younger brother. The motif of the younger brother succeeding despite all odds is prevalent in both scripture and folklore. Younger brothers are often depicted as unlikely heroes (Greenspahn 89–90). In Sam's case, his immaturity and his affinity for evil make us doubt him. His older brother is a more likely candidate for heroics due to his moral strength and stability. But in the end, Sam is the one who will defeat his alter ego Lucifer. It is no longer Michael, traditionally humanity's angelic savior, who will save the world. Instead, humanity saves itself from the malevolent angels. Michael shares Lucifer's contempt for humanity, but contrary to Lucifer has no mind of his own. So, when Michael is pulled to Hell together with Lucifer, we don't exactly shed a tear. By mirroring Lucifer and Michael, Sam and Dean illustrate the importance of free will. Both Lucifer and Michael ultimately resign responsibility for their actions, because they believe everything is destined. The Winchesters succeed because they believe in choice.

Twice in the season 5 finale, *Supernatural* invokes the idea of God testing angels and humans. The series has Lucifer asking Michael if their brotherly war is nothing more than "one of Daddy's tests?" In the final monologue, the narrator, Chuck Shurley, repeats the issue: "I'd say this *was* a test. For Sam and Dean. And I think they did alright." Since the series indicates that Chuck may be God, seasons 4 and 5 could be interpreted as God testing angels as well as humans. It seems as though *Supernatural*'s God knew the angels were flawed and that they disliked humans, and decided to test their faith. Most angels — in particular Michael and Lucifer — fail his test. The Winchesters pass because, in Chuck's words: "They made their own choice. They chose family. And, well, isn't that kinda the whole point?" In this series, it certainly is.

In a recent article on *Supernatural*'s use of religious motives, Line Nybro Peterson argues that the series transforms Christian motifs, yet one may wonder what "Christian" really means in this context. While

Supernatural's interpretation of angels is intriguing, it can be placed within certain trends in American popular culture. First, there is the narrative of apocalyptic and warrior angels, most recently portrayed in the Hollywood film *Legion* (2010). Second, we find an increasing sympathy for the figure of Lucifer, and third, angelic frustration either because of unhappiness with the situation in Heaven or a problem with God himself (Gardella, esp. 168–199, 231–236). With the exception of the first motif, these elements can hardly be described as Christian, certainly not as biblical. In these narratives, angels are no longer primarily messengers, the warrior function taking over almost entirely. In addition, the angels are not exactly benevolent toward humans.

Yet there is something special about *Supernatural*'s angels. Aside from an intriguing mix of Catholic and Protestant ideas, the angels' strong potential for evil, for becoming "fallen," is unique. They are warriors of the Apocalypse, but not warriors of good. Michael's depiction in particular is far removed from the Bible as well as tradition. Typically the most active warrior angel, he is surprisingly passive in this narrative. The angels' lack of independent thought, of an inherent understanding of what is truly "good," is at the center of their characters. In traditional Apocalypses, such as that of John or the earlier Henoch, it is always clear that there are good and bad angels fighting for either God or an evil principle. The same is true for many modern Apocalypses. But in *Supernatural*, the warriors of Good are human. Humans are morally superior because they will not be coerced into doing something that is "wrong" and have an inherent understanding of good and evil that seems to escape the angels. *Supernatural*'s angels serve to reinforce the heroic nature of the Winchester brothers by providing a strong contrast. So *Supernatural* does transform the angel motif, both in relation to the Bible and tradition, and popular culture. Historically speaking, the angel narrative has undergone multiple transformations, always with the goal of communicating a certain message and reinforcing values. *Supernatural* is a recent example providing a fresh approach to this popular — and entertaining — theme.[4]

Televisual Folklore
Rescuing *Supernatural* from the Fakelore Realm

Mikel J. Koven and Gunnella Thorgeirsdottir

Supernatural draws quite explicitly upon traditional folkloric forms, contemporary urban legends, and ghost stories. Unlike *The X-Files*, the series it is most often compared to (and appropriately, considering the number of personnel who worked on both series), when *Supernatural* draws upon traditional monsters it not only makes those connections explicit but fully recognizes that the audience is aware of the lore too. What *Supernatural* does uniquely, in the context of entertainment and horror, is to self-consciously play with the tradition of storytelling itself. Eric Kripke, the show's creator, is himself fully aware of this: "I've always wanted to do a show about urban legends and American folklore," Kripke noted. "That's always been an obsession. We have this American mythology that is as uniquely American as jazz and baseball, and it's as intricate as any world culture, but it's just not as well-known" (Pyle). Although the "American" premise is unnecessarily limited (and not necessarily accurate, as stories like these appear in cultures all over the world), Kripke makes explicit that he is fully aware of the materials from which he is drawing. This awareness shouldn't be surprising: *Supernatural* is only the latest in a long list of television series and movies that make use of folklore motifs to draw in the audience with a familiar yarn.[1]

Supernatural draws upon a wealth of cultural references — not only traditional folklore, but also horror movies and other aspects of popular culture — often simultaneously. Take, for example, the episode "Monster Movie" (4.5): the episode opens by exchanging the series' customary title credits for a dark metallic font upon darkened skies and in black and white. As the brothers ride into town, booming dramatic music is heard playing until Dean switches radio stations, thereby revealing that what we believe is non-diegetic music (the score that plays over a scene but not actually part of it), is, in fact, diegetic (part of the fictional world of the show). The viewer is cued to see this episode initially as stylistically different to other episodes of the show (monochrome cinematography, change in title font, and music), but that initial viewing position is turned around through metatextual play once the episode's narrative kicks in properly. Upon arriving in a small Pennsylvania town that is celebrating Oktoberfest, Dean and Sam are faced with a number of weirdly "moviesque" monsters, like Dracula and the Wolf Man, and an Egyptian Mummy has coincidentally just been delivered to the museum, sans documentation. Clearly "Monster Movie" is paying homage to the classic Universal horror films of the 1930s and 1940s. The episode plays with popularization and how the images many of us have of monsters from folklore are also, in turn, at least partially constructed from literature and classic movies. Even if a viewer has not actually read Bram Stoker or Mary Shelley nor seen the classic monster movies the episode is referencing, the *image* of these monsters has permeated popular culture so ubiquitously that they can be said to have re-entered folklore itself. As Larry Danielson put it, "films forcibly remind us of the roles modern media play in the re-animation, intensification, and distribution of folk narrative" (219).

Folklore permeates the series from beginning to end. The notebook the Winchester brothers carry, inherited from their father, is not just a guide to demon hunting, but also a mini-guide to contemporary folklore and urban legends in particular, like the file boxes behind

Mulder's desk, the literal "X-Files," which Leslie Jones saw as being almost an encyclopedia of urban legendry (78; see also Koven 69–81). However, John Winchester's notebook specifically, and the series' use of folklore more generally, are what folklorist Richard Dorson might have referred to as "fakelore" (see Dorson's *American Folklore* and *Folklore and Fakelore*, as well as Ball et al). For Dorson and a number of contemporary folklorists, fakelore is the antithesis of folklore; popular culture bowdlerizations rather than authentic products of the folk imagination. Fakelore, at least as Dorson intended it, is the intentional invention of "folksy"-like "lore," often for commercial or advertising purposes. It might look like folklore and sound like folklore, but it is inauthentic; the Brothers Grimm's *Kinder und hausmarchen* is authentic, the films of Walt Disney are not (see Zipes 1997). Authentic folklore materials, like urban legends, are easily denigrated as fakelore when popular culture, like television series, plays with materials. This essay argues that such a denigration of popular culture's use of folklore in general, and of *Supernatural*'s use of this material specifically, is far from fakelore.[2]

The arguments that posit television's use of folklore as fakelore only work if a particular use of folklore materials is seen to remove the item from its original context and present it as somehow separate from the culture that produced it. Dorson's primary examples for popularized fakelore are collections such as Benjamin Botkin's *A Treasury of American Folklore* (1944), which excerpt the items from their original contexts and often clean up the vulgar and occasionally obscene nature of the folk imagination. As Dorson himself warned, "beware of the adjectives 'charming' and 'delightful' when applied to folktales and folksongs. The fact is that much folklore is coarse and obscene, and in its true form is often meaningless and dull to the casual reader" (*American Folklore* 4). However, television writers who use folklore materials in their plots do not excerpt and decontextualize in this way — they may borrow from a culture's lore, and they may change the tradition to suit their own narrative purposes, but for every narrative these writers borrow, they *re*contextualize the folklore, not *de*contextualize it. *Supernatural* may borrow freely from world folklore, but by simply *using* it, they recreate it and return it to the cultural nexus from which it originally emerged. The question then becomes, not how is *Supernatural* folklore, or is *Supernatural* fakelore, but *for whom* is *Supernatural* folklore?

All groups, however such a group is defined, will have customs and traditions that its members are likely to recognize (Dundes 6). *Supernatural*, in drawing upon specific popular and folk culture referents, speaks to an alternative "folk group" watching the show (see Althusser). Because of the wide-ranging cultural contexts *Supernatural* is pillaging from, in order to maintain a consistent vision within the series, as is demanded by fantasy-genre television, the series needs to repackage the lore within the worldview and folklore culture of those who watch the series. The show's performance of folklore, the world in which these folk (and pop cult) monsters exist has to be immediately recognizable as "our world" (however that world is conceived). As Melissa Gray notes, Sam and Dean live in a world "whose essential reality we recognize." *Supernatural*'s use of folklore and popular culture is the primary connection to that recognizable reality — a recognizable reality that defines *Supernatural*'s worldview within a specific generational and cultural group.

The term we are suggesting here, "televisual folklore," is an attempt to bridge the folklore/fakelore debate for the representations of folklore within television drama. The term is a variation on Juwen Zhang's coinage "filmic folklore," which he defines as: "an imagined folklore that exists only in films, and is a folklore or folklore-like performance that is represented, created, or hybridized in fictional film" (267). For Zhang, popular cinema frequently represents folklore-like elements (narratives, customs, aspects of material culture, song traditions, etc.) which have no pre-existing tradition within the folk groups being represented; in other words, pure fakelore. While filmic folklore only exists in the movies, an aggregate of popular culture representations begins to behave like "actual" or "authentic" folklore.[3] Zhang notes "it is a re-enactment . . . but in a non-traditional milieu; it is performance . . . but in a non-traditional verbal or non-verbal context; it is artistic communication, but in non-traditional small groups . . . not to mention the role of filmmakers in such folklore performance; and, it is art, artifact, and artifice . . . but made and transmitted in non-traditional societies" (267).[4] The implication of Zhang's "filmic folklore" is that it is not fakelore, despite being popularized through the mass media. Instead, filmic folklore recognizes mass-mediated folklore as legitimately authentic.

When Zhang's filmic folklore is applied to television studies, the relationship between the authentic and the inauthentic is made even more problematic. Televisual folklore is often inauthentic even when it attempts, as much as it can, to reproduce as much of its original context as possible. The folklore must always be subservient to the form and the narrative of the television series itself. In a series such as *Supernatural*, where each week the Winchester brothers hunt, fight, and usually kill some folkloric monster, the television narrative demands some kind of concretized lore to literally represent the week's monster. The inchoate folklore must be, somehow, physically embodied. In cinema, despite the narrative demands on popular film, a movie can get away with more ambiguity and particularity than is possible within the production of a television series; the series must maintain a consistent (and standardized) diegetic story-world, whereas films can play with ambiguity more in treating each film as a stand-alone text. Most episodes of *Supernatural* follow a very basic structure: some kind of anomalous monster is stalking a community, the Winchester brothers hear about these strange deaths and travel to the besieged community in order to investigate, and then hunt a monster from folklore or urban legend (Bloody Mary, the hook-handed killer, a wendigo, a vampire, a ghost, a demon).

A television drama series, like *Supernatural* (or *The X-Files* before it), must concretize its monsters to some degree. Keeping all possible variant texts alive would make for very confused television (although it might be interesting to see someone try).[5] The monstrous antagonists the Winchester brothers fight, while they might be based on traditional legends, still must appear as single embodiments, not a combination of all the legends, and in this series, such incarnations may be accused of bordering "fakelore." *Supernatural*'s monsters *are* artificial fusions of many folkloric and popular culture variants; the problem here is that, by this fusion, the series could be seen to suggest its version is the "real" one.[6] Each week's monster, in addition to being recognized as having its own folkloric tradition, including variant texts across time and space, is concretized into an actual creature the Winchesters can fight. The diverse narratives around *Supernatural*'s monster of the week are dismissed within the storyline as errors in folk memory, and in so doing, those histories of narration and belief, including their divergence, are at least recognized by the series' writers. Usually it is Sam Winchester, the more scholarly of the brothers, who recognizes the variants by either consulting his father's Filofax of traditional legend or doing research online (although one hopes his research takes him beyond Wikipedia). It is worth noting that in at least one episode, "A Very Supernatural Christmas" (3.8), Sam gets it wrong: while it appears that a "psycho Santa" is stalking a particular community and leads to Sam's investigation of the Black Peter/Zwarte Piet tradition in European folklore, the actual monsters turn out to be a couple of pagan gods who are annoyed no one believes in them anymore.

The issue of folkloric authenticity, however, lies less in the belief traditions of the episodes' actual monsters (i.e., the episode's content) than it does in the contemporary American context of supernatural television. When *Supernatural* premiered in 2005, the original premise of the series was focused on urban legends specifically. The episode titles of the first few episodes made explicit reference to the legends the narratives were based on: "Wendigo" (1.2), "Bloody Mary" (1.5), and "Hook Man" (1.7). As the series caught on, the episode titles changed to titles such as "Bugs" (1.8) and "Route 666" (1.13), making more and more explicit its intertextual play to the series' audience. By examining that intertextual play through a simple examination of the episode titles, a clear impression of *Supernatural*'s audience emerges with enough commonality that we can tentatively identify the folk group for whom this recontextualized and televisualized folklore is intended.

Episode titles that make explicit reference to the legend text on which they are focused fall out of favor very quickly in *Supernatural*'s development. While some episode titles may echo a legend or a legendary belief tradition (i.e. "Route 666" and in this case the reference may equally be a jokey reference to "Route 66" — recorded by the likes of Johnny Mathis, Chuck Berry, and the Rolling Stones), by and large these allusions do not continue beyond the halfway point in season 1, and by season 2, almost all the monsters the Winchesters hunt derive more from popular culture than folk tradition. Certainly by the beginning of season 2, *Supernatural*'s writers begin their game of intertextual play in earnest. Episode titles begin to reference film titles, classic rock songs, and a variety of esoteric popular culture references, all of which point to whom this body of modern lore is being recontextualized for.

The episode titles that reference film titles tend to refer to horror movies, as one would expect from a horror TV series: "Hell House" (1.17) is a shortened reference to *The Legend of Hell House* (1973) and "Something Wicked" (1.18) is likewise an abbreviated echo of *Something Wicked This Way Comes* (1983). However both "Hell House" and "Something Wicked" are further references to the novels the films are adaptations of, by Richard Matheson (1971) and Ray Bradbury (1962) respectively. Both Matheson and Bradbury are popular authors within the horror fan communities.[7] That one episode reference should follow the other sequentially suggests that this connection is not accidental. As a horror series, *Supernatural* frequently makes reference to horror cinema: we've already mentioned the episode "Monster Movie," and while some titles obviously evoke popular horror movies, like "I Know What You Did Last Summer" (4.9), others are more esoteric, like "Children Shouldn't Play With Dead Things" (2.4), an allusion to the relatively obscure (at least for non-horror fans) film directed by Bob Clark in 1973. While

"My Bloody Valentine" (5.14) is a reference to the original George Mihalka slasher film (1981), it equally invokes the 2009 remake that starred *Supernatural*'s Jensen Ackles.[8] This kind of intertextual play, alluding to other, sometimes esoteric horror films, is unsurprising in a genre as intertextual as horror; however the references to non-horror films in the episode titles are even more interesting.

Some title references can be dismissed as general pop culture awareness (like "The Usual Suspects," 2.7[9]), but others begin to play with their referents, splicing the film title with the *Supernatural* diegesis (i.e., "The Curious Case of Dean Winchester," 5.7; "Sam, Interrupted," 5.11; or "Weekend at Bobby's," 6.4). Still other film title references begin to suggest a strongly eclectic nexus of cinematic referents: "Bad Day at Black Rock" (3.3, based on the 1955 John Sturges thriller) or "Death Takes a Holiday" (4.15), which evokes a relatively obscure 1934 melodrama starring Frederic March. If *Supernatural*'s writers are eclectic in their horror tastes, they are likewise eclectic in their cinematic tastes too. Should series writers simply have been playing an elitist game likely to go over the heads of most of the audience, then it is unlikely the show would have survived. Instead, these references are equally recognized, shared, and understood by *Supernatural*'s fans too — the writers trust that those who watch *Supernatural* are equally eclectic in their viewing habits beyond the saga of Sam and Dean.

A tremendous number of episode titles make reference to classic rock music, and those references also reflect a certain eclecticism beyond the stereotype of the heavy metal headbanger. While some of the references are to songs by The Who ("The Kids Are Alright," 3.2), The Doors ("The End," 5.4), Black Sabbath ("Heaven and Hell," 4.10), Pink Floyd ("Dark Side of the Moon," 5.16), Iron Maiden ("Two Minutes to Midnight," 5.21), and The Rolling Stones ("Time Is on My Side," 3.15; "Sympathy for the Devil," 5.1; and "Exile on Main Street," 6.1), other references are to Robert Johnson ("Crossroad Blues," 2.8, an episode about the Johnson legend wherein he sells his soul to the Devil at the crossroads), Albert King ("Born Under a Bad Sign," 2.14), Johnny Cash ("Folsom Prison Blues," 2.19), and even Whitney

Houston ("I Believe the Children Are Our Future," 5.6). Given the dominance of classic rock both in the episode titles and on the soundtrack itself, it is safe to assume the Whitney Houston reference is intended ironically, but that irony only works for an audience that understand the cultural logic of the series' musical allusions. By far *Supernatural*'s most referenced rock band in the episode titles is Led Zeppelin: while five episodes directly reference songs by Zeppelin, "Hammer of the Gods" (5.19) alludes to the title of the band biography by Stephen Davis (1985), whereas "Swan Song" (5.22) refers to a Zeppelin-owned record label founded in 1974. In the season 5 finale (and the final episode under the leadership of Eric Kripke), Sam and Dean need to defeat both the Archangel Michael as well as fallen angel Lucifer, and the logo for Swan Song Records was of a falling angel. The "Swan Song" reference and its appropriateness to the season's conclusion, would only be recognized by those audience members with the esoteric knowledge of Led Zeppelin and its record label, much like the irony of the Whitney Houston reference.

More immediate than the names of episodes are the allusions Sam and Dean (although usually Dean) make when they are passing themselves off as priests, police, FBI agents, or whatever disguise they assume in order to get access to police reports, grieving families, or pre-autopsied bodies. Frequently, the Winchesters take on the name of rock performers: Father Simmons and Father Frehley (from KISS in "Nightmare," 1.14),[10] U.S. marshals Gibbons and Beard (from ZZ Top in "Croatoan," 2.9), FBI agents Tyler and Perry (from Aerosmith in "Yellow Fever," 4.6), agents Geddy and Lee (Geddy Lee from Rush, in "It's the Great Pumpkin, Sam Winchester," 4.7), Coach Roth (from Van Halen, in "After School Special," 4.13), agents Marley and Cliff (Reggae stars Bob Marley and Jimmy Cliff in "Dead Men Don't Wear Plaid," 5.15), etc. In at least five of the episodes, Sam and Dean take on the names of members of Led Zeppelin — Agents [Jimmy] Page and [Robert] Plant in "I Believe the Children Are Our Future" or John Bonham in "The End" (5.5). Not only do the writers of the series connect with our experiences with music, but the other characters in the episodes have decent record collections too: in at least two episodes, Dean is called on his alias by someone who recognizes the musical reference being made.

When not taking on classic rock aliases, Sam and Dean occasionally take on film references which operate in much the same way as allusions. So, for example, in "Heart" (2.17), a werewolf story, the Winchesters become Detectives Landis and Dante: John Landis directed *An American Werewolf in London* and Joe Dante made *The Howling* (both in 1981). In "Long-Distance Call" (3.14), their aliases are Mr. Campbell and Mr. Raimi, references to the frequent collaborations between director Sam Raimi and actor Bruce Campbell, most famously in the *Evil Dead* movies (1981, 1987, and 1992). "Family Remains" (4.11) offers a reference to County Code Enforcement Officers Barbar and Stanwyck (an allusion to Golden Age Hollywood star, Barbara Stanwyck).

It is in a final category of episode title allusions — rather diverse and eclectic pop culture references — that the folk group defined by *Supernatural* spectatorship can be properly identified. In the titles, a wide range of popular culture is evoked — from Judy Blume teen novels ("Are You There God? It's Me, Dean Winchester," 4.2), *Sesame Street* books ("The Monster at the End of This Book," 4.18), children's music ("Free to Be You and Me," 5.3) and a variety of experiences with other television programs, from childhood through to adulthood: "A Very Supernatural Christmas" (3.8), "Ghostfacers" (3.13, a parody of the many reality TV ghost hunting shows), "It's the Great Pumpkin, Sam Winchester," "After School Special," etc. But other kinds of pop cultural eclecticism begins to creep in: "Malleus Maleficarum" (3.9), for example, is a 15th-century treatise on witchcraft that the Inquisition used to torture and murder hundreds of people accused of witchcraft; "Metamorphosis" (4.4), while a common enough expression, given *Supernatural*'s esoteric referencing, could easily be a Kafka allusion; and there are not one, but two references to American avant-garde filmmaker Kenneth Anger: "Hollywood Babylon" (2.18) was Anger's 1958 book outlining the scandals of Tinseltown, and "Lucifer

Rising" (4.22), his controversial film from 1972 with its connections to Charles Manson's cult. Such references indicate a highly literate and well-educated corpus of writers, certainly, but as we noted previously, the show couldn't have been successful if those references went over the heads of most of the audience.

Consider the episode allusion "Jump the Shark" (4.19): while the allusion is most likely to the popular culture buzzphrase identifying a TV show that has lost its credibility due to a single irreversible plot contrivance (like Fonzie "jumping the shark" on water-skis at the beginning of *Happy Days*' fifth season) and popularized by Jon Hein on his webpage jumptheshark.com (now entirely co-opted by *TV Guide*), the phrase was also used as an episode title on *The X-Files* (9.15) in 2002. So, while the allusion is to the pop culture buzzword, it is equally an allusion to the *Happy Days* episode, and, given the shared personnel between *Supernatural* and *The X-Files*, probably to that latter show too.[11] The multiple allusion webs that spread out with each reference are complex and eclectic. Their diversity is further reflected by the multiple readings one can make of them. For example, while we may interpret the episode title "Sin City" (3.4) as a reference to the Frank Miller comics or the Miller and Robert Rodriguez–directed film based on those comics (2005), the reference could equally allude to the AC/DC song (from the band's 1978 album *Powerage*). Which allusion is intentional? The question is moot; within the popular culture nexus of the series' "folk group" in which the allusion-webs operate, the title refers to all of them simultaneously.

The wide range of allusions in *Supernatural*'s episode titles suggests to us an in-group communication for those who grew up on a diet of (largely) American popular culture from (mostly) the 1970s. The kind of pop-culture knowledge required for this reference-nexus is largely experiential, rather than studied. The prominent use of such popular culture references, Daniel Chandler shows, is

> a particularly self-conscious form of intertextuality: it cred-
> its its audience with the necessary experience to make sense

of such allusions and offers them the pleasure of recognition. By alluding to other texts and other media this practice reminds us that we are in a mediated reality, so it can also be seen as an "alienatory" mode which runs counter to the dominant "realist" tradition which focuses on persuading the audience to believe in the on-going reality of the narrative.

Whereas many shows rely only on denotation, hand-feeding the audience the explanations for all allusions presented, *Supernatural* depends mainly on connotation, trusting in the viewers' socio-cultural and personal associations to figure out the allusions for themselves. According to Peterson, the intertextuality serves to "ascribe legitimacy to *Supernatural* by placing the show in [a recognizable] popular culture history" (5.1) — that is, a popular culture history for those who grew up in the 1970s.

Supernatural's generational target audience, however, is up for some debate; Louisa Stein argues that the audience for *Supernatural* is younger than we are suggesting. She refers to the target audience as the Millennial audience, reaching back no further than the Generation Y and Generation Me age groups, that is, those who were born between the late '70s and the late 1990s (1.6). She bases her reading of the audience demographics primarily on the broadcast context for *Supernatural*, the CW, for whom the primary market is understood to be that Millennial generation. We base our assumption of the target audience, partially on our own generation (we were born in the late '60s and early '70s, and reject the suggestion we're too old for *Supernatural!*), but also on the aggregate of cultural experiences the series plays with. While it is certainly possible, if not likely, that Millennial, Y, and Me generations can listen to classic rock music and watch old movies, the other category identified, that of 1970s American popular culture evoked as childhood nostalgia is more ingrained, not learned. The references *Supernatural* makes to this generation are too obscure and too experiential for any group other than Generation X to catch.

The term we are proposing here — televisual folklore — addresses the concerns folklorists and cultural studies scholars have with television fictions as disseminators of traditional narrative (as well as other forms of tradition culture). Unlike typical popularization or fakelore, television series like *Supernatural* play with the lore quite consciously. *Supernatural* avails itself to and transforms contemporary legend materials from which it draws. Following on from Zhang's coinage of "filmic folklore," which we suggest should stand beside televisual folklore as a concept, the grammar and syntax of popular culture need to be recognized as an aggregate of cultural experiences. By understanding the cultural experiences as performance (i.e., on television), we can begin to redraft the imaginary boundaries that define identity in our postmodern worldview.

Supernatural evokes the fear and the thrill of horror movies, playing on stories, motifs, and genres with which the audience is already aware from both popular culture and traditional folklore. But in addition to the key narrative motifs and tales the series dramatizes, it also addresses that narrative performance. Such performance demands an appreciation of the diverse materials woven together; not that such recognition is mandatory, but understanding its roots offers a greater appreciation of its construction. These folkloric stories are recontextualized, like the popular culture allusions, into the new fabrics, into new stories. While the narratives themselves may no longer return to their original contexts, the stories, rather than simply seeing this appropriation as a kind of televisual museology, are recontextualized into an alternative cultural group context.

Far from inauthentic "fakelore," the actual cultural context from which *Supernatural* emerges is our cultural context: 30- and 40-somethings who grew up in the 1970s on a steady diet of North American popular culture. Like the films of Quentin Tarantino, *Supernatural* demands of its audience a cultural awareness of diverse signifiers from horror (and non-horror) movies, classic rock, and popular culture. However, as they are presented as emerging from the cultural contexts of Generation X-ers, *for* Generation X-ers, the cultural authenticity is assured. When it comes to *Supernatural*, Zhang's "filmic folklore" becomes our "televisual folklore." The series' use of folklore is self-conscious, not creating an artificial "folksy"-like narrative, but presenting the legends in a new, contemporary way, as an organic and dynamic extension of the process that legend tellers and their audiences have undertaken since storytelling began.

Part 6

Cruel Capricious Gods

Auteurs, Fans, Critics

Sympathy for the Fangirl
Becky Rosen, Fan Identity, and Interactivity in *Supernatural*
Brigid Cherry

Dean: Check it out, there's actually fans! [. . .] There's Sam
girls and Dean girls and . . . What's a slash fan?
Sam: As in Sam-slash-Dean. Together.
Dean: Like together together?
Sam: Yeah.
Dean: They do know we're brothers, right?
Sam: Doesn't seem to matter.
Dean: Oh come on, that's just sick!
"The Monster at the End of This Book" (4.18)

In March 2010, TV.com ran a feature by staff writer Tim Surette entitled, "TV's
Craziest Fanbases . . . With Video Proof." Surette contrasts being a
"pretty big TV fan" — for example, someone who watches a season of
Supernatural episodes over a weekend — with being a "hardcore fan";
in his estimation, the former is acceptable, the latter is considered
mentally unstable. So, what exactly (for Surette) marks a fan out as
hardcore? Predominantly, this status is reserved for those who write

fan fiction or make fan films. While the article is clearly intended to be ironic, the dismissive attitude and tone taken are common in the media and therefore contribute to the development of a discourse that alienates the markedly intense or devoted fan, especially those fans who take part in the creation of what Abigail Derecho has termed archontic literature. This is what she defines as "a virtual construct surrounding the text, including it and all texts related to it" (65). Fan fiction forms part of an archontic literature since it pointedly locates itself within the world of the archontic text: fanfics are "variations that explicitly announce themselves as variations" (65). As archontic texts, fan fictions are not subordinate, appropriative, or derivative; rather they are part of an archive that expands upon the originating text. The language used by Surette in reference to these fan writers — "creepy, scary, insane" — sets them apart. They are a "different breed" from those he approves of, those "normal" excessive consumers dedicating entire weekends to watching TV. In fact, Surette makes clear he is not talking about *"the entire fan base for a particular show, just the extremes"* (his italics); "normal" fan behavior is used as a yardstick to place the "hardcore" fan safely at arm's length.

Although not made explicit, gendered stereotyping underlies Surette's scale of extreme fandom, whether he's referring implicitly to male fans (excessive consumers) or subordinate female fans (archontic writers). *Supernatural* tops his list of nine shows as having the craziest fanbase. It is given an "insanity level" of "10 out of 10, call the National Guard" — the only series in the list to receive the maximum rating. Even those Surette considers "normal" *Supernatural* fans are described as "completely bats*** insane." His overt revulsion is caused by the Wincest fan fiction — the Sam-slash-Dean pairing that also alarms Dean in the epigraph to this paper — and to a Dean-slash-Castiel (or Destiel) kink meme in which Castiel has a crab claw for a hand.[1] Surette's readers need to be shielded from these "weirdest" of fans who exhibit "clinical" behavior in the production of "perverse" and "X-rated" material to which he will not even provide a link: "I don't want to be responsible for you gouging you [sic] eyes out or developing an aversion to crab cake. . . . Just don't say I didn't warn you."

Surette does not explicitly make reference to gender, but since slash fiction writing is predominantly a feminine form of fan production, his distaste (however tongue-in-cheek) is thus reserved for female fans. All fan production (the article focuses on fan films of various kinds) crosses the boundaries of normal/insane, but it is erotic or intimatopic[2] female fan fiction writing in particular that he distances himself from. Such flippant responses to these kinds of archontic writing can be seen as examples of the male fandom marginalizing female fans. Certainly, a heterosexist discourse can be identified elsewhere in Surette's article, with examples of fan production involving normative heterosexual pairings being placed lower down on his insanity scale: for example, the Brennan and Booth shipper fic community[3] earns *Bones* a mere "4 out of 10, uncomfortably eccentric." Heterosexual pairings in fan fiction may still be beyond Surette's personal boundary, but they are relatively safer and more acceptable (to the male fan's comfort levels) than slashed and — worse — incestuous pairings.

Supernatural encodes similar responses within the text. On discovering that they are the subject of the Supernatural series of novels in "The Monster at the End of This Book," Dean is as alarmed as Surette when he learns of the fans who slash his fraternal relationship with Sam. At the end of the exchange reproduced in the epigraph, Dean flips the laptop screen down and pushes it away from him, calling it — like Surette — "sick." For him, it is abject and must be repressed. Dean's reaction is undoubtedly intended (albeit again ironically) to reflect the anticipated response of the average (male) fan or viewer on learning of the activities of the slash fiction communities (now on public display with the Internet having facilitated the proliferation of fan writing); it is a source of disgust and amusement.

This rejection could be read as contributing to the ongoing subordination of female slash communities, but that both Dean and Surette think it should be repressed begs the question of why the production team went on to focus much more intently on it in this and later episodes. This knowing acknowledgment of *Supernatural*'s female fandom is also a development of the metatext that encourages those female fans' interactions with the text (or at least those who appreciated the representation), primarily through projected interactivity played out in fan fiction.

Amber Davisson and Paul Booth — drawing on James Gee's account of the relationship between a player and a virtual character in a video game — suggest that, in order to understand the complicated identity play occurring in online fan cultures, "one needs to conceive of the three identities that are present in the activities [of fans] — the fan, the character, the community" (41). They propose that fan fiction gives the writer control over the relationship through their play with the character's traits, actions, and environment. In this way the fan brings the projected identity close to their own identity. A deeper understanding of fan activities can be gained from research into the ways fans communicate and interact with characters. This can be achieved through analysis of fan fiction in combination with textual analysis and empirical studies of the fandom (although it is certainly not the only approach that can be made). What makes *Supernatural* such a productive series to address in this respect are its metatextual elements: by incorporating fan characters into the show, the interactivity does not only operate in one direction (by acknowledging the fans, the production team interacts with them), and for some fans this intensifies the interactive relationships they develop with the characters. This consideration of projected interactivity with *Supernatural*'s fan-characters explores the communication and agency taking place within the text, the fan community, and the fan fiction.

Representations of Fans

Supernatural has always been in dialogue with its fandom. Representations of fans began early in the series and include the fanboys and one fangirl in the episodes "Hell House" (1.17), "Ghostfacers" (3.13), and "It's a Terrible Life" (4.17), the fans of stars, historical icons, and celebrities in "Fallen Idols" (5.5), the female novel fan community — publisher-fan Sera Siege in "Monster" and "super-fan" Becky Rosen in "Sympathy For the Devil" (5.1) and "The Real Ghostbusters" (5.9) — and fan convention attendees, also in "The Real Ghostbusters." Sam and Dean themselves are encoded as fans of popular culture.

Given the recent inclusion of fans and fandom in American television drama (since 2005 major crime series including *Bones*, *CSI: Miami*, *Numb3rs*, *Psych*, and *Cold Case* have produced episodes set around fan conventions), it is unsurprising that *Supernatural* also includes representations of fans. The recurring characters Ed Zeddmore and Harry Spengler, introduced in "Hell House," are constructed with several typical fanboy characteristics. Dean assumes their website HellhoundsLair.com is "streaming live out of mom's basement," and they use references to cult texts as expletives ("sweet *Lord of the Rings*"), refer to *Buffy the Vampire Slayer* as a life manual ("Be brave. WWBD . . . What Would Buffy Do?"), collect McFarlane Dragons and Spawn action figures that are still in their original packaging ("What a shocker!" Dean remarks sarcastically), and want to become famous so that they can have "sex — with girls" (something normally unavailable to the stereotypical fanboy). Maggie, the female member who joins the team in "Ghostfacers," has an interest in science and technology and is responsible for the team's gadgetry; despite a potential romance with Harry, she is depicted as one-of-the-fanboys. Similarly in "The Real Ghostbusters" the majority of convention-goers are in costume (though with metatextual irony, almost all as Sam or Dean).

These fanboys buy merchandise and are full of cultural knowledge; one is depicted as a nitpicker, pointing out detailed weaknesses in the novels' plots (the 'naysayer' or anti-fan being a common trajectory of fan behavior[4]). The fans are also subordinated by Sam and Dean in these episodes. In "Hell House" they play pranks on Ed and Harry and disparage them as "amateurs." In "The Real Ghostbusters," the fans are "freakin' annoying," and Dean tells the Sam-fan Barnes that it "must be nice to get out of your parent's basement, make some friends." However, as a counterpoint Dean is also faced with the positive values of fandom, Demian, the fan engaging in Dean cosplay[5], tells him he is wrong:

> I'm not sure you get what the story's about. In real life he sells stereo equipment, I fix copiers. Our lives suck. But to be Sam and Dean, to wake up every morning to save the world, to have a brother who would die for you, well who wouldn't want that?

Moreover, Demien and Barnes reveal that they became a couple after meeting in a chatroom. Although these fan representations contain ironic jibes at fandom, these are not straightforwardly negative. Moreover, Sam and Dean negotiate trajectories of fandom themselves.

In "Hell House," Dean links Sam's knowledge of magical sigils — a kind of cultural currency which could be equated with fan knowledge of the text — to "never get[ting] laid" and suggests that the ghost attacked Sam because of his feminine traits. Dean's cultural competencies, on the other hand, are in the form of knowledge of rock music (he recognizes the Blue Öyster Cult symbol the teenagers have used to make an old farmhouse look haunted). Dean's fan interests represent a more acceptable (and mainstreamed) trajectory of fandom that does not threaten his working class masculine posture (Wright). The tensions between different trajectories of fans are also emphasized in "Fallen Idols," an episode about "super famous, super pissed-off ghosts killing their super-fans." When a James Dean fan mentions "Little Bastard" — the car in which the actor died — Dean (Winchester) is in awe: "I am definitely checking this out," he says. Sam, however, does not recognize the James Dean reference, but he is depicted as an admirer of Gandhi — a different kind of idolization, as is the Civil War buff's enthusiasm for Abraham Lincoln. Dean's remarks to Sam after he is attacked by Gandhi — "You couldn't have been a fan of someone cool?"; "That is good, even for you that is good"; and "Just when I thought you couldn't get any geekier" — suggest that intellectual fan interests are of a different quality than pop culture ones (James Dean is an interest that does not conflict with Dean's masculine traits).

Also subordinated in this episode are the teen fans of Paris Hilton, a different fan trajectory again. And despite all these fan interests being much the same to the "backwoods forest god" in that any worship is better than none — "Adoring fans stroll right in the door. . . . So, they worship Lincoln, Gandhi, Hilton . . . Whatever, I'll take what I can get." — celebrity fandom is regarded as particularly low. In a comment on celebrity culture, *Supernatural* has Hilton (self-referentially playing the god in her image) stating: "This is what passes for idolatry, celebrities? What have they got besides small dogs and spray tans?"

Undoubtedly, *Supernatural* encodes several trajectories of fans and fandoms, and, in common with other American television drama, suggests hierarchies of fan behaviors — almost all other fan trajectories are valued higher than young women's adoration of celebrities. Overall, there is much potential for fans to recognize themselves, not only in fan-characters but also in the leads.

It is within this continuum of representations that female fandom — and the archontic work of female fans — is also finally recognized in "Monster." (Not only is the female fan rarely acknowledged in other American television drama, she is barely represented at the fan convention in "The Real Ghostbusters," which is odd given the context of the *Supernatural* novels having a female fan following.) As a representative of female fandom, Becky the slash fiction writer (and to a lesser extent Sera the publisher-fan) is a problematical representation. Borrowing a phrase from an interview with Misha Collins, who plays Castiel, JulesWilkinson describes this as being "trapped inside a box of mirrors with the show's writers and the unicorn and pony of our creative endeavors" ("Box of Mirrors" 1.1). Becky opens up spaces for negotiating the relationship between fan identity and character identity.

Female Fandom and Community

The producers and creative personnel on the series have frequently discussed and related to fan opinions and activities. In an interview in *TV Guide* series creator Eric Kripke stated, "We are conscious and aware of our fans. We're making the show for the fans. [. . .] When we make missteps, we pay attention to the fans and we course correct. So, fans, I love you all, but stop worrying" (Ausiello). In the context of the *Supernatural* metatext, however, it is not simply that the producers are considering the responses of the fans and adapting the narrative as a result, but that they go beyond the normal boundaries of the fiction by writing those fans, their responses, and the archontic writing they produce into the text itself through characters such as Becky and Sera. This is significant for fan studies, since not only do fans become manifest in the text, but those characters develop the potential for fans to participate interactively with representations of themselves.

As already established by Henry Jenkins (*Textual Poachers*), fans involve themselves in the creative process by re-mediating and rewriting the text. Fan production exists at the heart of an intertextual relationship with the originating text, but over and above this it works against the nature of media's one-way communication and creates potential social interactions between fans and fictional characters, often in an attempt to meet the fan's own needs (Geraghty). As Anne Kustritz points out, fan writing often serves to make the relationship with the characters more intimate by turning them into real people (375).

Fans have, of course, responded to representations of female fandom and slash writing in online discussion sites. Reactions have been spread across a large number of online communities, but key among these is the Television Without Pity site, not least since it is apparently the one that has been appropriated by the production team for the fan site Sam and Dean look at in "Monster." Fans note that the site has the same sage green color scheme as TWoP and Dean reads out a post written by Simpatico, the username of an actual TWoP member. In fact, several real-life posters in the episode discussion thread refer to this "shoutout."[6] The posts written in response to the metatextual references in "Monster" were overwhelmingly positive about it, though a very small number (less than 5%) reported being resentful, feeling mocked, or cringing, or of the opinion that what happens in fandom should stay within fandom.[7] Simpatico herself took part in the discussion. Depicted as a naysayer in the episode, the fictional Simpatico calls the demon storyline "trite, clichéd, and overall craptastic." The actual Simpatico does not dispute the fictional Simpatico's assessment, though she does "nitpick" the authenticity of the language, saying: "HEY! I have *never* made use of the word 'crap-tastic.' Trite, clichéd, 'steaming pile of shit,' 'cringe-inducing,' 'holy crap can this show get any worse,' yes; but not 'craptastic.' That's a ridiculous word."

On TVGuide.com (TV Guide News 2009), supervising producer Sera Gamble states that writer Julie Siege was "very even-handed in that she managed to take hilarious jabs at the writers, the fans, and the boys. [. . .] But if there was any doubt that we have a sense of humor about ourselves, this ought to clear it up."

While self-reflexive jokes by writers at their own expense (there are several of these encoded in the character of Chuck Shurley, for example) may be acceptable since they are under the control of the writers themselves, it is more problematic when these are directed at fans with no control and no warning. Laura Felschow's discussion of the slash community's responses to the metatextual elements in this episode opens up debates about the (im)balance of power between producers and fans. Simpatico makes a important point about how this imbalance could be potentially damaging:

I wasn't hurt. Just shocked and bemused that they picked me of all people. [. . .] I could understand someone whose passionate opinions had not been slowly crushed over three seasons by their favorite show's rampant mediocrity being hurt by this, though. Circa season 2, when I still deeply gave a damn? I might have cried myself to sleep. But not before cursing the ground Kripke walked on, coming to the realization that life is a fruitless endeavor, and swallowing a bottle of Tylenol PM, making sure to mail my suicide note to Vancouver beforehand. [. . .] Good thing they didn't give me a shoutout then, eh?[8]

ᕈ With this development the production team is not just representing generic fans, as it did with the Ghostfacers, but responding to specific instances of negative responses by female fans and to specific individuals. Clearly, care needs to be taken with the writing of such representations, and it is understandable that some fans might react negatively. Nevertheless, the majority of posters on TWoP, including Simpatico, enjoyed the representations of fans in the episode and found it amusing (particularly in the context of much wider representations of fan trajectories as outlined above). Regardless of the potential impacts of the writers making "hilarious jabs" at the fans, the fans themselves seem able to negotiate these fan-character identities productively. Becky appears in only two episodes (and is mentioned in a third without appearing) but she has piqued the interest of fan fiction writers who have appropriated the character.

Projected Interactivity

Her walls covered in posters and blowups of the novel covers, her desk and computer adorned with feminine accessories, neatly arranged in contrast to Chuck's untidy living space, Becky's introduction in "Sympathy" is a mirror image of Chuck's in "Monster," speaking lines of her fic aloud as she writes and going over a phrase until she finds the right word. If Chuck is a self-referential encoding of the writer into *Supernatural*, perhaps the writers are also suggesting that the fan fiction author is not so very different from themselves. Moreover, when Chuck phones Becky to ask her to take a message to Sam and Dean, his contact with her implies a moment of celebrity, a fan's dream perhaps of connecting with the characters and being recognized by the "powers that be."

In one respect, Becky is stereotyped as the crazed, sexualized female fan. She writes fan letters to Chuck, sends him gifts of marzipan, and declares that she is his "number one fan." She is similarly breathless, gasping, and speechless when she sees Sam, has a quiver in her voice when she manages to speak, and she keeps touching him, eyes closed and gasping open-mouthed in a semblance of orgasm. She is resigned to being mocked, saying, "I know that *Supernatural*'s just a book, okay? I know the difference between fantasy and reality." But Becky's quickness to accept that "it's all real" (as Chuck tells her) with an ecstatic "I knew it!" is nevertheless a representation of projected interactivity. The characters for her *have* become real. Furthermore, this can be correlated with feelings of cultural ownership: if the Winchesters are real, they cannot "belong" to Chuck as author. This encodes the kinds of fan activity (and kinds of fan) that remain uncourted by the culture industries according to Gray, Sandvoss, and Harrington (4). The way in which these fans — and prime among these are the female slash communities — overlook the culture industries' claims to legal ownership of the text is given legitimacy here when the author (Chuck) hands authority over the characters to the fan (Becky).

Although the representation itself has multiple possible meanings — she can be read as an unwelcome stereotype, or as a knowing nod to the fan — the recognition that she is permitted to play with the characters may perhaps help to explain why the majority of respondents on the TWoP episode thread who mention Becky found the characterization amusing and enjoyable. Fans said that:

> "The fangirl's fanfic was creepy to hear on my TV. But [. . .] it was funny." (oneder)
> "Fangirl attack . . . That was both creepy and hilarious at the same time." (greeneyedgal)
> "The fanfic girl had me rolling from her first scene to the end." (randomnation)
> "Becky the fangirl made me laugh in horror and glee. I heart you a little more for that Kripke." (UKchickforlife)

Although some fans seem to be experiencing something uncanny in the familiar portrayal of themselves, they did appreciate the character. Furthermore, some fans actually wondered whether Becky was based on someone from their community:

> "That has to be based on a real fan, with all the 'feeling Sam up' stuff. :)" (omaroca)
> "Ok, which one of you was the basis for Becky?" (kcblue86)
> "There is a Becky who helps run Winchester Radio (I believe) . . ." (Gwonk)
> [in reply] "Eeee! Thank you! That is me! If they named this Becky after me, I am thrilled! Plus, I'm a huge Sam!Girl!" (SisterSpooky)

There is a sense of community bonding over the representation, as when SisterSpooky says, "I promise I'm not as crazy as *that* Becky and I've never written fanfic!" and GigglingKat replies, "LOL Sister-Spooky. I notice you don't deny rubbing Sam's chest though. . . ." There is no evidence that these fans feel insulted by this representation; rather they seem proud to be the basis of it, and it works to make the character real through these shared relationships.

The Fan Metatext Fic

It is this recognition that has contributed to the appropriation of the character in Becky fanfic, itself a re-appropriation of the fan back from the producers. One key example illustrates the way in which fans develop projected interactions with the character. "Becky the Castiel Fangirl," a fanfic story by ShatteredSiren, occupies the interface between character identity and fan identity. A 17-year-old who works part-time in a library and wishes to study literature at university,[9] ShatteredSiren clearly recognizes herself in Becky. She says that *Supernatural* is her current favorite fandom and identifies points of similarity with characters who are significant for her as a fan: "I, like

Dean, love pie," she writes in her fanfiction.net profile[10]; "I, like Castiel, have blue eyes and do that head-tilt thing"; and she declares herself like Becky "a slash-addicted fangirl." Thus, elements of characterization and performance — tastes, mannerisms, and pastimes — enable interactivity with the characters, Becky in particular. ShatteredSiren says in her email interview that "It is disturbingly easy to write Becky. Maybe because she is so much like me. . . ."

One fan who responded negatively on TWoP thought Becky was "grating and embarrassing. Such an idiot. [. . .] Not a flattering portrayal of fangirls" (cieley). There is a sense here in which the brief portrait given in the episode is insufficient in capturing the depth, complexity, and intelligence of the real fan writer. Rather than rectifying any potentially negative representation of Becky (perhaps to intellectualize her), however, ShatteredSiren's writing gleefully embraces and plays up her emotionality. Becky "hyperventilate[s] down the phone" to Sam, giggles, gives "long shrill scream[s]" and makes noises that "faintly sounded like a kettle boiling" (Becky chapter 1). The fic thus exaggerates the traits Becky is given in the original text, effectively reclaiming the character (and therefore her own autonomy) back from the writers.

Writing the fic also allows ShatteredSiren to develop the narrative arc of the characters with whom she most identifies. Her fic is set after the events of "The Real Ghostbusters" when Chuck and Becky had begun a relationship. It moves Becky's story forward, taking the story beyond the romantic happy ending of a canon pairing that was left untold (the majority of the Becky fanfics are set in this moment) and depicting her living with Chuck. Furthermore, in Becky chapter 3, she also gives Becky a final scene as redress for her being written out in "Swan Song" (5.22) with a single line of dialogue: "It didn't work out," says Chuck. "I had too much respect for her." In the introduction to this chapter, ShatteredSiren writes that it "had to be done, poor Becky got no happy ending." In the chapter, Becky objects to Dean settling down with Lisa and forces Chuck (God) to get Dean and Castiel back together. Becky's happy ending is to watch omnipotently along with Chuck.

Similarly, in "Becky Is Not Writing This Story," Grey_Bard (a

28-year-old with interests in a wide range of fan texts) sets Becky up with Gabriel after she has split with Chuck:

> So she called Castiel and next thing, she has Gabriel on her couch, eating kettle corn and laughing. [. . .] Then he started critiquing her NC-17 scenes in detail with *visual aids.* Archangel illusion powers are the BEST! And then . . . things went from there.

These examples are not unusual in extending the text and giving more depth to characters, but as fan metatext fics (a self-applied generic label) they also engage with the notion that since fan activity is acknowledged within the series' narrative, fan discourses are now canonical. While the author writing herself into her own fan fiction as a thinly disguised original character (in the Mary Sue style) is generally derided (in fact Grey_Bard directly parodies this in her fic: "Becky is TOTALLY the Mary Sue of her own life, and you know what? It is SO AMAZING."), Becky as a fan-character gives permission for the writer to draw on both her own inner life and her participation in fandom within her fic.

In Becky chapter 2, ShatteredSiren has Becky sharing her insider knowledge with her fellow fans:

> Becky typed furiously on her keyboard, fingers tapping in rhythm to her frantic heartbeat.
> OMG, she typed, Destiel is totes canon!
> No way! said Saltluver14 almost instantly.
> Yeah rlly! Carver Edlund just MSN'ed me and showed me spoilers!
> She wasn't about to say she was actually dating Carver Edlund himself, the fandom would go crazy.

Fan chat is thus incorporated into the fiction and just like the real fans, ShatteredSiren's Becky shares the fan community's views. In Becky chapter 1, she is established as disliking other female characters ("I kept in the Anna storyline which Becky hated me for," Chuck tells Sam, while Becky scowls and says, "I hated that book. When Anna touched the hand print on your arm I died a little inside") and she prefers to slash the text (Sam flicks through a copy of Chuck's latest novel, "coming to a page that was dog-eared, with Becky's frantic writing saying that this was the scene where Dean and Castiel had met"). ShatteredSiren thus fulfills a hope that the fan can influence the writer (which, as the quote from Kripke above suggests, already happens).

In fact, Chuck's novel now includes slash-style writing, such as "[Castiel's eyes] were shockingly large and the deepest blue Dean had ever seen, almost mesmerizing him in their cerulean depths" and "Castiel turned, his blue eyes almost hypnotizing Dean. His expression was pleading yet calm" (Becky chapter 1). In the fic, Becky plots to get Dean and Castiel together (and succeeds); the fan not only gets to influence the writer, but she can also mirror Chuck (already an echo of the series' writers) in becoming a "capricious god" who can control the characters' lives. In Becky chapter 2, the fans' influence is underscored as Chuck completes his latest novel:

> [A]s he typed the words THE END with some degree of satisfaction, he knew that Becky would be delighted with this one. The first time any of his visions had hinted towards romance between the hunter and the angel had really happened here. He knew that with this book published there would be no denying the chemistry between the two.

↓ Even more significantly, there is a suggestion in other Becky fanfic of the fan's motives in the act of writing itself. In "Peanuts," Lassiter (who writes Wincest and has an interest in a range of shipper groups) uses Chuck to defend the archontic work of the fanfic writer. He "used to ask [Becky] why she doesn't just write her own stories, but she says these *are* her own stories, of my stories, which aren't even mine anyway, but are handed down from God. 'Every story is just a fic of another story,' she says with her typical conviction." This clearly expresses the claims of the fans to cultural ownership of the text. As Jenkins notes (*Convergence Culture*), fan participations are increasingly central to the production decisions shaping the current media landscape, and it is therefore not surprising that fan culture is now frequently represented in American television drama (not only *Supernatural*, but the crime drama mentioned previously). However, this still leaves a major question around archontic writing that overlooks the culture industries' legal ownership of the text. The metatextual elements of *Supernatural* give permission to re-mediate the fan-characters since they are already appropriated from the fans themselves.

While it is to be expected that some fans might feel maligned or exposed due to the "hilarious jabs" at their expense and to the imbalance of power between producers and fans that this represents, others embrace the possibilities of projected interactivity that are opened up. According to Kristina Busse and Karen Hellekson (25), fandom is an act of performance involving dialogue, community, and intertextuality. Working at the interface between fan identity and character identity, the writers of Becky fanfic articulate their own desires (for example, for the Destial relationship) and counter the abject status of "extreme" fandom as stereotyped by Surette and others through knowing humor and irony of their own. Although space has not permitted a fuller study of the *Supernatural* fandom and its responses to Becky, this attempt to conceptualize the relationships between the fan and the text, between the producer and the fan, and between the fan and the fan-character, illustrates the fact that we might not always have to offer sympathy to the fangirl.

Crossing Over
Network Transition, Critical Reception, and *Supernatural* Longevity
Karen Petruska

Sometimes we feel we're
the best-kept secret since the Manhattan Project.
Eric Kripke, creator of Supernatural

Chicago Tribune television critic Maureen (Mo) Ryan, watched the first few seasons of *Supernatural* inconsistently.[1] In response to pleas from fans of the show that she give the program a second chance, Ryan wrote, "I don't dislike the show, but I just don't watch it that much" (Ryan, "A *Supernatural* Holiday"). One year after writing that, Ryan declared she had changed her mind. She explained, "Sometimes in their fourth seasons, shows start to sag, slow down, and coast. *Supernatural* has done the opposite — it's gotten even more interesting. I know Thursday nights are crowded, but . . . I look forward to watching it each week" (Ryan, "Shows You Should Be Watching"). From her perspective, *Supernatural* achieved something unique in its fourth season by becoming an even stronger series.

The achievement is more remarkable, however, when one considers all the obstacles *Supernatural,* a series that has repeatedly defeated the odds, had to overcome to reach that fourth season. Born on the WB network, *Supernatural* became the only WB program to debut in 2005 that survived its freshman class to earn a second season.[2] During its first year, this genre series about two brothers who hunt ghosts and demons premiered alongside three major network science fiction programs, including *Invasion, Threshold,* and *Surface,* all of which would be canceled. *Supernatural* also survived a network merger, a writers' strike, and being scheduled on Thursday, the most competitive night for broadcasters. Despite these challenges, *Supernatural* has persisted into its sixth season.

Mo Ryan was not the only critic to rediscover *Supernatural* during its fourth season. *TV Guide's* Matt Roush had followed the program during its first season and remembers being "pretty enthusiastic" about the series, but he lost track of it after its move to Thursday nights midway through the first season.[3] As Roush explained, he works for a major mass-market publication so his job is to stay current on the major television shows, and *Supernatural* did not rank first in his Thursday lineup. Then in 2009, Roush wrote in a blog post, "I took the plunge with the goal to catch up with *Supernatural* in time to enjoy this year's pivotal and possibly climactic fifth season of apocalyptic mayhem alongside the loyal fans. It's the best decision I made all year" (Roush, "My Supernatural Summer"). Roush and Ryan have both admitted in the past a preference for genre programs, so their hesitation to view *Supernatural* more faithfully deserves some consideration. What about this program's fourth season encouraged these critics to revisit the series? Ryan describes *Supernatural* as crucial for the CW: "it is like a foundation stone; you don't think about it, but you need it there." With so little support from critics and without achieving the highest ratings on the CW, why has this program become a mainstay of the CW network?

Supernatural boasts a devoted, passionate fan base, and many scholarly studies — for example an issue of *Transformative Works and Cultures* devoted exclusively to the series — apply a fan studies methodology, looking at the fandom itself (Tosenberg). The support of fans is certainly one factor in the program's success; however, other factors have contributed to its long run as well. I will examine the secret to *Supernatural*'s longevity through two complementary approaches: media industry studies and critical reception analysis.[4] To learn more about the program's critical reception, I conducted interviews with the critics mentioned above who are also fans of the program, Mo Ryan and Matt Roush. Their expertise and insider knowledge of network promotions and decision-making provide insight into industrial factors that have supported *Supernatural*. Beyond fan support, two overlooked factors have enabled the success of *Supernatural*.

First, in opposition to the traditional reading of the cw's relationship with *Supernatural*, I contend that *Supernatural*'s success has depended in part on its affiliation with a fledgling network. Alice Jester, a blogger and long-time advocate of *Supernatural*, tends to be critical of the cw in her blog posts, citing a lack of network promotional support as damaging to the show's growth. Laura E. Felschow seconds this critique of the cw in her essay about the relationship of *Supernatural* fans with the show's producers, complaining that "the wb/the cw did not put much weight behind promoting its product" (5.2). Challenging this assumption of the cw's failure to nurture *Supernatural*, I will demonstrate that the network has proven an asset for this series rather than a liability. Second, I will analyze how new media technologies have played a strong role not only in *Supernatural*'s history but also the cw's network strategies. Contextualizing the place of criticism within the broader industrial economic and programming practices of the cw, I will highlight the interplay of forces that contribute to success on broadcast television.

The Evolution of the CW Network: *Supernatural* Persistence

In January of 2006, Warner Bros. Entertainment and CBS Corporation "shocked virtually everyone in the tv industry" with the announcement that the wb network, owned by Warner Bros., and the United

Paramount Network (UPN), owned by CBS, would merge to form the CW (Klaassen). Reportedly the result of a dinner conversation between CBS President Les Moonves and WB Entertainment Chairman Barry Meyer, the merger made quite a bit of sense despite its suddenness (Simmons). Both the WB and UPN networks targeted a similar demographic of young adults, so combining them spared each netlet the competition the other posed.[5] Dawn Ostroff, President of UPN, became President of the CW and quickly set to work selecting programs from both UPN and the WB to continue on the CW. *Supernatural* had outperformed its other first-season companions on the WB, but that did not guarantee it a spot on the CW lineup because Ostroff stated she wanted to introduce some new programming for the CW's inaugural year (Porter). In the end, *Supernatural* became one of only five programs from the WB to continue on with the CW ("Is glass half-empty").[6]

One *Supernatural* asset was its pedigree. Produced by Warner Bros. (Warner), *Supernatural* became an asset due to an agreement between CBS and Warner to share ownership of media properties airing on the CW that were produced by either company (Bill Carter). Both companies thus shared a stake in nurturing *Supernatural*'s progress. Yet co-ownership in and of itself did not guarantee Ostroff's decision to accept *Supernatural* as part of the CW's inaugural season. *Everwood*, another Warner-produced program, was canceled by Ostroff, outraging its avid fanbase. Unlike *Everwood*, *Supernatural* satisfied a stated goal of the CW network to create an ideal "flow" for its viewers.[7] Her decision not to pick up *Everwood*, Ostroff explained, was clear: "We looked at what shows had duplication. In other words, were viewers watching both shows? That was a big consideration in putting the schedule together" (Porter). *Everwood* failed to make the cut because it did not share an audience with other series on the schedule. *Supernatural*, however, offered an ideal pairing with the similarly fantasy-oriented *Smallville*.

In 2006, Ostroff pledged that the CW schedule "will have a flow . . . the shows are all there, there's a built-in following" (Atkinson, "Ostroff Meditates"). She refers here to a conscious effort by the CW to build on proven success in its debut season. This is a key strategy of brand building. As described by Douglas B. Holt, a brand arouses a host of images and identifications in the mind of a consumer. As Holt writes, brands are "symbols that people accept as a shorthand to represent important ideas," and they accumulate meaning over time (1, 3). For the CW, trying to establish their own, unique brand from the disparate identities of two former netlets, familiarity and consistency became a primary asset (Lisotta, "Slamming"). Flow became a means to achieve this. Ostroff hoped that viewers who visited the CW network to watch a familiar show would stay to watch an unfamiliar one. It also helped the CW to address its target audience, women aged 18 to 34, by distributing programming suited to their tastes and interests. As Matt Roush notes, "The CW is selling to a particular demographic — they are not interested in the general audience." Branding acted as an invitation to this audience.

As mentioned, for *Supernatural*, flow meant it had an obvious partner in its lead-in, *Smallville* (Porter). Both programs featured male leads and therefore might extend the CW's reach beyond the target female demographic. Those who watched *Smallville*, a strong performer on the WB since 2001, were seen as likely to stick around to watch *Supernatural* as well ("Rising from the Ashes"). Because of *Supernatural*'s affinity with *Smallville*, it was picked up by the CW to help establish its brand. "The CW is basically one step away from cable," Roush explains. "Cable will stick with a show." Like a cable station, the CW targets a niche audience and has more patience with newer programs.

Supernatural paid off for the CW immediately. During its second season premiere (its first airing on the CW), *Supernatural* earned a rating that increased 46% from the rating *Everwood* earned in the same time slot one year prior. (Kissell). Thanks to pedigree and affinity, *Supernatural* survived the challenge of the network merger.

Supernatural hit a few speed bumps in its third season. Now promoting its second year of existence, the CW tried to reinforce its brand with new programming like *Gossip Girl*. During the 2007–2008 season, older programs like *Supernatural* and *Smallville* took a backseat to a promotional push that prized newness. An unnamed spokesperson for the network commented to *Advertising Age* that as the cw's focus on its target demographic of young women intensified, "[we] intend ultimately to own that audience" (Atkinson, "Road"). *Gossip Girl* spoke to this audience. Another challenge arrived with the writers' strike later that season, delaying production and hampering ratings growth for many programs. *Supernatural*'s average Season 3 audience — just under 3 million viewers — was its lowest yet. Despite the decrease, *Supernatural* demonstrated consistency. Beginning the third season with 2.97 million total viewers, *Supernatural* ended the season with an even 3 million ("Ratings").[8]

A number of factors combined in 2009 to provide *Supernatural* with genuine security, knowing it was unlikely to be canceled. Although the fourth season is frequently thought to be the series' best, *Supernatural* did not retain a secure position on the cw schedule simply by sustaining a level of quality. Most significantly, the cw's own future seemed more secure. Bruce Rosenblum, president of the Warner Bros. Television Group, marked a shift by noting that journalists no longer began interviews with questions about the future of the network: "I think the built-in assumption and the expectation is that the cw is here to stay" (Adalian, "The CW Lives!"). In March 2009, *Television Week* reported that the cw had awarded early renewal notices to six of its programs, including *Supernatural*. All of the programs were produced "in house," backed by either Warner Bros. Television or CBS Paramount Television Network. Once again, *Supernatural*'s pedigree helped it stand above other programs airing on the cw. In addition, *Supernatural*'s ratings with its target audience were up 8% (Adalian, "The CW Lives!").

All of the programs given early renewal that year also shared another similarity: they were all cited in the press release issued by the cw as "syndicable assets" — media programs offering the potential to provide subsequent income beyond advertising dollars accrued with each initial airing (Adalian, "The CW Lives!"). Aside from syndication, in which a program reaps additional income for its producers by being sold to individual television stations to air in repeats, programs also earn more income from franchising their brand through ancillary products. Because *Supernatural* had this potential, Warner Bros. Television signed a two-year development deal with *Supernatural* creator Eric Kripke in June 2008 (Schneider, "WBTV Deal"). This alliance assured *Supernatural* of two more seasons airing on the cw. It also gave the half-owner of the cw a stake in its subsequent offshoots, which today include a comic book series, a magazine, and a web series called *Ghostfacers* (Schneider, "Ghost").

With its financial stake in *Supernatural* confirmed, the cw made a strong and unusual promotional push — a direct overture to television critics. "The cw did a really smart thing in season 4. I think they realized they had something special on their hands," Mo Ryan explained. In addition to sending critics the first two episodes of the upcoming fourth season of *Supernatural*, they packaged the disc with a King James Bible, including a bookmark in the Book of Revelations, a nod to the season's theological and apocalyptic themes. This promotion intrigued the *Chicago Tribune*'s Ryan enough to inspire her to act on her increasing curiosity about the program and commit to the entire fourth season: "I thought it was pretty clever. It made me think perhaps there is something more timely going on with this program." Matt Roush agrees, "The cw was heading into a big storyline. It was an impetus to catch up." With the Bible campaign, the cw recommitted itself to *Supernatural* by inviting the most high-profile fans — television critics — to reconnect with a program at its peak. Though in past seasons, hip programs like *Gossip Girl* might have attracted more attention, it seems the cw did indeed realize *Supernatural* deserved continued support and that critics could help provide it.

For underdog netlets like the cw, critical accolades offer legitimacy, something the cw and its forebears have lacked. Put simply, the wb, upn, and now the cw struggle to get respect.[9] Consider the example of *Buffy the Vampire Slayer*, a critically acclaimed program on the wb network. When addressing her lead role on *Buffy*, actress Sarah

Michelle Gellar commented to *Rolling Stone* in 2000 that her program was written off by many viewers and industry experts because of its subject matter and its network host, the wb: "You try being on a mid-season replacement show on the wb called *Buffy the Vampire Slayer* and see how much respect you get" (Udovitch). Positive reviews can counteract the low cultural status of a genre program. For example, after Roush praised *Supernatural* on his blog for *TV Guide*, he heard from fans of *Supernatural* who were "gratified" to see someone of his stature acknowledge the quality of the series. Ryan notes the special influence of print publications. "I got some response from *Supernatural* fans that were just excited to see their show in print — print can grant legitimacy in a way the web does not." The praise of Roush and Ryan — critics for major print publications — supported fan claims that *Supernatural* is deserving of praise. It also reinforced the cw's support for the show.

When I introduced the possibility of the cw being a liability for a show such as *Supernatural*, Ryan nevertheless disagreed. She argued the problem for a cw show involves money, not taste. "There's always that voice in the back of my head going, 'Well, it's the wb/cw, is it really going to be that good?'" Ryan admitted thinking. But then she explained further, "[Big network shows] have a budget, they have money, they have special effects." For Ryan, the disadvantage of the cw is that it simply does not have the same resources as larger networks, meaning its shows have to work harder to achieve the same ends in most cases. Then again, Ryan also believes the cw can be an asset to a program like *Supernatural*: "If you aren't the ten million dollar a week show on the high-profile network, you're not going to have executives crawling down your throat every time you try to do something innovative."

There are pros and cons to being a cw show, but it seems for *Supernatural* the association has largely worked to its advantage. Because the cw was new and needed time to establish itself, *Supernatural* was able to develop gradually, improving each season by deepening its characters' struggles and increasing the risks taken with the program's mythology. With its young, attractive stars and its natural fit with *Smallville*, *Supernatural* advanced the branding initiative undertaken by the CW to attract a target demographic of young adults. Because both parent companies, Warner Bros. Television and CBS, owned a stake in the program, it made sense to continue with a program that offered additional value through ancillary product lines. Ryan offers the CW "kudos" for its support of *Supernatural*, yet the issues of ownership and economics factor heavily into their commitment to the program.

Technology and the CW: *Supernatural* Innovation

Another factor supporting *Supernatural*'s longevity is the CW's willingness to experiment with new technologies, most prominently with its ambitious advertising innovations. Though the CW demographic offers automatic value to sponsors for its youth and purchasing power, the network has made itself more attractive to sponsors by offering them new ways to engage with this audience. In 2006, they developed content wraps, mini-programs sponsored by a particular advertiser, meant to block the use of the fast forward button on DVRs (Bauder). In 2007, they innovated again with the "cwicki," a 10-second commercial meant to stand apart from the usual 30-second spot (Steinberg, "CW Shatters"). The network's willingness to experiment with form has paid off: the network demands higher advertising rates than either the WB or UPN did the year before (Hibberd, "On Target").

The CW's advertising innovation is motivated by more than a need for building sponsorship. The CW is also deeply invested in the time-shifting and multiple-platform viewing habits of its young demographic. Because its viewers often do not watch programs through traditional means, sitting in front of the television as programs air live, its rating numbers have been notoriously low. *Gossip Girl* is perhaps the most famous example of a CW "hit" lagging in the ratings.[10] But all of the CW programs benefit from ratings that factor in DVR viewing. In season 4, *Supernatural* regularly received a boost of 500 to 750 thousand viewers from Nielsen's time-shifting numbers ("Ratings").[11] For the CW, it is not enough to cater to the viewers reflected in Nielsen's live ratings. "We are trying to straddle old media and move into new media, just like our audience is," Executive Vice President for Marketing Rick Haskins notes (Lisotta, "CW Free to be"). The fact that the CW targets such a particular, tech-savvy audience has encouraged the CW executives to accept new methods of evaluating success. Thus while *Supernatural* has low ratings compared to series on larger networks, the consistency of the program's ratings, as well as their significant growth through DVR use, makes it a hit through the eyes of the CW executives. A program like this may have died a quick death on another network, but with the net benefits of the intersection of new technologies and young audiences, it has been able to persist and grow.

It is important to remember that in ratings discourse the numbers themselves only tell a small part of the story. *Supernatural*'s ratings are impossible to understand outside the context of its industrial programming history. For example, its ratings during the first season dropped from a high of almost 6 million to a low of 3 million. Yet the ratings only fell so dramatically after *Supernatural* was shifted from Tuesday night following *Gilmore Girls* to a much tougher ratings night on Thursday following *Smallville*. Despite these challenges, *Supernatural*'s ratings during the first season made it a "hit" compared to the other members of its freshman class, like *Just Legal*, a Jerry Bruckheimer–produced legal drama that was canceled after only three episodes.

The DVD is another type of technology facilitating *Supernatural*'s ability to reach new audiences. Many shows have benefited from DVD releases, *24* perhaps being the most prominent for the 24-hour binges it inspired (Pamer). According to Ryan, though, *Supernatural* is a program particularly well suited to intensive DVD consumption. Describing the show as an "anthology," Ryan suggests that the program offers enough variety to sustain a viewer through concentrated viewing experiences. Adds Matt Roush, the program's depth and nuance also become clearer through DVD viewing: "If you watch *Supernatural* during a condensed time, each episode builds its cumulative power."

For both Ryan and Roush, *Supernatural* on DVD provided them the opportunity to catch up with the series. It also introduced them to the particular values of the program, including its complexity and character depth. "I just look back, and I'm kind of embarrassed that I missed [the show] the first time around," Ryan admits. The DVD allowed Ryan to correct that oversight. The DVD has made the program familiar to a wider audience and offered countless opportunities to join the series as a viewer.

After its fifth season, Eric Kripke stepped down as the showrunner for *Supernatural*, handing the reins to longtime producer, Sera Gamble. Kripke had drafted a five-series arc for the series, which culminated in the threat of the Apocalypse. After completing this vision, he has, perhaps wisely, invited Gamble to develop her own. Gamble's intended arc for the program is not yet clear, but *Supernatural*'s future is less fuzzy. At the 2010 Television Critics Association summer session for the CW, Dawn Ostroff confirmed that she thinks that *Supernatural* will go on for many more years, saying that "everyone feels that there's a lot more juice in the characters" (Prudom). With a new showrunner and a new night, Friday, a long-time television graveyard, *Supernatural* once again faced challenges in its sixth season. Nevertheless, it remains a financial asset for the CW and financier-producer Warner Bros., continuing to draw a faithful audience across multiple viewing platforms as it produces consistent, critically championed programming each season. *Supernatural* has a history of beating the odds, but this isn't due to luck. Instead, its success owes much to good timing and to the coming together of various forces that worked to its advantage, including the birth of a fledgling network, the advances of viewing technologies, and the advocacy of all its fans, including prominent television critics.

Plagiarism or Props?
Homage to Neil Gaiman
in Eric Kripke's *Supernatural*
Laura Felschow

Neil Gaiman's work, ranging from *The Sandman* graphic novels, to children's tales such as *Coraline*, to acclaimed adult novels like *American Gods* and *Neverwhere*, combines "elements of science fiction, Gothic horror, dark fantasy, age-old legend, ancient mythology and biblical allegory in modern-day settings" (Burns and Hunter). While this description applies to much of Neil Gaiman's corpus, it also, not coincidentally, succinctly and conveniently sums up Eric Kripke's *Supernatural*.

At the San Diego Comic-Con *Supernatural* panel in 2007, Kripke informed the audience of his adoration of Neil Gaiman. "I was hoping I would meet [him here at Comic-Con] because he's a huge influence on *Supernatural*, between *American Gods* and *Sandman*" (Boris 2). The earlier seasons of *Supernatural* draw on Gaiman's work in style and spirit, yet one would be hard pressed to pinpoint particular moments cribbed directly from Gaiman's canon. In seasons 4 and 5, however, Gaiman fans began to notice characters and storylines that seemed quite close to characters and storylines they'd read in novels like *American Gods* and *Good Omens* (the latter of which Gaiman co-authored with Terry Pratchett).

As the series progressed, a narrative that once showed superficial Gaiman fingerprints began to exhibit the hand of Gaiman quite clearly, and some viewers began to feel as if *Supernatural* had lost some of its own originality. By working through *Supernatural*'s five complete seasons, it will become evident how the question of the influence of Gaiman's graphic and prose novels becomes more complex. Are the Gaimanesque elements of *Supernatural* an homage to the writer's work or televisual plagiarism?

Wink-Wink, Nudge-Nudge: Metafiction and Neil Gaiman

There is a certain irony to the question, for Neil Gaiman's success and critical acclaim is in part due to the way he borrows characters and ideas from previous works and turns them into something new and exciting. His graphic novel series *The Sandman* (1989–1996), which chronicles the trials and tribulations of Dream (a.k.a. Morpheus and many other names) and his relations with his six siblings — Death, Destruction, Desire, Despair, Delirium, and Destiny — drew upon a wide range of sources and scattered them across the breadth of its complicated and vast narrative. In his essay "Dreamland," Steve Erickson offers this description of *The Sandman* chronicles:

> An open-ended epic, the narrative, and the stories within it, and the stories within the stories, move from the atriums of ancient Greek myth to the veldt of African folklore, from the French Revolution to modern-day Manhattan, from the tale of a man who has decided never to die to the bodiless head of Orpheus begging someone to kill him, from Shakespeare making the terrible bargain that will transform him from hack to genius, to Thomas Paine muttering in his jail cell about the ideal that betrayed him, from a novelist who locks his muse in his attic, defiling her for black inspiration, to a convention of serial killers in the American South with a guest of honor who swallows people's eyes.

In *The Sandman* we encounter biblical figures such as Lucifer, Eve, Cain, and Abel, and comic book heroes like Batman, John Constantine, and Clark Kent. On every page the reader will meet familiar figures from history or imagination. The Sandman himself is an appropriated character from a previous DC series from the 1970s written by Joe Simon and Michael Fleisher and illustrated by the legendary Jack Kirby, while the renderings of Morpheus in Gaiman's version recall pop culture icon Robert Smith of The Cure or, at times, Gaiman himself. *The Sandman* is not the only Gaiman work that looks at the literary past through a postmodern lens. *Good Omens* takes the Book of Revelations and satirically turns it on its head; *Stardust* draws water from the creative fountain of Victorian fairytales; and *Neverwhere* is a twist on Narnia in modern London, with humdrum accountant Richard Mayhew adventuring through secret doors to a dangerous world that exists underneath the city. *American Gods* chronicles the travels of ex-con Shadow as he is caught in the crossfire of a war between old gods of mythology and new gods of modern technology as they battle for America's soul in the heart of the country's midwest. Gaiman's entire oeuvre, from *Coraline* to *Interworld* to *Anansi Boys*, contains threads of stories previously told, notions already formed, and ideas written and re-written, all stitched together masterfully to create a colorful patchwork quilt that seems at once old and new.

Gaiman's penchant for metafiction — or drawing attention to the artifice of storytelling itself — consistently references the works of others. About drawing upon Chaucer's *Canterbury Tales* for *Sandman Vol. 8: World's End*, Gaiman states, "If you're going to steal, you might as well do so from a great source" (Bender 176). Gaiman's list of influences is seemingly endless, steeped in late-Victorian/early-Edwardian literature, science fiction, and fantasy, as well as comic books. He lists G.K. Chesterton, James Branch Cabell, C.S. Lewis, Will Eisner, Frank Miller, Alan Moore, and many others as authors who shaped his artistic approach. Gaiman has no qualms about recycling and reusing what has come before.

As Chris Dowd states, Gaiman "throws slabs of mythology, fairy tale, and horror onto the autopsy table and cuts into them like a mad scientist, turning them inside out to see how they are built. And then he beckons us closer to have a look at the carcass and shows us something we could never have seen otherwise" (104). Gaiman expands on this approach: "You're working in a medium in which enough stuff has entered popular culture that it becomes part of the vocabulary or what we can deal with. The materials of fantasy, the materials of science fiction, the materials of horror, it's pop culture. It's tattooed on the insides of our retinas" (Grossman). He continues, "I learned that we have the right, or the obligations, to tell the old stories in our own ways, because they are our stories, and they must be told" (Rauch 117).

So if Gaiman's own work is a pastiche or mash-up of folklore, mythology, history, and other literature, why should it matter if *Supernatural* winds up borrowing from Gaiman's texts? The answer lies in the manner in which *Supernatural* switches from approaching their world with a Gaimanesque attitude to attempting to force a combination of Gaiman's worlds with its own.

"*Star Wars* in truck stop America": *Supernatural*'s Storytelling

Gaiman's *American Gods* is described as containing "both the magical and the mundane, a fantastic world of divine beings and bizarre happenings and a world full of prisons, rundown roadside attractions and quaint small towns" (Gaiman 2001, Discussion Questions). This could just as easily be a blurb on the back of a *Supernatural* DVD cover or a promotional paragraph for the CW series in *TV Guide*.

Neil Gaiman is by no means the only influence on Eric Kripke and the rest of the *Supernatural* writing team. The show has also been described as a cross between Joseph Campbell's hero structure and the film *An American Werewolf in London,* or as Kripke puts it, "*Star Wars* in truck stop America" (Langton). Seasons 1 and 2 of the program focus on brothers Sam and Dean Winchester as they crisscross the American heartland in search of their missing father and the supernatural creature responsible for the death of both their mother and Sam's girlfriend, Jessica. The monster-of-the-week storylines overlaid with the overarching mythology of Sam's possible connection to the demon terrorizing their family provide ample opportunity to reinterpret urban legends and ghost stories for a new generation while simultaneously appealing to something more grand and epic. A wide variety of sources contribute to *Supernatural*'s tales.

In her essay "Keepers of the Lore," Shanna Swendson delves into the use of myths and legends in the first two seasons of the program: "Sam and Dean," she writes, "are just as likely to run into the truth behind a story spread by the Internet as they are to run into ancient legends, and often the ancient and the modern mingle. There are traditional horror story subjects like ghosts, vampires, and werewolves, and then there are the stranger things that go bump in the night" (252). Indeed, the first season dispatches major urban legends and modern folklore quite quickly — the pilot features the Winchester boys dealing with a Woman in White/phantom hitchhiker amalgamation, and episodes 5 and 7 utilize familiar slumber party tales "Bloody Mary" and "Hook Man" respectively. Other episodes deal with Native American curses and lore ("Wendigo," 1.2; "Bugs," 1.8), while modern technology is combined with myth and religion in other episodes such as "Phantom Traveler" (1.4) and "Hell House" (1.17). Scandinavian gods, tricksters, faith healers, vampires, werewolves, revengeful ghosts, backwoods cannibals, shapeshifters, changelings, zombies, witches, death omens, demons, exorcisms . . . many different roads are explored as Kripke & Co. take the Winchester brothers on their tour of strange America.

The act of storytelling occurs time and time again, with Sam and Dean continually referencing the handwritten journal their father left them and Sam's research skills frequently leading him to set aside a heavy, dusty tome or click on an Internet site and turn to his brother while saying, "Well, according to lore . . ." *Supernatural* constantly draws upon a vast reserve of not only myth and legend, but also the myriad books, television shows, and films that have likewise drawn upon such concepts in the past. Eric Kripke comments on the writing staff's attention to detail by pointing out that they always try to reference myths and stories that already exist in popular culture: "We try very, very hard [to make sure] that the references in the show are accurate, that the legends that they deal with do exist out there somewhere. Even the throw-away references . . . those are always accurate and real stories that you can look up" (Langton). He adds, "Basing things in real life legend, it makes things feel more permanent, it makes things feel more mythic and sort of grounds it in this beautiful way, that there's a tradition that's hundreds and hundreds of years old" ("Mythologies of *Supernatural*"). In essence, *Supernatural* actively seeks to avoid creating something from nothing, instead opting to root itself in stories that are "Google-worthy."

The commonality between Gaiman and *Supernatural* is not just in this postmodern approach; they also share a melancholy tone. In the introduction to "Death: The High Cost of Living," singer/songwriter and close Gaiman friend Tori Amos observes that Gaiman's *Sandman* series is about "fragmented, busted-up people finding their common bond," while literary critic Steve Erikson adds that a sense of loss pervades the work — "loss of friendship, loss of love, loss of innocence, loss of certainty, loss of identity, loss of the past, loss of the soul . . . until Death transacts the last and greatest loss of all" (5–6). A viewer of *Supernatural* might readily recognize how this applies equally to its narrative, for loss is a recurring imperative to act for both Sam and Dean. Throughout the course of the show, the boys lose their mother, their innocence and childhood, their chance at normal lives, their girlfriends, their father, and, repeatedly, one another in various ways. Dean even loses his soul — literally. Their main mission in hunting is to stop others from facing the same staggering losses they themselves have suffered in the face of supernatural forces.

Despite these similarities in tone and style, it is not easy to point a finger at a single episode in seasons 1 through 3 and identify an idea or storyline derived directly from Gaiman's work. Yet as early as March 2007, when the show was still in its second season, a Livejournal community, spn_gaiman, was created to promote a *Supernatural*/Neil Gaiman crossover "ficathon" as well as to archive fiction that had already been written by fans earlier in 2006. A *Good Omens/Supernatural* crossover archive can also be found at fanfiction.net. Clearly, some *Supernatural* fans were onto the fact that Gaiman's oeuvre had a strong influence on the program — some even before Kripke publicly acknowledged it. But it was in seasons 4 and 5 that fans with Gaiman in their library and *Supernatural* on their television could most clearly see the connection.

Paved with Good Intentions: Angels, Demons, an Anti-Christ, and an Apocalypse

Season 4 kicks off with Dean being raised from Hell by the stoic and mysterious angel Castiel. What follows is a two season–long debate over where the truth lies and the nature of good and evil/Heaven and Hell. "We take the Book of Revelation and tweak it and twist it to fit our world," series writer Jeremy Carver states in the season 4 special feature "The Mythologies of *Supernatural*." What Carver does not say is that, more than before, *Supernatural* draws more heavily on *American Gods*, *Neverwhere*, and *Good Omens* for source material.

Gaiman and Pratchett's *Good Omens* tells the story of a prophe-sized end of the world due to come about at the hands of an 11-year-old Antichrist, Adam Young. As the Four Horsemen take to the streets on their motorcycles, Aziraphale, an angel with an affinity for rare books, and Crowley, a demon with a love of booze, speed, and fine suits, decide that they might actually like the world and humanity and don't care for it to end just yet.[1] Expected enemies become friends, supposed allies become dangerous foes, and even God's plan is not foolproof. This is also a recurring theme in seasons 4 and 5 of *Supernatural*.

As Sam explores his demon-killing powers at the behest of alleged demon ally Ruby, Dean is urged by the angels of Heaven to stop his brother from going astray and to help them in their mission to avert the Apocalypse. In the end, both angels and demons are shown to be traitors and deceivers; the supposed faces of good are merely masks. The angels desire the Apocalypse just as much as the demons from

Hell, and both sides use their powers of manipulation to maneuver the brothers into positions to ensure this disastrous outcome. Episodes such as "Heaven and Hell" (4.10), "On the Head of a Pin" (4.16), "The Monster at the End of This Book" (4.18), "When the Levee Breaks" (4.21), and "Lucifer Rising" (4.22) all pivot around the treacherous nature of these heavenly and hellish cohorts.[2] Even Castiel, who is for the most part helpful to the boys, double-crosses them when he sets Sam free from blood detox in "When the Levee Breaks." Other angels such as Uriel, Anna, Michael, and Raphael all attempt to destroy the Winchesters rather than be of assistance or comfort. Similarly, in "99 Problems" (5.17) a young lady purporting to be a prophet of the lord is in fact the Whore of Babylon, there to wreak havoc and bring mayhem and death to all in a small town.

The Archangel Zachariah, in particular, continues to be a constant threat to the Winchesters, second only to Lucifer among season 5's major villains. In this case, the two-faced angel is more reminiscent of the Angel Islington of Gaiman's *Neverwhere*. Similar to *Supernatural*, that novel also "bursts with contrasts of what-is-real and what-is-not-supposed-to-be-real-but-is. An angel of light proves to be the most monstrous villain of all" (Brahen 141). Zachariah, who first presents himself as an ally to the Winchesters, is revealed at the end of season 4 to have his own agenda in helping to bring about the Apocalypse, and he plagues Sam and Dean across the entirety of season 5, beginning in "Sympathy for the Devil" (5.1) and continuing through "The End" (5.4), "Dark Side of the Moon" (5.16), "Point of No Return" (5.18), "Two Minutes to Midnight" (5.21), and "Swan Song" (5.22).

There are other ways in which the story of the Angel Islington of *Neverwhere* connects to *Supernatural*'s narrative. Islington is trapped inside a cage in the underworld and attempts to manipulate that story's hero and heroine, Richard and Door, into giving him the means of escape by first making them think they are helping the side of good. Richard and Door go on a long perilous journey and overcome many obstacles, only to realize that they have been tricked. While Door and Richard see through the angel's ruse and emerge victorious, Sam and

Dean are not so fortunate at the end of *Supernatural*'s fourth season. The demons Lilith and Ruby successfully trick Sam into killing Lilith in order to "stop Lucifer," when in reality Lilith sacrificing herself by Sam's hand sets Lucifer loose upon the world.

As God, Lucifer, and the angels begin to play a larger role in *Supernatural*'s mythology, both Sam and Dean question the savagery to which they bear witness nearly every day of their lives. Dean most especially rails against the idea of a god who would allow so many to suffer and perish. Gaiman's story "24 Hours" from *The Sandman Vol. 1: Preludes & Nocturnes*, in which a serial killer tortures and murders innocent customers in a diner, also concentrates on "the problem of evil, and the failure of moral and ethical systems to address it. For this slaughter has no meaning, no higher explanations of why God would allow such a thing to happen" (Rauch 126).[3] When Sam and Dean come face-to-face with God's representative, Joshua in "Dark Side of the Moon," they are informed God will not speak with them and he will intervene no further. To this Dean angrily retorts: "So he's just going to sit back and watch the world burn?" and refers to God as "just another deadbeat dad with a bunch of excuses."

Again, these commonalities between Gaiman's work and the *Supernatural* world are at this point more thematic and abstract than concrete. It is one thing to state that such-and-such element from the series reminds one of Gaiman. A case just as easily could be made that the series' attitude or overall storylines echo that of *Buffy the Vampire Slayer*, for instance. But in Season 5, the situation ceases to be "this reminds me of . . ." and turns into "Hey, that's *exactly* like . . ."

Case in point: "I Believe the Children Are Our Future" (5.6) features a young boy named Jesse who is of demonic parentage, his mother having been possessed by a demon at the time of his birth. This gives the mischievous lad a number of unique powers that permit him to unknowingly bring things from his imagination to life. Soon, children are getting sick from eating Pop Rocks and drinking soda, joy buzzers are electrocuting people to death, and someone's face really *is* freezing like that. Castiel informs Sam and Dean that Jesse is the Anti-Christ and possesses the ability to kill angels with a single thought. His mother has gone through great effort to hide him from demonic and heavenly agents, and until Jesse inadvertently discovered his powers, she had been successful. While Castiel believes that the boy must be killed or he will become an unstoppable tool on the side of evil, Sam and Dean think that Jesse will be able to make the right choices. In the end, Jesse is convinced and removes himself from the equation by going into hiding and telling no one, not even his mother, where he is going.

A child Anti-Christ with unique gifts who, in the end, makes the right choices in the face of evil? Jesse may as well have been named Adam Young, who, in *Good Omens*, is a spirited troublemaker who nonetheless opts not to "mess people around." When Metatron, the Voice of God, informs him that Armageddon may be a "temporary inconvenience, but that should hardly stand in the way of the ultimate good," Adam eventually replies:

> I just don't see why everyone and everything has to be burned up and everything. [. . .] An' not even for anything important. Jus' to see who's got the best gang [. . .] But even if you win, you can't really beat the other side, because you don't really want to. I mean, not for good. You'll just start all over again (334).

Adam goes on to say: "I don't see why it matters what is written. Not when it's about people. It can always be crossed out" (337). Dean echoes this sentiment by dubbing himself, Sam, and Castiel "Team Free Will" and stating with typical Winchester flair: "Screw destiny. Right in the face" ("The Song Remains the Same," 5.13; "Point of No Return").

Jesse is not the only character from *Supernatural* that has its roots in *Omen*'s pages. The demon Crowley, who enters the series in "Abandon All Hope" (5.10) and returns in "The Devil You Know" (5.20) and "Two Minutes to Midnight," is a smooth-tongued, sharply dressed wheeler-dealer with a British accent, expensive tastes, and a desire to help the Winchesters avert the Apocalypse. He makes his first appearance in an abandoned parking lot underneath a looping tangle of busy highways.

The Crowley of *Good Omens* is also a smooth-tongued, sharply dressed wheeler-dealer with a British accent and expensive tastes, and one of his "better achievements" is the M25 orbital motorway in London, "generally agreed to be among the top contenders" as evidence of the "hidden hand of Satan in the affairs of Man" (13). While the Crowley of *Supernatural* has a greater penchant for violence than the Crowley of Gaiman and Pratchett's book, in almost all other respects, they are so similar that there is little doubt that the character is meant as a direct homage to *Good Omens*.

While some might likewise think that Castiel could be the angelic equivalent of the book's Aziraphale, Crowley's Apocalypse-preventing angelic partner is a bit too carefree. Castiel only resembles Aziraphale overall in his growing preference for humanity and, in particular, as Castiel begins to lose his angelic powers and copes in decidedly human ways such as moping and getting drunk ("99 Problems"). Unlike the case for the two Crowleys, the equivalency of Aziraphale to Castiel is a dicey proposition.

＊ But angels and demons are not the only creatures *Supernatural* has in common with Gaiman. There is one last episode that seems to have stepped right out of Gaiman's pages and on to the television screen.

Hammer of the *American Gods*

I know how gods begin, Roger. We start as dreams. Then we walk out of dreams into the land. We are worshipped and loved, and take power to ourselves. And then one day there's no one left to worship us.

The Sandman: Brief Lives, 5.20

"Hammer of the Gods" (5.19) serves as a prime example for those who think that *Supernatural* may be treading on territory covered by

Gaiman. In his seminal novel *American Gods*, deities such as Anansi, Anubis, Bast, Czernobog, Kali, Loki, Odin, and the Zorya, as well as folklore heroes such as Paul Bunyan, Johnny Appleseed, and mythic creatures like leprechauns, populate the small towns and big cities of America. Like the gods that sometimes weave their way through *The Sandman*'s pages, these have been all but forgotten by America's people, who instead now worship the new gods of media and technology. At a strange roadside attraction well off the beaten path, the old gods gather to plan their war to recapture what they feel is rightfully theirs.

In "Hammer of the Gods," the gods Baldur, Ganesh, Kali, and many others gather at a strange roadside motel to plan their war against Lucifer and his oncoming Apocalypse. The gods conspire to bring the Winchesters to their odd convention and plan to use them as bait to bring Lucifer to their doorstep. While *American Gods* pits old gods vs. new, "Hammer of the Gods" places gods of many of the world's religions against the perceived arrogance of the Judeo-Christian theology within the context of *Supernatural*'s world, which is threatening apocalyptic destruction with no regard for the fact that their religion is not the only religion. The episode serves as a self-reflexive criticism of *Supernatural*'s heavier reliance on Judeo-Christian ideas since the beginning of season 4, but the pantheon of gods storyline also reminded many of Gaiman's novel. This prompted *CinemaSpy* writer Blaine Kylio to suggest: "If Sam and Dean are going to be confronting the likes of Anubis, Thor, and Kali — because she's bound to make a return, right? — in season 6, maybe Gaiman should be brought in at least as a consultant, if not a full-on writer/producer."

It's an interesting thought, and it brings about an important question. Since Gaiman's body of work would not exist as it is today if not for other bodies of work, if not for other writers' characters, plots, and ideas, how would Gaiman feel about *Supernatural* liberally borrowing from his texts? Drawing on his published statements, it seems he would not be too bothered and may even be flattered. He states:

People writing within a certain genre are always going to overlap with ideas — some of which they glean from others and some of which they come up with themselves. And that's a good thing. It's only in this unfortunate era when some people seem to think that all ideas must spring brand new from a virgin mind that the idea of sharing, building on the works of others and creating new derivative works are seen as being bad (Manick).

If Gaiman's work is derivative — if *Good Omens* draws on Chesterton (and surely also parodies demonic children movies like *The Omen* and other biblically inspired books, TV shows, and movies not mentioned herein) — then is not *Supernatural* just another link in the chain? Is borrowing from *Good Omens* and *American Gods* that strikingly different or worse than the tone and spirit of Gaiman that tinges earlier seasons? Some *Supernatural* fans familiar with Gaiman aren't bothered by the obvious allusions to his work in season 5. Long-time fan Krystina writes: "Overall, I thought the similarities between the recent seasons of *Supernatural* and *Good Omens* were pretty amusing. It just felt as if Sam and Dean had traveled through the *Good Omens* world from time to time" (personal communication, 27 September 2010). Another fan, Amanda, holds the opposite opinion: "I'm glad I wasn't the only one who wasn't impressed by the *Good Omens* rip off. I felt like it was too . . . detailed to be homage" (personal communication, 19 November 2009). She adds later, "I couldn't help but be overwhelmingly reminded of the original material and how much better it had been handled there" by Gaiman and Pratchett (personal communication, 4 October 2010).

It is doubtful anyone in Gaiman's camp will be contacting their lawyers very soon, but whether or not the fans are crazy about the creative decisions being made in the writers' room is less clear. In the end, all of Kripke's interest in Gaiman may have an unexpected payoff. In early September 2010, *The Hollywood Reporter* broke the news that Warner Bros. TV is in the process of acquiring the television rights to *The Sandman* series and that the top candidate to write and produce the show is in fact none other than Eric Kripke. While at this point it is unclear whether Gaiman will participate in bringing *Sandman* to the small screen, maybe Kripke will get to meet Neil Gaiman after all.

Now: The Road Ahead, or the Chapter at the End of This Book

David Lavery

> Many die too late, and some die too early. Yet
> strange soundeth the precept: "Die at the right time!"
> *Friedrich Nietzsche,* Thus Spake Zarathustra

> When the author walks onto the stage,
> the play is over.
> *C. S. Lewis,* Mere Christianity

In *Supernatural's* season 5 we are not 100% certain Chuck is indeed God, but we certainly do meet Death itself, one of the Four Horsemen of the Apocalypse. In a brilliant sequence in "Two Minutes to Midnight" (5.22), cut to Jen Titus's cover of Ralph Stanley's classic "Oh Death," he arrives in a finned 1960s Cadillac on a Chicago street, where he has come to destroy the city as part of Lucifer's apocalyptic plans. Later, he will sit down in a Chicago pizza parlor with Dean Winchester, who has come to prevent obliteration of the Windy City. I am willing to wager that in the history of television, no conversation as profound as this one, written by *Supernatural*'s executive producer (and season 6's showrunner) Sera Gamble, has ever taken place:

> Death: You have an inflated sense of your importance. To a thing like me, a thing like you. . . . Think how you'd feel if a bacterium sat at your table and tried to get smart. This is one little planet in one tiny solar system in a galaxy that's barely out of its diapers. I'm old, Dean, very old. So I invite you to contemplate what if any significance I find in you. Eat!
>
> Dean: I got to ask, how old are you?
>
> Death: As old as God — maybe older. Neither of us can remember any more. Life, death, chicken, egg, regardless, at the end I'll reap him too.
>
> Dean: God? You will reap God?
>
> Death: Oh yes. God will die too, Dean.
>
> Dean: This is way above my paygrade.

Death will make even God his victim in the demythologized *Supernatural*verse, will reap even the anything-but-supreme being. Or is it a remythologizing? The notion of a divine power under the thumb of more powerful, more archetypal, and possibly more ancient cosmic forces is a very ancient, Greek mytheme.

Once, metaphysics was above television's pay grade, but no more. Now we have series god Eric Kripke acknowledging, "You haven't lived until you are in the writers' room and you talk about God's motivation in a scene." Here, in series television, on the cw, such ontological matters not only drive a story arc but are grounded, in a way philosophy and theology could never hope to imitate, in *our* reality, in human time. In the *Supernatural*verse Death decides not to carry out the deep-dish eradication brewing in the scene outside the window in the back of the frame. The reason? A city that has given the world such pizza does not deserve annihilation. To him, we may be the equivalent of bacteria, but our crust is to die for.

Death does not claim Chicago, but at the end of the season "he" did "reap" series creator Eric Kripke, a willing victim, who had predetermined *Supernatural*'s life expectancy. Kripke's series was envisioned as a five-season narrative telling the story of the Winchesters' roles, beginning in childhood, in the Apocalypse, the end-point in the Judeo-Christian tradition of history itself. According to C.S. Lewis, who had that history in mind and not just the aftermath of a drama, "When the author walks onto the stage, the play is over" (65). And when the author walks offstage? What follows that? How are wayward sons to carry on? Now the series has carried on, had a sixth season, and is entering its seventh. Without Chuck, without Kripke, did it jump the shark or never come down? Did it miss the opportunity to "die at the right time"? "The way I look at it," Chuck proclaims in "The Real Ghostbusters" (5.9), "it's really not jumping the shark if you never come back down." AK (after Kripke) has *Supernatural* returned to earth?

Supernatural AK (After Kripke)

When Kripke left the series he took with him, it would seem permanently, Carver Edlund, a.k.a. Chuck, who disappeared in a puff at the end of season 5. Also exiting the *Supernatural* writers' room was half of the origin of Chuck's pseudonym, Jeremy Carver, who had become the showrunner of the SyFy reboot of *Being Human*, the BBC's "werewolf, vampire, and ghost become roommates" series. Carver had authored/co-authored twelve important, and often metatextual episodes of *Supernatural*, including "Sin City" (3.4); "A Very Supernatural Christmas" (3.8); the *Groundhog Day* homage "Mystery Spot" (3.11); "Long-Distance Call" (3.14); the time-traveling, backstory-supplying "In the Beginning" (4.3); the inventive and hilarious "Changing Channels" (5.8), in which the most meta show on television became even meta-er; and, in his final *Supernatural* script, "Point of No Return" (5.18).

However, half of Carver Edlund — the Edlund half — did return for season 6. Ben Edlund had joined the writers' room one year earlier than Carver in season 2. By most measures, season 1 had been a success.

Though by no means off the charts, the ratings were good enough for renewal by the WB (see Karen Petruska's essay on pages 219–229), and most episodes seemed more than adequate realizations of Kripke's gameplan. That ten writers (Hatem, Milbauer, Burton, Nave, Coakley, Ross-Leming, Buckner, Callaway, Knauf, and Ehrman) would not return for season 2 nevertheless suggests Kripke and company felt the need for some new blood. A key addition to the staff was Edlund, who came over to *Supernatural* after cancellation of *Point Pleasant* (2005).

According to friend and collaborator Joss Whedon (he and Edlund wrote *Titan AE* and worked together on *Angel* and *Firefly*), Edlund possesses "a sensibility that's so left of center" (*Firefly: The Official Companion* I 9). The strange mind who gave us the comic book superhero The Tick and authored the unforgettable vampire-as-a-puppet *Angel* episode "Smile Time" and the delightfully offbeat "Jaynestown" installment of *Firefly* contributed mightily to the Kripke years. According to former television writer Jeffrey Stepakoff, "[W]hat most showrunners really want is a writer who has a fresh and distinctive voice; but at the same time, they want a writer who can suppress his or her fresh and distinctive voice and conform to the voice of the series" (77). Edlund's was clearly one such voice — an innovative collaborator whose tendency toward the metafictional would become, with the full sanctioning of Kripke, one of the series' trademarks.

Edlund has contributed 16 episodes to date, including "Hollywood Babylon" (2.18), a script indebted to the *Scream* films and the season 7 *X-Files* episode "Hollywood A.D." (7.17); "Ghostfacers" (3.13), in which Sam and Dean find themselves in the middle of an actual haunted house with the clueless makers of a public access paranormal reality show; the purely "Edlundian" "Monster Movie" (4.5), featuring a shapeshifting murderer who assumes the form of 1930s movie monsters; "Wishful Thinking" (4.8); "The End" (5.4); "My Bloody Valentine" (5.14); and Edlund's final Kripke-era episode, "The Devil You Know" (5.20). Chuck may be no more, Carver Edlund may have split, Kripke and Carver may have moved on, but *Supernatural* is likely to remain Edlundian until the very end.

Season 6 of *Supernatural* would end up in the hands of Sera Gamble. Part of the series' creative team since its first season, Gamble has been a key writer throughout authoring 23 episodes including the ghost story "Dead in the Water" (1.3); the werewolf tale "Heart" (2.17); the alternative-reality exercise "It's a Terrible Life" (4.17); the Brad Pitt-film-evoking "The Curious Case of Dean Winchester" (5.7); and, of course, "Two Minutes to Midnight" (5.21). Gamble's increasing centrality to the series can be seen in her writing assignments throughout its run. In seasons 1 and 2, she was assigned both the third and penultimate episodes. By season 3, both the second and next-to-last were put in Gamble's capable hands, and she retained that assignment for the remainder of Kripke's years as showrunner. In season 6, now the executive producer in charge, Gamble would take over the role of author of the season premiere, while again writing episode 21, yielding the assignment of the finale to the returning Kripke.

Interviewed by Sci-Fi Wire after "Dark Side of the Moon" (5.16), an episode in which Sam and Dean are killed and go to Heaven, Edlund was already contemplating the implications of *Supernatural*'s aversion to death. "As it turns out," Edlund observed, "we've decided that Sam and Dean are going to die many times. This is a terrible plight," he suggests. "It's a terrible thing when nobody lets you die. They might imprison you forever or take over your body or they might torture you, but you can't get out of the game. That's Sam and Dean's problem" (Huddleston). It may be *Supernatural*'s problem too.

Supernatural Season 6

The essays in this book — all but this one — were written between seasons 5 and 6 of *Supernatural* and are almost entirely unaware of AK — After Kripke — developments. This epilogue, however, was written after the first season of Sera Gamble's *Supernatural* had come to an end and the prospect of a second had become a reality. If *Supernatural* had ended with Kripke's "The End," what would we have missed? What would have never been? (The question almost seems like a *Supernatural* episode, does it not? Something along the lines of "What Is and What Should Never Be," 2.20; or "It's a Terrible Life," 4.17.)

- Sam Winchester, along with a family member, being brought back from the dead ("Exile on Main St.," 6.1).
- The Yorkie that terrified Dean in "Yellow Fever" (4.6) reprising his role ("Exile on Main Street").
- Many, many more episode titles (all 22, in fact) riffing on amusement parks ("Frontierland"); fiction ("Appointment in Samarra" and "And Then There Were None"); movies ("The Third Man," "Weekend at Bobby's," "Live Free or TwiHard," "You Can't Handle the Truth," "All Dogs Go to Heaven," "Clap Your Hands If You Believe," "Caged Heat," "Unforgiven," "Mannequin 3: The Reckoning" [either one of the series' best or worst titles], "The French Mistake," "The Man Who Would Be King," "The Man Who Knew Too Much"); music ("Exile on Main Street," "Like a Virgin," "My Heart Will Go On," "Let It Bleed"); television ("Two and a Half Men" and "Family Matters").
- Castiel, decidedly less funny than in seasons 4 and 5, ruling out Moses as the possible perpetrator of a crime performed with a staff ("The Third Man," 6.3).
- The children of the djinn in "What Is and What Should Never Be" seeking revenge against Dean ("Exile on Main Street").
- A civil war breaking out in Heaven, pitting the forces of Castiel against those of Raphael ("The Third Man").
- A delightful *Rosencrantz and Guildenstern Are Dead*ish episode, directed by none other than Jensen Ackles ("Weekend at Bobby's," 6.4).
- The Winchester boys crossing the Atlantic (a first) in order to find the human remains of Crowley ("Weekend at Bobby's").

- Dean becoming a vampire (though he is later cured) ("Live Free or TwiHard," 6.5).
- The knowledge that Castiel's true form is "approximately the size of [the] Chrysler Building" ("Family Matters," 6.7).
- Dean nuking Tinkerbell in a microwave ("Clap Your Hands If You Believe," 6.9).
- A scene choreographed to David Bowie's "Space Oddity" ("Clap Your Hands If You Believe").
- An unlicensed medical practitioner played by Freddy Krueger (Robert Englund) ("Appointment in Samarra," 6.11).
- "The French Mistake" (6.15), the most meta episode of any television series ever, written, of course, by Ben Edlund, in which, to protect them from an angelic hit man, Balthazar teleports Sam and Dean out of the *Supernatural* diegesis entirely, turning them into Jared Padalecki and Jensen Ackles.
- Balthazar rewriting history solely for the purpose of killing Céline Dion's career ("My Heart Will Go On," 6.17).
- Sam and Dean time-traveling to the Old West ("Frontierland," 6.18).
- Castiel's transformation from powerful but adorable trench-coated angel to darksider, resulting in the OMG (literally) development that ends the season ("The Man Who Knew Too Much," 6.22).

We would have missed, in other words, an uneven season, rich with identifiable *Supernatural* DNA — a season in search of a purpose (and a Big Bad: was it Soulless Sammy? Grandfather Samuel Campbell? Crowley? The Mother of All?). Twenty-two episodes that seemed in some way a season-long reboot. Not surprisingly, on three different occasions, characters (including "Bobby Singer," the alternate universe version of *Supernatural*'s actual executive producer and go-to director) are heard muttering "season 6 . . ." almost as if it were a cross between an interrogative and an expletive.

Though no longer series god, Eric Kripke was not entirely absent from Sera Gamble's *Supernatural*. In the über-self-referential "The French Mistake" "Kripke" shows up on the Vancouver set, fresh from finally selling his idea for *Octocobra*, only to be brutally slaughtered in a *Desperado* (Robert Rodriguez, 1995) homage by a shotgun wielding Virgil. His metadeath evidently left the actual Kripke unscathed, for he would return yet again, this time as the author of "The Man Who Knew Too Much" (6.22). It was Kripke, then, who made — that is, *imagined* — Castiel into a god.

So what will the next 22 episodes look like? Will the prayers of unhappy fans and snarky recappers (on Television Without Pity, The Onion TV Club) lamenting the series' abandonment of its early monster-of-the-week format for a leap into hyper self-awareness be answered? Is it possible that season 6 was intended as a way of finding a way back to the beginning — to the *Supernatural* from which some fans and critics wish it had never deviated in the first place?

Stacey Abbott and I, along with this book's contributors, promise to gather again outside these pages, first to discuss season 6 and, then, when the new season begins, regularly reassess and reimagine, pondering whether our readings still hold water, taking a look down the road ahead. Join us at http://tvgoestohell.blogspot.com/ for a lively post-mortem and running commentary on season 7.

Seasons 1–6
Supernatural Episode Guide
Stephanie Graves

Season 1
Ep. # | Episode Title | Air Date | Writer | Director

1.1 | Pilot | 9/13/05 | Eric Kripke | David Nutter
Dean Winchester shows up on his estranged brother Sam's doorstep, asking for help in locating their father, John, a man driven by a vendetta to find the creature that killed his wife, Mary, 22 years prior. Following their father's trail, they investigate a ghostly woman in white who takes revenge on unfaithful men traveling along a desolate highway.

1.2 | Wendigo | 9/20/05 | Teleplay: Kripke; Story: Ron Milbauer and Terri Hughes Burton | Nutter
Following coordinates left in John's journal, Sam and Dean investigate a cyclical pattern of disappearances in the Colorado woods. Rather than a grizzly, the brothers encounter something much more lethal — a wendigo.

1.3 | Dead in the Water | 9/27/05 | Sera Gamble and Raelle Tucker | Kim Manners

With no real leads on their father's whereabouts, Sam and Dean head to Lake Manitoc, Wisconsin, where they look into a series of suspicious drownings happening in — and around — the lake.

1.4 | Phantom Traveler | 10/4/05 | Richard Hatem | Robert Singer

When Dean receives a call from a friend of his father's, the brothers head to Pittsburg to investigate a plane crash. However, they get more than they bargain for when the cause of the crash seems to be a demon who is now systematically hunting down the remaining survivors.

1.5 | Bloody Mary | 10/11/05 | Teleplay: Milbauer and Hughes Burton; Story: Kripke | Peter Ellis

In Toledo, Ohio, Sam and Dean investigate the death of a man whose eyes exploded, and find the manner of his death tied to the spirit of a young woman who can travel from mirror to mirror.

1.6 | Skin | 10/18/05 | John Shiban | Robert Duncan McNeill

Sam drags a reluctant Dean along to St. Louis, where one of his college friends has been accused of murdering his girlfriend. When another woman is killed by her husband, the brothers discover that a shapeshifter has been assuming the identity of other people — and Dean is next on his list.

1.7 | Hook Man | 10/25/05 | Shiban | David Jackson

In Iowa, the Winchesters look into a mysterious death, the circumstances of which mimic the legend of the Hook Man.

1.8 | Bugs | 11/8/05 | Rachel Nave and Bill Coakley | Manners

Sam and Dean investigate mysterious deaths at a new housing development in Oklahoma, and they discover something strange is happening with the insect population.

1.9 | Home | 11/15/05 | Kripke | Ken Girotti

Sam convinces Dean to accompany him to their hometown of Lawrence, Kansas, by revealing he has been having prophetic dreams — one of which centers on their old house.

1.10 | Asylum | 11/22/05 | Richard Hatem | Guy Bee

Receiving coordinates in a text message from their father, Sam and Dean check out Roosevelt Asylum, an abandoned hospital and the site of a patient riot years earlier. But the ghosts of the patients aren't the ones terrorizing the asylum.

1.11 | Scarecrow | 1/10/06 | Teleplay: Shiban; Story: Patrick Sean Smith | Manners

The brothers finally get in touch with their father, who tells them it's not safe to be together and sends them instead to Burkitsville, Indiana. Butting heads with his brother, Sam takes off in search of John, while Dean checks out the series of disappearances in the too-charming town, which revolve around an apple orchard guarded by a sinister scarecrow.

1.12 | Faith | 1/17/06 | Gamble and Tucker | Allan Kroeker

Dean is electrocuted during a fight, and the damage to his heart means he has a short time to live. Desperate, Sam takes Dean to a genuine faith healer, and Dean is cured. But the boys soon discover that the healing comes at a cost.

1.13 | Route 666 | 1/31/06 | Eugenie Ross-Leming and Brad Buckner | Paul Shapiro

Dean gets a call from Cassie, an old flame in Mississippi, and the brothers head there to investigate tales of a giant black truck that seems to be linked to a series of racially motivated murders — with Cassie next on its list.

1.14 | Nightmare | 2/7/06 | Gamble and Tucker | Phil Sgriccia

Another of Sam's precognitive dreams leads the Winchesters to Saginaw, Michigan, to investigate what appears to be a suicide; when they arrive, they discover a family member who exhibits some eerie similarities to Sam.

1.15 | The Benders | 2/14/06 | Shiban | Ellis

After Sam goes missing while the brothers are checking on disappearances in Hibbing, Minnesota, Dean teams up with the local sheriff to search for the missing people. But in the backwoods, they encounter a surprising culprit.

1.16 | Shadow | 2/28/06 | Kripke | Manners

In the course of checking out grisly murders in Chicago, Sam and Dean run into Meg, who Sam met at a bus station when he briefly split from Dean.

1.17 | Hell House | 3/30/06 | Trey Callaway | Chris Long

Investigating tales of a haunted house, Sam and Dean encounter Harry Spangler and Ed Zeddmore, "ghost hunters" who run a website that details the legend of the house.

1.18 | Something Wicked | 4/6/06 | Daniel Knauf | Whitney Ransick

Children in Fitchburg, Wisconsin, have been falling into mysterious comas, and John sends Sam and Dean to investigate. Dean recognizes the handiwork of a shtriga — a witch who steals someone's life force — because, unbeknownst to Sam, the Winchesters have tangled with it before.

1.19 | Provenance | 4/13/06 | David Ehrman | Sgriccia

Mysterious murders in upstate New York draw Sam's attention, and the brothers discover the murders are related to a painting that is hiding a dark secret.

1.20 | Dead Man's Blood | 4/20/06 | Cathryn Humphris and Shiban | Tony Wharmby

When a fellow hunter is murdered by vampires, Sam and Dean check out his cabin, where they are surprised by their father's arrival. They team up to track down the vampires, who have stolen an object of legend that John has been searching for — one that can kill the thing that murdered Mary.

1.21 | Salvation | 4/27/06 | Gamble and Tucker | Singer

The whole Winchester family heads to Salvation, Iowa, where Meg has started killing off people John cares about — and swears to continue doing so until he surrenders the Colt to her.

1.22 | Devil's Trap | 5/4/06 | Kripke | Manners

With their father taken by Meg, Sam and Dean seek help from Bobby Singer, a friend and fellow hunter. But when Meg arrives the brothers find themselves in deeper jeopardy than before.

Season 2
Ep. # | Episode Title | Air Date | Writer | Director

2.1 | In My Time of Dying | 9/28/06 | Kripke | Manners

In the hospital following the Winchesters' terrible car crash, Dean finds his body in a coma and his spirit being stalked by a phantom entity. Meanwhile, John makes a horrifying deal with Azazel, the yellow-eyed demon.

2.2 | Everybody Loves a Clown | 10/5/06 | Shiban | Sgriccia

After cremating John's body, Sam and Dean track down Ellen Harvelle, proprietor of Harvelle's Roadhouse — a hub for hunters like themselves. Resident mulleted genius Ash starts compiling John's collected data, while the brothers investigate a series of murders that seem to be tied to something Sam truly fears — a clown.

2.3 | Bloodlust | 10/12/06 | Gamble | Singer

Sam and Dean look into a series of cattle mutilations and decapitations in Montana, and at the morgue they discover the severed heads have fangs. While searching for the vampire nest they meet Gordon, another hunter, whose agenda conflicts with theirs.

2.4 | Children Shouldn't Play with Dead Things | 10/19/06 | Tucker | Manners

While visiting their mother's grave, the brothers notice the nearby grave of Angela Mason is surrounded by dead plants. Their investigation turns up a series of murders, the victims all tied to Angela.

2.5 | Simon Said | 10/26/06 | Ben Edlund | Tim Iacofano

Ash's research points Sam and Dean to Guthrie, Oklahoma, where they meet Andy, a young man with powers similar to Sam's. Andy seems to be behind a series of suicides, until Sam and Dean discover Andy and Sam are not the only ones with special powers.

2.6 | No Exit | 11/2/06 | Matt Witten | Manners

Back at the Roadhouse, Jo Harvelle has information on a rash of disappearances from an apartment building in Philadelphia, but her mother, Ellen, forbids her from going. Jo doesn't listen and discovers that ghost-hunting is a lot more dangerous than she thought.

2.7 | The Usual Suspects | 11/9/06 | Humphris | Mike Rohl
While investigating murders that seem to be ghost related, Dean is arrested for the crime. Sam manages to elude the police, and Dean convinces one of the detectives to work with Sam. Together they realize the ghost wasn't punishing the inmates, but warning them of something far worse.

2.8 | Crossroad Blues | 11/16/06 | Gamble | Steve Boyum
The brothers look into black dog sightings, one of which is tied to an apparent suicide. A local bar — situated at a crossroads — is at the epicenter of the occurrences, which echo the Robert Johnson legend.

2.9 | Croatoan | 12/7/06 | Shiban | Singer
Another vision of Sam's — this time, of Dean shooting an unarmed man — leads the brothers to Rivergrove, Oregon, where they find "CROATOAN" carved on a pole and a mysterious blood-borne virus infecting the local population.

2.10 | Hunted | 1/11/07 | Tucker | Rachel Talalay
When Dean finally reveals what John's final warning to him was, Sam angrily takes off in search of others afflicted with the same psychic powers. However, Gordon — who has discovered Sam's "gift" — is now hunting Sam.

2.11 | Playthings | 1/18/07 | Witten | Charles Beeson
Sam and Dean check into mysterious deaths at an inn in Cornwall, Connecticut, currently inhabited by three generations of the family. They soon realize the inn has one extra inhabitant they hadn't noticed.

2.12 | Nightshifter | 1/25/07 | Edlund | Sgriccia
A string of peculiar robberies in Milwaukee prove to be perpetrated by another shapeshifter, and while trying to locate it, Sam gets locked inside a bank with a vigilante security guard who thinks

the crimes are the work of a "mandroid." To complicate matters, FBI agent Victor Henriksen arrives, intent on capturing the Winchesters.

2.13 | Houses of the Holy | 2/1/07 | Gamble | Manners

In Providence, Rhode Island, Sam and Dean investigate a rash of murders committed by people who claim an angel commanded them to kill evildoers. Dean suspects it is not an angel but an avenging spirit.

2.14 | Born Under a Bad Sign | 2/8/07 | Humphris | J. Miller Tobin

When Sam wakes up in a hotel room covered in blood with no memory of the past week, he and Dean retrace his steps; what they find is a dead hunter and security footage showing Sam killing him. However, Sam is not what he appears to be.

2.15 | Tall Tales | 2/15/07 | Shiban | Bradford May

Sam and Dean investigate a series of bizarre occurrences on a college campus that seem straight out of a tabloid. With no leads, and crippled by bickering, they call Bobby.

2.16 | Roadkill | 3/15/07 | Tucker | Beeson

A woman swerves to avoid a figure in the road and crashes. After the crash takes a ghostly turn, she manages to flag down the next passing car, which happens to be the Impala.

2.17 | Heart | 3/22/07 | Gamble | Manners

In San Francisco, the brothers look into what they suspect is a series of werewolf attacks. Sam falls for the woman they believe is the next target, but soon must make a heartwrenching decision.

2.18 | Hollywood Babylon | 4/19/07 | Edlund | Sgriccia

Sam and Dean pose as production assistants to investigate a death on the set of a horror film, which they find was faked for publicity — but soon, producers start actually dying.

2.19 | Folsom Prison Blues | 4/26/07 | Shiban | Rohl

Sam and Dean get themselves arrested in order to dispatch an angry spirit that is killing people at the county jail. Unfortunately, Henriksen learns of their arrest and wants the Winchesters in his custody.

2.20 | What Is and What Should Never Be | 5/3/07 | Tucker | Kripke

Dean is surprised to find himself leading a perfect life in his hometown, engaged to a beautiful woman, with Sam engaged to Jessica and his mother living nearby. Yet he suspects it isn't real, and must decide which "reality" he wants to be in.

2.21 | All Hell Breaks Loose, Part 1 | 5/10/07 | Gamble | Singer

Sam disappears, and Dean seeks Bobby's help; they go to the roadhouse for answers but find it burned down and Ash dead inside. Meanwhile Sam finds himself in a ghost town, left to fight for his life with a group of others who have similar psychic powers.

2.22 | All Hell Breaks Loose, Part 2 | 5/17/07 | Teleplay: Kripke, Story: Kripke and Michael T. Moore | Singer

Desperate to find a way to undo Sam's death, Dean makes his own deal with the crossroads demon. He and Sam use the Colt to do something that will put the rest of the world in peril.

Season 3

Ep. # | Episode Title | Air Date | Writer | Director

3.1 | The Magnificent Seven | 10/4/07 | Kripke | Manners

Dean, with only one year to live after his demon pact, is living it up Winchester-style, while Sam is searching for a way to get Dean out of his deal. Meanwhile, seven demons — each embodying one of the Deadly Sins — are wreaking havoc in Nebraska.

3.2 | The Kids Are Alright | 10/11/07 | Gamble | Sgriccia

A series of freak accidents in Cicero, Indiana, gives Dean an excuse to drop in on Lisa, an old flame, but he arrives in the middle of a birthday party — for her eight-year-old son Ben, who bears a striking similarity to Dean.

3.3 | Bad Day at Black Rock | 10/18/07 | Edlund | Singer

When John's storage unit is robbed, the brothers track down the thieves — hired by Bela Talbot, a procurer of supernatural items — who stole a cursed rabbit's foot that gives amazing luck to the possessor . . . and imminent death should it be lost.

3.4 | Sin City | 10/25/07 | Singer and Jeremy Carver | Beeson
In Elizabethville, Ohio, Sam and Dean find the formerly quiet town rife with drinking, gambling, and violent deaths. Dean, trapped in a basement with a demon, finds himself having a surprising conversation about the nature — and cause — of evil.

3.5 | Bedtime Stories | 11/1/07 | Humphris | Rohl
When strange deaths crop up in Maple Springs, New York, Sam and Dean find that the murders echo fairy tales straight out of the Brothers Grimm. Sam issues an ultimatum to the crossroads demon.

3.6 | Red Sky at Morning | 11/8/07 | Laurence Andries | Cliff Bole
A series of ghostly ship sightings that precede drowning — on dry land — bring Sam and Dean to investigate, and they cross paths with Bela Talbot again.

3.7 | Fresh Blood | 11/15/07 | Gamble | Manners
While hunting a growing nest of vampires created by a vampire named Dixon, Gordon — escaped from prison and convinced Sam is the Antichrist — shows up hunting Sam.

3.8 | A Very Supernatural Christmas | 12/13/07 | Carver | Tobin
The brothers check out disappearances in Michigan that seem to be tied to the Christmas holiday and certain pagan traditions. Meanwhile Dean, eager to celebrate his last Christmas with Sam, recalls a Christmas from 1991, also spent in a hotel room with his brother.

3.9 | Malleus Maleficarum | 1/31/08 | Edlund | Singer
Sam and Dean head to Sturbridge, Massachusetts, to look into a mysterious death, and find themselves up against a coven of witches — whom even Ruby fears.

3.10 | Dream a Little Dream of Me | 2/7/08 | Teleplay: Humphris; Story: Gamble and Humphris | Boyum
When Bobby falls into a mysterious coma, Sam and Dean take African Dream Root in order to enter Bobby's dreams and track down the cause.

3.11 | Mystery Spot | 2/14/08 | Teleplay: Carver, Story: Carver and Emily McLaughlin | Manners

Investigating a man's disappearance at the Mystery Spot, a cheesy tourist trap, Sam finds himself reliving the same day over and over, *Groundhog Day*–style — and every day ends in Dean's death.

3.12 | Jus in Bello | 2/21/08 | Gamble | Sgriccia

Thinking they've located Bela, Sam and Dean bust into her hotel room — and find cops waiting for them. Henriksen shows up to eagerly book the Winchesters, but when the police station is barraged by a small army of demons, they must band together for survival.

3.13 | Ghostfacers | 4/24/08 | Edlund | Sgriccia

In a house haunted by a leap year ghost, Sam and Dean once again cross paths with the bumbling Ed Zeddmore and Harry Spangler, who have a crew of fellow ghost hunters and cameras along, eager to create a pilot for a reality TV show called *Ghostfacers!*

3.14 | Long-Distance Call | 5/1/08 | Carver | Singer

While investigating a rash of phone calls from the deceased in Milan, Ohio, Dean is shocked when he gets a call from his father, who claims he can help Dean get out of his contract.

3.15 | Time Is on My Side | 5/8/08 | Gamble | Beeson

Organ theft brings the brothers to Erie, Pennsylvania, where they are surprised to find not a zombie, but a doctor — one who has managed to keep himself alive since 1816.

3.16 | No Rest for the Wicked | 5/15/08 | Kripke | Manners

With the clock ticking on Dean's pact, the brothers go after Lilith, who holds the contract. Using Ruby's knife and Dean's 11th-hour ability to recognize demons, they infiltrate the house she is occupying — but time is running out and the hellhounds are on their way.

Season 4
Ep. # | Episode Title | Air Date | Writer | Director

4.1 | Lazarus Rising | 9/18/08 | Kripke | Manners
Dean awakes — not in Hell, but in a coffin. Clawing his way out, he seeks out Bobby, for whom he has no explanation; Dean learns he has been dead for four months, but claims to have no memory of Hell.

4.2 | Are You There, God? It's Me, Dean Winchester | 9/25/08 | Gamble | Sgriccia
After finding fellow hunters slaughtered, Sam, Dean, and Bobby are besieged by ghosts — all of victims they were unable to save.

4.3 | In the Beginning | 10/2/08 | Carver | Boyum
Castiel sends Dean back in time to 1973 in Lawrence, Kansas, where he meets a young John Winchester and his girlfriend Mary Campbell — who is far more like her sons than Dean ever imagined.

4.4 | Metamorphosis | 10/9/08 | Humphris | Manners
In an abandoned warehouse, Dean watches in horror while Ruby coaches Sam, who uses his psychic powers to kill a demon. However, Dean and Ruby must set aside their difference of opinion in order to track down a rougarou.

4.5 | Monster Movie | 10/16/08 | Edlund | Singer
In a black-and-white world, Sam and Dean investigate a vampire attack at Oktoberfest in Pennsylvania that appears more Bela Lugosi than genuine. When the Wolfman and a mummy are also spotted, they suspect something else is afoot.

4.6 | Yellow Fever | 10/23/08 | Andrew Dabb and Daniel Loflin | Sgriccia
A series of suspicious heart attacks brings the brothers to Rock Ridge, Colorado, where a ghost sickness is infecting people, causing them to be scared to death — and Dean has managed to contract the illness.

4.7 | It's the Great Pumpkin, Sam Winchester | 10/30/08 | Julie Siege | Beeson

Just before Halloween, Sam and Dean look into two mysterious deaths, and they find hex bags at the crime scenes. Realizing it's all a plot to raise Samhain, the Winchesters try to stop it before the angels take matters into their own hands.

4.8 | Wishful Thinking | 11/6/08 | Teleplay: Edlund; Story: Edlund and Lou Bollo | Singer

A reported haunting in the women's shower at a health club piques Dean's interest, but once in town, he and Sam notice other things that are very much out of the ordinary.

4.9 | I Know What You Did Last Summer | 11/13/08 | Gamble | Beeson

Sam and Dean try to protect a young woman named Anna, an escaped mental patient who can overhear angels talking, and whom the demon Alastair is searching for. Meanwhile, Sam finally tries to explain to Dean why he trusts Ruby.

4.10 | Heaven and Hell | 11/20/08 | Teleplay: Kripke; Story: Trevor Sands | Tobin

Refusing to hand Anna over to the angels who intend to kill her, Sam and Dean hide her in Bobby's panic room. Pamela hypnotizes Anna to try to help her remember who she is, and the answer reveals why both the angels and the demons want her.

4.11 | Family Remains | 1/15/09 | Carver | Sgriccia

The Winchesters investigate a gruesome murder that they suspect is the work of a malevolent spirit bound to a house, but something more horrifying.

4.12 | Criss Angel Is a Douchebag | 1/22/09 | Siege | Sgriccia

With Sam resisting Ruby's advice to hone his powers, the brothers look into the strange death of a magician's rival.

4.13 | After School Special | 1/29/09 | Dabb and Loflin | Adam Kane

Posing as a janitor and a gym teacher, Sam and Dean revist their old high school, where a series of violent occurrences seem to be caused by a ghost that has a personal grudge against Sam.

4.14 | Sex and Violence | 2/5/09 | Humphris | Beeson

A rash of murders in Bedford, Iowa, are committed at the urging of exotic dancers. Though Dean is ecstatic to be on a case involving strippers, what they discover is something else entirely.

4.15 | Death Takes a Holiday | 3/12/09 | Carver | Boyum

Sam and Dean investigate a town where nobody is dying — despite fatal wounds. They find that Alastair has taken Reapers hostage in order to break another seal.

4.16 | On the Head of a Pin | 3/19/09 | Edlund | Rohl

Dean is taken by Uriel and Castiel, who want him to use the skills he picked up in Hell to torture information out of Alastair.

4.17 | It's a Terrible Life | 3/26/09 | Gamble | James L. Conway

In another alternate reality scenario, Dean Smith, Director of Sales at Sandover Bridge and Iron, and Sam Wesson, a cubicle-dwelling tech support guy, unexpectedly team up when a ghost starts killing off employees.

4.18 | The Monster at the End of This Book | 4/2/09 | Teleplay: Siege; Story: Siege and Nancy Weiner | Rohl

While investigating a haunting, Sam and Dean discover a series of books titled *Supernatural*, which chronicles every detail about their lives since the woman in white. They track down Chuck Shurley, the author — who turns out to be something rather unexpected.

4.19 | Jump the Shark | 4/23/09 | Dabb and Loflin | Sgriccia

Sam and Dean get a call on John's phone from someone in Windom, Minnesota, named Adam Milligan, who claims to be John's son — and whose mother has recently gone missing.

4.20 | The Rapture | 4/30/09 | Carver | Beeson

After Dean is contacted by Castiel in a dream, the brothers meet him at a warehouse that shows signs of battle — and Castiel no longer in his vessel's body.

4.21 | When the Levee Breaks | 5/7/09 | Gamble | Singer

With Sam locked in Bobby's panic room detoxing from demon blood and only a few seals left for Lilith to break, Bobby and Dean argue over whether Sam should be fighting.

4.22 | Lucifer Rising | 5/14/09 | Kripke | Kripke

While Sam and Ruby track down Lilith and get Sam amped up on demon blood, Dean is taken to a tacky waiting room by the angels, where he is told he will be sitting this one out.

Season 5
Ep. # | Episode Title | Air Date | Writer | Director

5.1 | Sympathy for the Devil | 9/10/09 | Kripke | Singer
Lucifer's cage now open, Sam and a leery Dean try to track down the archangel Michael's sword before the demons get it, and Bobby is driven to make a great sacrifice to prevent it.

5.2 | Good God, Y'all! | 9/17/09 | Gamble | Sgriccia
With Bobby in a wheelchair and Castiel off searching for God, Sam and Dean go help Rufus, another hunter. They arrive to find the handiwork of one of the four horsemen of the Apocalypse.

5.3 | Free to Be You and Me | 9/24/09 | Carver | Miller Tobin
Afraid he can't be trusted, Sam splits off from Dean, but his past catches up with him when a group of hunters tries to force him to use his powers. Meanwhile, Dean and Castiel search for Raphael, who they think might have information on God's whereabouts.

5.4 | The End | 10/1/09 | Edlund | Boyum
When Sam asks to rejoin Dean, Dean refuses, and when he wakes the next morning, Dean finds himself five years into the very bleak future, where he comes face to face with the consequences of his decision.

5.5 | Fallen Idols | 10/8/09 | Siege | Conway
When people in Canton, Ohio, are murdered in ways that seem tied to their idols, the brothers suspect ghosts tied to personal objects in the wax museum are behind it.

5.6 | I Believe the Children Are Our Future | 10/15/09 | Dabb and Loflin | Beeson
A series of strange occurrences — a man electrocuted by a joy buzzer, a tooth fairy taking all of a man's teeth and leaving 32 quarters, and kids hospitalized after mixing Pop Rocks and soda

— lead the Winchesters to a young boy with a very peculiar history
. . . and powers.

**5.7 | The Curious Case of Dean Winchester | 10/29/09 | Teleplay:
Gamble; Story: Jenny Klein | Singer**

Sam and Dean investigate a 25-year-old who dies of old age, and
they discover a powerful witch named Patrick is holding poker
games in which people bet years of their life.

5.8 | Changing Channels | 11/5/09 | Carver | Beeson

Lured in by a murder committed by the Incredible Hulk, the
Trickster traps Sam and Dean in TV Land.

**5.9 | The Real Ghostbusters | 11/12/09 | Teleplay: Kripke; Story:
Weiner | Conway**

Fangirl Becky tricks Sam and Dean, and they arrive at a hotel to find
themselves in the middle of a *Supernatural* convention, complete
with costumed fans participating in a role-playing game.

5.10 | Abandon All Hope . . . | 11/19/09 | Edlund | Sgriccia

Sam and Dean break into Crowley's house in search of the Colt,
and are surprised when he gives it to them and tells them where to
find Lucifer, who is trying to summon Death.

5.11 | Sam, Interrupted | 1/21/10 | Dabb and Loflin | Conway

Sam and Dean get themselves committed to a mental institution —
by telling the truth about the Apocalypse — in order to investigate
the deaths of several patients. Once inside, however, they begin to
question their own sanity.

**5.12 | Swap Meat | 1/28/10 | Teleplay: Siege; Story: Siege, Rebecca
Dessertine, Harvey Fedor | Singer**

A geeky teenage boy casts a spell that switches his body with Sam's,
and uses his new visage to visit a bar and pick up a woman. Stuck
in the teenager's body, Sam needs to undo the spell before the teen
can make a fateful deal with Lucifer.

**5.13 | The Song Remains the Same | 2/4/10 | Gamble and Weiner |
Boyum**

When rogue angel Anna goes back in time to 1978 to kill John and
Mary in order to avert the Apocalypse, Castiel takes Sam and Dean

as well, where they try to protect their future parents — and learn something interesting about their heritage in the process.

5.14 | My Bloody Valentine | 2/11/10 | Edlund | Rohl

⁂ After two people on a first date literally consume each other, Sam and Dean suspect a rogue cherub.

5.15 | Dead Men Don't Wear Plaid | 3/25/10 | Carver | John F. Showalter

Investigating reports close to Bobby's house of a man back from the dead, the brothers find that he is not alone — and among the newly risen is Bobby's dead wife.

5.16 | Dark Side of the Moon | 4/1/10 | Dabb and Loflin | Jeff Woolnough

Sam and Dean are killed by two angry hunters, and in Heaven they find themselves pursued by Zachariah while they seek out Joshua, Heaven's gardener.

5.17 | 99 Problems | 4/8/10 | Siege | Beeson

In Blue Earth, Minnesota, the Winchesters find a town teeming with demons — and a religious militia group that fights back, led by Pastor Gideon and his daughter Leah, who is not what she seems.

5.18 | Point of No Return | 4/15/10 | Carver | Sgriccia

As Bobby and Sam try to talk Dean out of his plan to say yes to Michael, Castiel appears with Dean and Sam's half-brother Adam, who they believe has been resurrected in order to serve as Michael's vessel.

5.19 | Hammer of the Gods | 4/22/10 | Teleplay: Dabb and Loflin; Story: David Reed | Rick Bota

At the Elysian Fields Hotel, Sam and Dean find themselves the unfortunate the center of attention at a meeting of pagan gods such as Odin, Baron Samedi, Mercury, and Kali — all who want to use the Winchesters as a means to bargain with the angels. But when Gabriel and Lucifer arrive, all bets are off.

5.20 | The Devil You Know | 4/29/10 | Edlund | Singer

Reduced to desperate measures, Dean accompanies Crowley in

an effort to capture Pestilence's head minion, who works at a pharmaceutical company — and who has a history with Sam.

5.21 | Two Minutes to Midnight | 5/6/10 | Gamble | Sgriccia
Sam and Dean track Pestilence to a convalescent home, where, with Castiel's help, they manage to dispatch him — but they must rush to stop a shipment of vaccines tainted with the Croatoan virus. Meanwhile, Bobby sells his soul to Crowley in exchange for Death's location.

5.22 | Swan Song | 5/13/10 | Teleplay: Kripke; Story: Eric "Giz" Gewertz | Singer
As Chuck finishes up the final chapter of his Winchester gospels, the brothers find themselves at the mercy of the Archangels, and they must make some earth-shattering decisions.

Season 6
Ep. # | Episode Title | Air Date | Writer | Director

6.1 | Exile on Main Street | 9/24/10 | Gamble | Sgricci
Dean, doing his best to live an apple-pie life with Lisa and Ben, is poisoned by a djinn — and is shocked to be rescued by Sam, who he believed was still trapped in Hell.

6.2 | Two and a Half Men | 10/1/10 | Adam Glass | Showalter
Sam calls Dean to help him protect a baby found at a murder scene from the shapeshifter that is after it — who happens to have a tie to the baby.

6.3 | The Third Man | 10/8/10 | Edlund | Singer
When three policemen in Easter, Pennsylvania, die in the manner of biblical plagues, Sam and Dean investigate and find it is in fact the work of a biblical weapon.

6.4 | Weekend at Bobby's | 10/15/10 | Dabb & Loflin | Jensen Ackles
Sam and Dean's troubles with a lamia take a back seat to Bobby's struggle to regain his soul from Crowley, all while contending with Rufus, his neighbor Marcy, and a relentless okami.

6.5 | Live Free or TwiHard | 10/22/10 | Brett Matthews | Rod Hardy

A vampire coven is targeting young girls with vampire obsessions, and the investigation becomes grim when Dean is bitten.

6.6 | You Can't Handle the Truth | 10/29/10 | Teleplay: Eric Charmelo & Nicole Snyder; Story: David Reed, Charmelo, and Snyder | Jan Eliasberg

A rash of suicides brings Sam and Dean to Calumet City, Illinois, where they find that each victim was driven to take his or her life after hearing hard, painful truths.

6.7 | Family Matters | 11/5/10 | Dabb & Loflin | Guy Bee

While tracking down an alpha vampire with Samuel and his group of hunters, Dean's distrust of both Samuel and Sam comes to a head.

6.8 | All Dogs Go to Heaven | 11/12/10 | Glass | Sgriccia

In Buffalo, New York, Sam and Dean have no choice but to follow Crowley's instructions to investigate a series of murders that have been chalked up to animal attacks.

6.9 | Clap Your Hands If You Believe | 11/19/10 | Edlund | Showalter

While Dean struggles with Sam's soullessness, the brothers investigate crop circles and disappearances in Elwood, Indiana, which many locals have been attributing to aliens.

6.10 | Caged Heat | 12/3/10 | Matthews & Klein | Singer

Crowley's machinations drive Sam and Dean to team up with both Castiel and longtime enemy Meg, but when they arrive at Crowley's compound they find he has an unexpected ally.

6.11 | Appointment in Samarra | 12/10/10 | Gamble & Singer | Rohl

Making a deal with Death in a last-ditch effort to rescue Sam's soul from Lucifer's cage, Dean agrees to take Death's helm for 24 hours. However, Sam has a different plan.

6.12 | Like a Virgin | 2/14/11 | Glass | Sgriccia

With Sam's soul precariously back in place, the brothers head to Oregon to look into the disappearance of several pious young women, where they encounter a creature of legend.

6.13 | Unforgiven | 2/11/11 | Dabb & Loflin | David Barrett

Sam receives a mysterious text message with coordinates, and he

and Dean head to Bristol, Rhode Island, to look into the matter —
but once they arrive, Sam realizes he has been there before.

**6.14 | Mannequin 3: The Reckoning | 2/18/11 | Charmelo & Snyder |
Jeannot Szwarc**
While investigating murders tied to the disappearance of a
seamstress in New Jersey, Dean gets a panicked call from Ben
begging him to return home.

6.15 | The French Mistake | 2/25/11 | Edlund | Beeson
In an attempt to hide the brothers from Raphael, Balthazar
transports Sam and Dean into the "real" world, where they are
actors Jared Padalecki and Jensen Ackles, starring in a show called
Supernatural.

6.16 | And Then There Were None | 3/4/11 | Matthews | Rohl
Sam, Dean, Bobby, and Rufus team up to investigate a rash of
killing sprees at a cannery. They suspect Eve is behind the murders,
but when they arrive, they run in to Samuel and Gwen.

6.17 | My Heart Will Go On | 4/15/11 | Charmelo & Snyder | Sgriccia
The Winchesters look in to a series of freak accidents, the victims
of which are all descendants of people who came to America on
an unremarkable ship called the *Titanic* — of which Balthazar is
pictured as a member of the crew.

**6.18 | Frontierland | 4/22/11 | Teleplay: Dabb & Loflin; Story: Dabb,
Loflin, & Jackson Stewart | Guy Bee**
After finding an entry in Samuel Colt's diary about killing a
phoenix, Sam and Dean convince Castiel to send them back to the
wild west of 1860 to locate the ashes — which can be used as a
weapon against Eve.

6.19 | Mommy Dearest | 4/29/11 | Glass | Showalter
Together with Bobby and Castiel, Sam and Dean head to Grants
Pass, Oregon, for the final showdown with Eve, who has infected
the entire town with hybridized monster mutations.

6.20 | The Man Who Would Be King | 5/6/11 | Edlund | Edlund
As the brothers search for Crowley — who, it turns out, is alive
after all — they discover Castiel has been keeping some very dark

secrets from them.

6.21 | Let It Bleed | 5/20/11 | Gamble | Showalter

While Bobby investigates a lead on H.P. Lovecraft having opened a door to Purgatory, Sam and Dean try to locate Lisa and Ben, who have been abducted by Crowley as insurance.

6.22 | The Man Who Knew Too Much | 5/20/11 | Kripke | Singer

When Castiel breaks down the wall in Sam's head that holds back his memories of Hell, Sam's mind shatters into pieces and he struggles to put his psyche back together. Meanwhile, Dean and Bobby track down Castiel and Crowley to try to stop them before they open the door to Purgatory.

Notes

Notes to the Introduction

1. *Route 66* was a popular television series in the 1960s that followed two young men as they traveled from job to job, town to town across the USA in their Corvette. Eric Kripke used this premise to pitch *Supernatural* as a series on urban legends told '*Route 66* style' (Knight, *Supernatural: The Official Companion Season 1* 6).

2. The effect is achieved by overlaying the contrast between light and dark with a desaturated color palette in which the color appears to have been drained from the image, an aesthetic choice appropriate to the series' seedy locations and its apocalyptic narrative.

3. See David Lavery's chapter in this volume for a discussion of Ben Edlund's contribution to *Supernatural*.

Notes to Abbott

1. Carver Edlund is itself a reference to *Supernatural* writers Jeremy Carver and Ben Edlund. See David Lavery's essay elsewhere in this volume.

2. See Hills ("Pleasure of Horror"), Brown and Abbott, Denison and Jancovich, Abbott and Jowett for further discussions of TV horror.

Notes to Beeler

1. Eric Kripke was born in 1974, Jensen Ackles in 1978, and Jared Padal-

ecki in 1982. Jeffrey Dean Morgan, who plays John Winchester, was born in 1966 and would have been too young to appreciate the series' music when it first appeared. The one exception among the recurring characters is Jim Beaver (Bobby Singer), who was born in 1950 and would have been the appropriate age for the initial target audience of the music.

2. In her article "Virtual Reality and Cult Television," Gwenllian-Jones points out that cult television may be categorized by its location format. These formats are travelogue, nodal, combination, and portal. Travelogue series have the protagonists move through an ever-changing landscape, while nodal formats anchor the series to one place while guests come and go. Combination series have a moveable node that travels through a changing landscape. Portal series have a link to an alternate world. I believe that *Supernatural*, like *Star Trek*, fits her definition of a combination series, with the Impala serving as a moving node.

3. Overdriven sounds are characteristic forms of electronic distortion used to produce a buzzy, screaming, or fuzzy effect.

4. Cutting to the beat is a video editing technique that synchronizes shot transitions with the beat of background music.

5. Will Brooker's article "Living on Dawson's Creek: Teen Viewers, Cultural Convergence, and Television Overflow" presents a comprehensive view of the integration of various media in the experience of watching a contemporary television series.

6. The fact that Jason Manns is actually a friend of Jensen Ackles, the actor who plays Dean in the series, makes this negative reaction to the contemporary music serve as a hermeneutic reference for those fans who follow the lives of the actors closely. (MacKenzie interview with Jason Manns)

7. The title is probably a quotation from the English translation of Dante's *Divine Comedy*. "Abandon all hope, ye who enter here" is the inscription above the gates to Hell. Its relevance to the plot of the episode is obvious. There is a song by Aesop Rock with the title "Abandon All Hope" but it is the wrong genre and period to be part of the series' thematic.

Notes to Jowett

1. *The Lost Room* (2006) pushed this notion to the extreme: the title refers to a motel room that exists only in another dimension.

2. Except when essential to the plot, as in "I Know What You Did Last Summer" (4.9) and for comic effect in "The Curious Case of Dean Winchester"

(5.7), when the young maid comments on the magically aged Dean's "adorable" flirting.

3. *American Psycho*, a novel by Bret Easton Ellis, published 1991, was adapted for cinema in 2000, directed by Mary Harron (USA). *Fight Club*, by Chuck Palahniuk, published 1996, was released as a film in 1999, directed by David Fincher (USA).

4. The same might be said of a car, but the Impala has abiding associations, a history, having been in the Winchester family for decades, as emotively presented in the voice-over narration of "Swan Song" (5.22).

5. See S. Brown in this volume for a discussion of the family in 1970s horror films.

6. "After School Special" (4.13) combines the investigation of deaths at a high school with flashbacks to Dean and Sam's past when they attended this school for a time.

Notes to Burnell

1. The term "white trash" can inspire great pride as well as great shame depending how it is being used and by whom. Throughout this paper, my aim is not to offend. However, I also do not wish to sterilize the history and emotions linked to this phrase.

2. There is, however, a shift in fandom, both *Supernatural* and fandom as a whole, wherein "social issues" are being highlighted and discussed. However, as of this writing, these conversations of "social issues" and "white knighting," as this shift in the critical lens is often referred to in fandom, is relatively new in formation and rather peripheral.

3. One notable exception, of course, is the season 1 episode "The Benders," which appears to be a direct homage to *The Texas Chainsaw Massacre*.

Notes to Brown

1. See L. Jowett in this volume for a discussion of the role of the motel in *Supernatural*.

2. The song also appears in a key scene in *The Exorcist*, where Father Karras confesses to his superior that he may have lost his faith, partly due to guilt over having left his mother alone.

3. See S. Beeler in this volume for further discussion of the role of music in *Supernatural*. Kansas and Styx perform the songs on which the title of this chapter is based, respectively "Carry On Wayward Son" and "Renegade."

Notes to Palmer

1. From "Commentary with Complex Chinese Characters" (2.20), *Supernatural* DVD.

2. The demon Alastair (Christopher Heyerdahl) taunts Dean in "On the Head of a Pin" (4.16) about torturing him in Hell for 30 years; thus, time moves far slower for the damned than it does for the living.

3. Some of the series' key female antagonists have included Meg Masters (later revealed to be the demon Azazel's daughter) (Nicki Aycox); Ruby (Katie Cassidy 2007–2008, Genevieve Cortese 2008–2009); Bela Talbot (Lauren Cohan); and the prime mover, Lilith (Rachel Pattee, Sierra McCormick, and Katherine Boecher).

Notes to Calvert

1. The *Supernatural* CW Lounge message boards record negative fan reaction to the characters Bela, Ruby, Jo, and Lisa (in threads like "Did Bela seem like a snob to you?" during season 3, or "When is Lisa leaving," which began immediately after the end of season 5); Eric Kripke calls the comments on Ruby "brutal" (Kripke, "Lucifer Rising" Commentary). This kind of reaction seems to be absent or reduced in relation to the male recurring characters Bobby and (especially) Castiel, who is frequently singled out for praise in online discussions. In March 2011, hits on the Castiel character page on the *Supernatural* wiki outnumber those for Dean and Sam.

2. In the "Lucifer Rising" DVD commentary, Eric Kripke is specific in calling the show "a horror movie."

3. "The Angel in the House" is the title of a poem by Coventry Patmore (1854), later targeted by Virginia Woolf, who declared, "Killing the Angel in the House was part of the occupation of a woman writer" (151).

4. This latter remark grows in meaning through the series, from a fairly straightforward interpretation in "Houses of the Holy" (2.13) to something far more ominous in "The Song Remains the Same."

5. Though the depiction of Mary as "Angel of the House" is troubled by later revelations in season 4 ("In the Beginning," 4.3), Mary herself has far more of an investment in maintaining this identity than is evident at the series opening.

6. I note that cult actors Julie Benz and Tricia Helfer take on these particular "damsel" roles (in what Jeffrey Bussolini has called "intertextuality of casting").

7. The presence of another cult actor, Amber Benson, as the vampire Lenore may also help to confuse the viewer's identification of "good" and "bad" characters in this episode.

8. I note additionally that behind each of these "female" demons is a "male" demon: Azazel behind Meg, and Lucifer behind Ruby.

9. Fans were wrong-footed by interviews in which writers and actors stressed Ruby's efforts to do good, and some fans came closer to Ruby's true aim — "I'd really rather they show her having some kind of ulterior motive" — as they criticized and rejected the possibility that Ruby might be "a demon with a heart of gold" (Cortese, "mikek21m" and "shannon01" comment postings).

10. While fans were generally unhappy about the relationship between Sam and Ruby, their reaction had a moral foundation. Fans insisted that Sam would not trust a demon, and to have this happen was a form of character assassination, "destruction of Sam's character," "an insult to everything Sam's family went through trying to protect him"(Cortese, "mousitsa" and "shannon01" comment postings).

11. Bela's "angry sex" comment upset many fans (TV.com Q&A, comment postings) but in context this comment only highlights the way Bela's character is presented in a position of power and control; in this case, she seems to succeed in discomfiting Dean, even if only momentarily.

12. Casting could have something to do with some issues over Jo's character. The character is played by a young, blonde actor and has none of the edge of a Bela or Ruby (or even of a Buffy or an Echo, a Sydney or a Starbuck). However, as I note, there are connections between Jo and developments in the character of Mary in season 4.

13. In the fantasy world created for Dean by the angel Zachariah, his mother is Ellen and his sister is Jo ("It's a Terrible Life," 4.17).

Notes to Elliott-Smith

1. For the purposes of this article I want to distinguish "queer" here as a sexually counter-normative identity in general and "gay" in relation to my discussion of contemporary male homosexual identity connected with gay male fans of *Supernatural*.

2. Jose Munoz defines disidentification as a practice by which subjects outside of a racial or sexual majority negotiate with dominant culture by transforming, reworking, and appropriating ideological impositions from

the mainstream. In terms of gay male identification, the subject simultaneously recognizes himself in the image of a hypermasculine ideal (symbolized in its purest form in the straight male) but also acknowledges that it is different *from* his homosexual self.

3. Sara Gwenllian-Jones defines slash fiction as deriving from the punctuating slash '/' that emerged from the "Kirk/Spock" or "K/S" erotic fan fiction inspired by the *Star Trek* television series (1966–1969). Gwenllian-Jones continues that, "Scholarly studies of slash have tended to emphasize its romantic male/male manifestations. Usually authored by heterosexual women, such stories subvert or overturn conventional gender constructs as male bodies and male sexuality are described in terms of profound emotional connection and sensual surrender" (81).

4. Dean's seemingly bittersweet reunion with Lisa at the end of season 5 ("Swan Song," 5.22) merely offers another false denouement, as the appearance of an apparently vengeful, resurrected Sam outside the couple's white picket fenced home signals a further destruction of heteronormative domestication.

5. This is not to suggest that there are no male authors, "as in the early years of slash, the majority of slash writers are heterosexual women, however a significant minority of male fans also write slash, and the male to female ratio varied across different fandoms" (Gwenllian-Jones, "Sex Lives" 80). The non-specificity of gender on slash fiction internet forums makes it more difficult to be certain about author's gender, rendering it more queer. Indeed, Wincest fiction is itself referred to within the show's narrative in the inclusion of Becky Rosen ("Sympathy for the Devil," 5.1; and "The Real Ghostbusters"), a young female slash fiction author who posts queer erotic stories about Sam and Dean inspired by Carver Edlund's (Chuck Shurley's) serialization of the Winchester brothers' adventures in his own books.

6. The "Ghostfacers" phenomenon now extends to official *Supernatural* spinoff webisodes, which contain, among other things, a short "A Ghostfacers' Christmas' Secret Santa video" in which the team members offer gifts to each other. In it the specter of Corbett looms large as his name is included in the team's pinned-up stockings. The team's only female member, Maggie, reiterates the Ghostfacers' creed: "We face the ghosts where the others will not, whether Catholic, Jew, or Queer. . . ." Despite this affirmation, though, Corbett's memory lingers on; in future episodes his Ghostfacers' replacement is female intern Ambyr.

Notes to García

1. "In 1953, the term diegesis was revived by Etienne Sourlau to describe the 'recounted story' of a film, and it has since achieved wide usage in literary theory. 'Diegesis' has come to be the accepted term for the fictional world of the story" (Bordwell 16).

2. In this respect, we employ the narratological terminology introduced by Genette, Gaudreault, and Jost.

3. All of the aliases used by Winchester are listed in the *Supernatural* Wiki.

4. "*Supernatural* draws on Southeast Asian visual tropes of horror" (Peirse 263).

5. Umberto Eco defines *kitsch* as the inability of a quote to adapt to its new context: "A styleme that has been abstracted from its original context and inserted into a context whose general structure does not possess the same characters of homogeneity and necessity as the original's, while the result is proposed as a freshly created work capable of stimulating new experiences" (201).

6. Like the self-references that make up the fake trailer for *Hell Hazers II* or the self-mockery of "Jump the Shark" (4.19), an episode in which a new Winchester suddenly appears out of the blue.

7. The 2007–2008 Writers Guild of America strike affected *Supernatural* by cutting season 3 from 22 episodes to only 16. There was a big break from "Jus in Bello," aired on February 21, and "Ghostfacers," aired on April 24.

Notes to Giannini

1. "Hammer of the Gods" (5.18) involves the gods of many of the world's religions attempting to put aside their theological differences in order to band together and stop the Apocalypse. While the represented gods include Kali, Ganesh, Odin, Baldur, Zao Shen, and Mercury, their characterization is problematic at best. Kali, when warned by the Archangel Gabriel that all of them are powerless against Lucifer, rages against the "arrogance" of "westerners," claiming, "We were here first."

She goes on to argue that if anyone has the right to destroy the earth, it is she and all the earlier gods. Despite this attempt to acknowledge a polytheistic worldview, these gods — some from Western mythology, others from current religions such as Hinduism — are all portrayed as cannibals. The entirety of the implications of such a representation are too numerous to do justice to in this article, but there is one point in such a portrayal that I will emphasize: much as all of these religions are lumped into the demonic category, their portrayal as such represents another sacrifice to *Supernatural*'s overarching idea of humanism/humanity as the center and religion in and of itself as occasionally ridiculous and often actively bad.

2. Sam states this explicitly in "Sex and Violence" (4.14). He tells Dean: "You're holding me back. I'm a better hunter than you are. Stronger, smarter; I can take out demons you're too scared to go near." While this is said under the influence of a siren that manipulated the brothers into attempting to kill one another, Sam's previous and subsequent behavior reinforces his words.

3. In season 2, Special Agent Victor Hendrickson makes this connection explicit; he describes their father John Winchester as "ex-marine, raised his kids on the road, cheap motels, backwoods cabins. Real paramilitary survivalist type. I just can't get a handle on what type of whacko he was. White supremacist, Timmy McVeigh, to-may-to, to-mah-to" ("Nightshifter," 2.12). As many demons infected a human host, Sam and Dean would inevitably leave a trail of dead bodies in their wake. As few were aware of the demonic reasons for these deaths, the Winchesters came to the attention of both local ("The Usual Suspects," 2.7) and federal ("Nightshifter," 2.12; "Folsom Prison Blues," 2.19; "Jus in Bello," 3.12) authorities.

4. In the episode "In the Beginning" (4.3), it is revealed that Mary (Campbell) Winchester, the boys' mother, comes from a long line of hunters.

5. Jimmy's knowledge also parallels him with most of the hunting community within *Supernatural*, in that most hunters became so because of exposure to demonic threats that often resulted in the loss of loved ones.

6. In "Wishful Thinking" (4.8), Dean and Sam must deal with a wishing well that actually grants wishes. When Dean ask whether Sam would wish to be "some big yuppie lawyer with a nice car and a white picket fence," Sam denies it, claiming that he's "not that guy anymore" and that all he wants is "[the demon] Lilith's head on a plate, bloody."

7. Martin Luther referred to the Catholic Church (and the pope in particular), as the Whore of Babylon (see: Edwards, "Apocalypticism Explained").

8. In "Two Minutes to Midnight," as Dean and the horseman Death share a pizza in Chicago, Death tells Dean that at some point he will "reap God."

9. My thanks to Monnie Neely for her insights on the series and Matthew Amason for technical assistance.

Notes to Wimmler and Kienzl

1. A competent overview of angels in American popular culture is given in Gardella.

2. See O'Rourke, Klitenic Wear, and Aquinas for an insightful analysis of this theme.

3. A good read concerning the angels' reaction to Adam's creation in Judaism and Islam is Chipman, Leigh N.B. "Adam and the Angels: An Examination of Mythic Elements in Islamic Sources." *Arabica* 49.4 (2002): 429–444.

4. We would like to thank Theresia Heimerl for her valuable comments on an earlier version of this article.

Notes to Koven and Thorgeirsdottir

1. Space does not permit further development or discussion of the many television programs that draw upon folklore and traditional storytelling. This topic will therefore need to wait for another paper.

2. In addition to the Dorson and Ball et al pieces, see Bendix, Kirshenblatt-Gimblett, and Newall for how more contemporary folklorists have challenged Dorson's assumptions regarding authenticity and fakelore. Sullenberger also addresses how popular television (in his case, television advertisements) use folklore to transform the lore itself, and not simply bowdlerize it.

3. Examples of this phenomenon could include how contemporary and modern Pagans use Robin Hardy's *The Wicker Man* (1973) as a template for their own rituals (see Koven 25–35), or how an awareness of werewolf lore is heavily dependent upon Hollywood lycanthropes, rather than traditional witchcraft metamorphosis narratives and, in turn, become problematized in *Ginger Snaps* (John Fawcett, 2000) (see Miller). These examples are, of course, in addition to the Chinese films Zhang discusses in his article, such as *Raise the Red Lantern* (Yimou Zhang, 1991).

4. Each of the points Zhang identifies in his definition of filmic folklore refers to traditional definitions of folklore within the academic study of folkloristics, intended as a rebuttal to such modern folklorists as Roger Abrahams, Richard Bauman, Dan Ben-Amos, and Elliott Oring.

5. *The X-Files* episode "El Mundo Gira" (4.11) attempts this to some degree (see Koven 73–79).

6. Such a suggestion would imply the impossibility in the viewer to distinguish between fiction and reality, and maybe such an audience member

shouldn't be watching TV in the first place.

7. There is an even greater level of allusion abstraction here, as Bradbury took *his* title from one of the witches' lines in Shakespeare's *Macbeth* ("by the pricking of my thumbs, something wicked this way comes") and Matheson from Shirley Jackson's 1959 novel *The Haunting of Hill House*.

8. The title is also a reference to the British-Irish "shoegazer" band, My Bloody Valentine, and although the band took its name from the Mihalka film, this does further demonstrate how cyclical these webs of allusions can be.

9. But even this allusion is at least double: referring to Brian Singer's 1995 film, but also potentially to *Casablanca* (1942), the classical Hollywood film which Singer's film alludes to.

10. There is potential irony here in having a priest share the name with the KISS bass player, since Simmons is Jewish.

11. As of June 2008, the term "jump the shark" appears to have been replaced by a new pop-cult term, "nuke the fridge" in reference to the (absurd) moment in *Indiana Jones and the Kingdom of the Crystal Skull* (2008) when Indiana Jones (Harrison Ford) survives a nuclear test blast by hiding in a lead-lined refrigerator (see Nicholl and Lecca).

Notes to Cherry

1. The term "kink meme" refers to a LiveJournal posting with explicit sexual content. "Claw" was originally posted to the blindfold_spn community and can be found at http://ibroketuesday.livejournal.com/45025.html.

2. The term is used by Woledge (2006) in reference to fanfics dealing with intimacy.

3. 'Shipping' is a term derived from the word relation*ship* and is used in relation to fans ("shippers") who yearn to see a relationship develop between two characters.

4. The term 'trajectory' is borrowed from Busse (2006). She suggests that fan studies should distinguish between "different trajectories that combine into levels of fannishness." For Busse, these different trajectories might incorporate being a singular fan, participating in a fan community, or enacting fannish behavior (perhaps without even self-identifying as a fan), as well as whether people consider themselves to be a fan of a particular text, a member of a fandom, or a fan per se.

5. Cosplay, an abbreviation of costume play, is the fan activity of dressing

in costume as a favourite character and often involves elements of role play. Cosplay frequently takes place at fan conventions, though it may also take place during other social events, charity work, or everyday life.

6. This essay draws on postings to Television Without Pity, Live Journal, Blog Talk Radio, Fan Fiction.net, Archive of Our Own at the following URLs:

http://forums.televisionwithoutpity.com/index.php?showtopic=3184017&st=360

http://forums.televisionwithoutpity.com/index.php?showtopic=3188896&pid=12962985&st=450

http://www.blogtalkradio.com/winchester_radio

http://www.fanfiction.net/s/5736895/1/Becky_the_Castiel_Fangirl

http://grey-bard.livejournal.com/79246.html

http://archiveofourown.org/works/78987

7. See Schmidt for a more detailed discussion of these negative responses.

8. Simpatico's response to the shout-out is indicative of fans' complex and sometimes contradictory emotional reactions and behavior. Interestingly, she states in an aside that her earlier negative comments about the series "left permanent scars on [the production teams'] psyches." This clearly states a belief that the fans' criticisms can affect the creative personnel and thus maintain a degree of power in the imbalanced relationship with the culture industries.

9. Information given in interview carried out via email.

10. See http://www.fanfiction.net/u/2167489/Shattered_Siren.

Notes to Petruska

1. Ryan announced on August 14, 2010, that she was leaving the *Chicago Tribune* to join *AOL Television* as their television critic.

2. Other series that premiered on the WB with *Supernatural* in 2005 included *Just Legal, Related,* and *Twins.*

3. For its first 16 episodes, *Supernatural* aired on Tuesday nights after *Gilmore Girls,* a series on which *Supernatural* star Jared Padalecki had played the character Dean.

4. For more about media industries studies, see also *Media Industries: History, Theory, and Method,* edited by Jennifer Holt and Alisa Perren.

5. The term "netlet" implies a smaller network. A netlet produces and distributes programming like networks do, but on a smaller scale.

6. The other programs from the WB that transitioned to the CW included *Gilmore Girls, One Tree Hill, Smallville,* and *7th Heaven.*

7. "Flow" is a key term in television studies. Raymond William described planned flow as the "the defining characteristic of broadcasting" in 1974. This pronouncement has been fiercely debated ever since (see also Ellis and Corner). CW executives use the term more broadly. While television scholars consider flow as the interplay of segmented programming along with interstitial texts, like commercials and promos, Ostroff seems to mean only how one program leads into another.

8. There is not space in this chapter to provide a more detailed analysis of the writers' strike's impact upon the ratings of *Supernatural* and other programs, but the significant point here is that *Supernatural*'s audience proved loyal. After an all-time low of 2.2 million viewers for "Ghostfacers" on April 24, 2008, the ratings fluxuated until the show earned a solid 3 million viewers for the season finale on May 15, 2008. In other words, the audience lost due to the interruption of the strike had largely returned to the series by the end of the season.

9. Matt Roush jokes that he and other critics used to refer to UPN as "the Used Parts Network" because their programming was recycled from other networks.

10. In the spring of 2008, the CW removed full episode replays of *Gossip Girl* from the network's website to persuade viewers to tune in live and boost ratings. Fans were outraged and the network re-instituted the web replays (Steinberg, "Nets Try").

11. Ratings discourse is notoriously slippery, with its metrics failing to accurately reflect real-time viewership historically and today. See also Ien Ang's *Desperately Seeking the Audience* and Eileen Meehan's "Why We Don't Count."

Notes to Felschow

1. This satire is dedicated to G. K. Chesterton, who Gaiman credits with the essentials of the plot for *Good Omens*: The message of [Chesterton's] *The Man Who Was Thursday* can be summarized into: "God is the devil; everybody who thinks they are working for God may be working for the devil or vice versa. Do not take everything at face value and do not be surprised when all the masks come off." I think in many ways that was also the plot of *Good Omens* (Elder 73).

2. As Eric Kripke has stated that he planned a five-season-long story for

Supernatural (see Francich) and as he was head writer and executive producer for seasons 1 through 5, I will treat every episode as if under Kripke's
creative control and will not list individual writers or writing teams for story
or teleplay credit. This information can be found the episode guide on pages
253–272.

3. The "24 Hours" story also echoes "My Bloody Valentine" (5.14). In that
episode, one of the Four Horsemen, Famine, holes up in a diner and forces
all of its customers to feed themselves to death in exceptionally violent ways.

TV and Filmography

Television Shows

Alias (ABC, 2001–2006)

The Andy Griffith Show (CBS, 1960–1968)

Angel (WB, 1999–2004)

Battlestar Galactica (Sci-Fi, 2004–2009)

Being Human (BBC, 2008–)

Bewitched (ABC, 1964–1972)

Bonanza (NBC, 1959–1973)

Bones (FOX, 2005–)

Buffy the Vampire Slayer (WB, 1997–2001; UPN, 2001–2003)

Californication (Showtime, 2007–)

The Comeback (HBO, 2005)

CSI: Miami (CBS, 2002–)

Cold Case (CBS, 2003–2010)

Curb Your Enthusiasm (HBO, 2000–)

Dark Angel (FOX, 2000–2002)

Dawson's Creek (WB, 1998–2003)

Dexter (Showtime, 2006–)

Doctor Who (BBC, 2005–)

Entourage (HBO, 2004–)

Everwood (WB, 2002–2006)

Extras (HBO, 2005–2007)
Firefly (FOX, 2002–2003)
Friends (NBC, 1994–2004)
The Fugitive (ABC, 1963–1967)
The Ghost Whisperer (CBS, 2005–2010)
Gilmore Girls (WB, 2000–2007)
Gossip Girl (CW, 2007–)
Happy Days (ABC, 1974–1984)
The Incredible Hulk (CBS, 1978–1982)
Invasion (ABC, 2005–2006)
Just Legal (WB, 2005–2006)
Leave It to Beaver (CBS, 1957–1958; ABC, 1958–1963)
Lost (ABC, 2004–2010)
The Lucy Show (CBS, 1962–1968)
Medium (NBC, 2005–)
Millennium (FOX, 1996–1999)
Nip/Tuck (FX, 2003–2010)
Numb3rs (CBS, 2005–2010)
The Office (BBC, 2001–2003)
Point Pleasant (FOX, 2005)
Psych (USA Network, 2006)
Queer as Folk (Showtime, 2000–2005)
Route 66 (CBS, 1960–1964)
Sesame Street (Children's Television Workshop, 1969–2000; Sesame
     Workshop 2000–)
Singing Detective (BBC, 1986)
Six Feet Under (HBO, 2001–2005)
Smallville (WB, 2001–2006; CW, 2006–2011)
Surface (NBC, 2005–2006)
Threshold (CBS, 2005)
The Vampire Diaries (CW, 2009–)
The X-Files (FOX, 1993–2002)

Films
28 Days Later (Danny Boyle, UK, 2002)
Abbott and Costello Meet Frankenstein (Charles Barton, USA, 1948)
American Psycho (Mary Harron, USA, 2000)

Assault on Precinct 13 (John Carpenter, USA, 1976)

The American Nightmare (Adam Simon, USA, 2000)

An American Werewolf in London (John Landis, USA, 1981)

Army of Darkness (Sam Raimi, USA, 1992)

Back to the Future (Robert Zemeckis, USA, 1985)

Bad Day at Black Rocks (John Sturges, USA, 1955)

The Blair Witch Project (Daniel Myrick and Eduardo Sánchez, USA, 1999)

Boogeyman (Stephen T. Kay, NZ, 2005)

The Car (Elliot Silverstein, USA, 1977)

Casablanca (Michael Curtiz, USA, 1942)

The Cat and the Canary (Elliot Nugent, USA, 1939)

Children Shouldn't Play With Dead Things (Bob Clark, USA, 1973)

Christine (John Carpenter, USA, 1983)

The Curious Case of Benjamin Button (David Fincher, USA, 2008)

Death Takes a Holiday (Mitchel Leison, USA, 1934)

Deliverance (John Boorman, USA, 1972)

Desperado (Robert Rodriguez, USA, 1995)

Don't Look Now (Nicolas Roeg, UK, 1973)

Dracula (Tod Browning, USA, 1931)

Dracula: Dead and Loving It (Mel Brooks, USA, 1995)

Duel (Steven Spielberg, USA, 1972)

The Evil Dead (Sam Raimi, USA, 1981)

Evil Dead 2 (Sam Raimi, USA, 1987)

The Exorcist (William Friedkin, USA, 1973)

Fight Club (David Fincher, USA, 1999)

Firestarter (Mark Lester, USA, 1984)

Freddy vs. Jason (Ronny Yu, Canada, 2003)

Girl, Interrupted (Mangold, USA, 1999)

Ghost (Jerry Zucker, USA, 1990)

Groundhog Day (Harold Ramis, USA, 1993)

The Hills Have Eyes (Wes Craven, USA, 1977)

House on Haunted Hill (William Malone, USA, 1999)

House of Wax (Jaume Collet-Serra, Australia/USA, 2005)

The Howling (Joe Dante, USA, 1981)

I Know What You Did Last Summer (Jim Gillespie, USA, 1997)

It's a Wonderful Life (Frank Capra, USA, 1946)

Jaws (Steven Spielberg, USA, 1975)

The Last House on the Left (Wes Craven, USA, 1972)

The Legend of Hell House (John Hough, UK, 1973)

Legion (Scott Charles Stewart, USA, 2010)

Lucifer Rising (Kenneth Anger, USA, 1972)

The Mask (Chuck Russell, USA, 1994)

Midnight Run (Martin Brest, USA, 1988)

Modern Times (Charles Chaplin, USA, 1936)

My Bloody Valentine (George Mihalka, Canada, 1981)

My Bloody Valentine (Patrick Lussier, USA, 2009)

Night of the Living Dead (George Romero, USA, 1968)

A Nightmare on Elm Street (Wes Craven, USA, 1984)

The Omen (Richard Donner, USA, 1976),

The Others (Alejandro Amenábar, USA/Spain, 2001)

Poltergeist (Tobe Hooper, USA, 1982)

Psycho (Alfred Hitchcock, USA, 1960)

Red River (Howard Hawks, USA, 1948)

Ringu (Hideo Nakata, Japan, 1998)

Scream (Wes Craven, USA, 1996)

The Searchers (John Ford, USA, 1956)

Shaun of the Dead (Edgar Wright, UK, 2004)

The Shining (Stanley Kubrick, UK/USA, 1980)

Silence of the Lambs (Jonathan Demme, USA, 1991)

Sin City (Frank Miller and Robert Rodriguez, USA, 2005)

Something Wicked This Way Comes (Jack Clayton, USA, 1983)

Stagecoach (John Ford, USA, 1939)

Star Wars (George Lucas, USA, 1977)

Stay Tuned (Peter Hyams, USA, 1992)

The Texas Chainsaw Massacre (Tobe Hooper, USA, 1974)

The Thing (John Carpenter, USA, 1982)

Titan AE (Don Bluth/Gary Goldman/Art Vitello, USA, 2000)

Twilight (Catherine Hardwick, USA, 2008)

Up in the Air (Jason Reitman, USA, 2009)

The Usual Suspects (Bryan Singer, USA, 1995)

Van Wilder (Walt Becker, USA, 2002)

Contributors

Stacey Abbott is reader in film and television studies at Roehampton University. She is the editor of *Reading Angel: The TV Spin-off with a Soul* (I.B. Tauris, 2005) and *The Cult TV Book* (I.B. Tauris, 2010). She is the general editor for the Investigating Cult TV series (I.B. Tauris) as well as the author of *Angel* (TV Milestones, Wayne State UP, 2009) and *Celluloid Vampires* (University of Texas Press, 2007).

Stan Beeler is professor of English at the University of Northern British Columbia, Canada. His areas of interest include film and television studies, popular culture, and comparative literature. His publications include *Reading Stargate SG-1* (I.B. Tauris), *Investigating Charmed: The Magic Power of TV* (I.B. Tauris), and *Dance Drugs and Escape: The Club Scene in Literature Film and Television Since the Late 1980s* (McFarland).

Simon Brown is principal lecturer and director of studies for film and television at Kingston University. He is the co-editor with Stacey Abbott of *Investigating Alias: Secrets and Spies* (I.B. Tauris, 2007) and has also written on *Dexter*, *The X-Files*, and the Showtime network.

His other research areas are early cinema and the history of color cinematography.

Aaron C. Burnell graduated Warren Wilson College in 2009 with a Bachelor's degree in English Literature concentrating in continental critical theory. In 2011, he graduated Bowling Green State University with a Master's in American culture studies. He considers East Tennessee home and counts himself as one of those "smart rednecks."

Bronwen Calvert is an associate lecturer with the Open University in the North of England and subject area leader in Literature at the North East Centre for Lifelong Learning in Newcastle-upon-Tyne, U.K. Her current research and publication is on aspects of embodiment in science fiction and fantasy narratives.

Brigid Cherry is a senior lecturer in communication, culture, and creative arts at St. Mary's University College, Twickenham, U.K. Her research has focused on horror and science fiction fan cultures. Her film guidebook, *Horror*, was published by Routledge in 2009 and she is currently working on a monograph on *Lost* and an edited collection on *True Blood* for I.B. Tauris.

Darren Elliott-Smith is a film education coordinator and lecturer in film for the University of Hertfordshire. He programs and delivers film education for the Hertfordshire region for all ages and his specialist teaching includes horror, gender, and sexuality on film. His research involves the analysis of the emerging sub-genre of queer horror film (post-1995 to present) in Western film and television.

Laura Felschow holds a BFA in film from Syracuse University and an MA in media studies from the State University of New York at Buffalo. She has worked in the film/TV industry in New York City, Toronto, and Buffalo, and currently resides in Austin, Texas.

James Francis, Jr. received his Ph.D. in film and children's literature from MTSU. He has published works on Tennessee Williams, *Dexter*, horror, film noir, and creative writing. James is also an internationally published photographer. He spends his downtime watching *Supernatural* and *Psych*, and hopes television programming continues to challenge itself.

Alberto N. García is an associate professor of film and television studies at the University of Navarra (Spain). He is co-editor of *Landscapes of the Self: The Cinema of Ross McElwee* (2007), and author of *El cine de no-ficción en Martín Patino* (2008). He runs the popular weblog "Diamantes en serie," focused on American and British TV series.

Erin Giannini is a Ph.D. student at University of East Anglia. Her work focuses on product placement, the effect of new technology on broadcast television, and the shifts in the broadcast model in the past 10 years. She also enjoys justifying her television watching with the phrase, "It's research!"

Stephanie Graves has a Bachelor's degree in theatre and works as a lighting designer while pursuing her MA in English at Middle Tennessee State University, where she studies postmodernism, film, and cult media. She lives in Nashville, Tennessee, and is saving up for a '67 Impala.

Lorna Jowett is a senior lecturer in Media at the University of Northampton, U.K., where she teaches some of her favorite things, including horror, science fiction, and TV. Her research interests focus on genre, form, and representation across television drama, film, and literature.

Lisa Kienzl is studying religious studies and European ethnology at the University of Graz. In 2006 she spent one semester at the Department of Culture and Identity in Roskilde, Denmark. Currently she is head of the Students Representative Council and co-editor of its newspaper at the Faculty of Theology.

Mikel J. Koven is a senior lecturer and course leader in film studies at the University of Worcester. He has written extensively on the area of folklore and film and TV, including *La Dolce Morte: Vernacular Cinema and the Italian Giallo Film* (2006) and *Film, Folklore, and Urban Legends* (2008).

David Lavery is the author of numerous essays and reviews and author/co-author, editor/co-editor of numerous books including *The Essential Sopranos Reader* (University Press of Kentucky), *Joss Whedon: Conversations* (University Press of Mississippi), and volumes on such television series as *Twin Peaks, The X-Files, Buffy the Vampire Slayer, Lost, Deadwood, Seinfeld, My So-Called Life, Heroes, Gilmore Girls*, and *Battlestar Galactica*. He co-edits the e-journal *Slayage: The Journal of the Whedon Studies Association* and is one of the founding editors of *Critical Studies in Television: Scholarly Studies of Small Screen Fictions*. He has lectured around the world on the subject of television.

Lorrie Palmer is a Ph.D. candidate in film and media at the University of Indiana-Bloomington. Her work on cyborgs, superheroes, science fiction TV, Will Smith, Harold Lloyd, and genre/gender appears in *The Velvet Light Trap, Senses of Cinema, Bright Lights*, and *Camera Obscura*. (Also, a Dean girl.)

Karen Petruska is a doctoral candidate at Georgia State University with an interest in television studies, the media industries, new media, and feminist theory. Her dissertation spotlights the historic television critic as a lens to better understand aesthetic, technological, and industrial change.

David Simmons has published widely in the twin fields of American popular fiction and screen media. His recent work includes chapters on Hammer Studios and science fiction, *Xena: Warrior Princess*, and *Spartacus: Blood and Sand*. David is currently editing a collection on the television series *Heroes* for publication in 2011.

Gunnella Thorgeirsdottir is an Icelandic folklorist currently in the writing up stage of her Ph.D. researching the rituals and beliefs surrounding childbearing in Japanese society. An avid researcher of film and television culture, she is interested in the uses of folklore and the culture that surrounds them.

Jutta Wimmler was born in Graz (Austria) in 1985. She studied history and religious studies and has spent a year in the United States and a semester in South Africa. She is currently working as a research associate at the Department of Social and Economic History at the University of Graz.

Bibliography

Abbott, Stacey. "'I don't know what kind of man I am anymore': The Damaged Man in *Angel* and post-*Angel* Cult Television." Slayage International Conference on the Whedonverses. Henderson State University, Arkadelphia, AK. June 5–8, 2008. Featured Speaker.

— and Lorna Jowett. *Investigating TV Horror*. London & New York: I.B. Tauris (forthcoming 2012).

Ackles, Jensen and Jared Padalecki. "Supernatural 4: Eye of the Tiger and Comedy." The CW Source. <www.youtube.com/watch?v=BrLZaLT6il8& feature=fvw>.

Adalian, Josef. "The CW Lives!: How the 'Gossip Girl' Network Beat the Odds by Pleasing Its Parents." *Television Week*. March 2, 2009.

— and Michael Schneider. "The CW." *Daily Variety*. September 12, 2007: A12.

Alexander, Bethany. "No Need to Choose: A Magnificent Anarchy of Belief." Schweitzer 135–140.

Althusser, Louis. "Ideology and the Ideological State Apparatuses (Notes Towards an Investigation)." Marxists.org. <www.marxists.org/reference/ archive/althusser/1970/ideology.htm>. Accessed June 20, 2008.

Alvey, Mark. "Wanderlust and Wire Wheels: The Existential Search of Route 66." *The Road Movie Book*. Eds. Steven Cohan and Ina Rae Hark. London & New York: Routledge, 1997. 143–164.

"American Nightmare, The." Dir. Adam Simon. *The Hills Have Eyes* DVD, Anchor Bay, 2003.

Ang, Ien. *Desperately Seeking the Audience*. London & New York: Routledge 1991.

Aquinas, Thomas. *Die "Summa theologiae." Werkinterpretationen*. Berlin: de Gruyter, 2005.

Atkinson, Claire. "Ostroff Meditates on Enticing Tech-Savvy 18–34 Demo to the CW." *Advertising Age* 77.11. March 13, 2006. LexisNexis. Accessed August 20, 2010.

Atkinson, Claire. "Road to the Upfront: The CW." *Advertising Age*. April 2, 2007. LexisNexis. Online.

Ausiello, Michael. "Exclusive: *Supernatural* boss on why he stepped down and what's coming up (hint: monsters)." *Entertainment Weekly*. Online. July 15, 2010. Accessed July 25, 2010.

—. "*Supernatural* Exec: We Won't Be *One Tree Hill* with Monsters!" *TV Guide*. Online. July 21, 2007. <www.tvguide.com/news/Supernatural-Exec-We-8522.aspx>. Accessed July 13, 2010.

Awn, Peter J. and Annemarie Schimmel. *Satan's tragedy and redemption. Iblis in Sufi psychology*. Leiden: Brill, 1983.

Bacon-Smith, Camille. *Enterprising Women: Television Fandom and the Creation of Popular Myth*. Philadelphia: U of Pennsylvania P, 1992.

Ball, J., G. Herzog, et al. "Discussion from the Floor." *Journal of American Folklore* 72 (1959): 233–241.

Barth, John. *The Friday Book. Essays and Other Nonfiction*. Baltimore: Johns Hopkins UP, 1984.

Bauder, David. "New CW Network revives '7th Heaven' in first schedule." Associated Press. May 18, 2006.

Beeler, Stan. "There Is Nothing New in the Underworld: Narrative Recurrence and Visual Leitmotivs in *Charmed*." *Investigating Charmed: The Magic Power of TV*. Eds. Karin Beeler and Stan Beeler. London & New York: I.B. Tauris, 2007. 129–142.

Bender, Hy. *The Sandman Companion*. New York: DC Comics, 1999.

Bendix, Regina. "Tourism and Cultural Displays: Inventing Traditions for Whom?" *Journal of American Folklore* 102 (1989): 131–146.

Bersani, Leo, *Homos*. Cambridge: Harvard UP, 1996

—. "Is the Rectum a Grave?" *Is the Rectum a Grave? And Other Essays*. Chicago: U of Chicago P, 2010.

Bianco, Robert. "A critic's-eye view of networks' fall lineups." *USA Today*. May 19, 2008: 3D.

Bird, Sharon. "Masculinities in Rural Small Business Ownership: Between Community and Capitalism." *Country Boys: Masculinity and Rural Life*. Eds. Hugh Campbell, Michael Mayerfeld Bell, and Margaret Finney. University Park: The Pennsylvania U State P, 2006.

Bordwell, David. *Narration in the Fiction Film*. Madison: U of Wisconsin P, 1985.

Boris, Cynthia. "Eric Kripke: Satan's Head Writer." TV of the Absurd. July 25, 2007. <tvoftheabsurd.com/2007/07/25/eric-kripke-satans-head-writer>.

Borsellino, Mary. "Buffy the Vampire Slayer, Jo the Monster Killer." *In the Hunt*, 107–118.

—. "Super Women: *Supernatural*'s executive story editor Sera Gamble." Sequential Tart. 2006. <www.sequentialtart.com/article.php?id=345>. Accessed December 3, 2010.

Boss, Pete. "Vile Bodies and Bad Medicine." *Screen* 27.1 (1986): 14–26.

Botkin, Benjamin A. *A Treasury of American Folklore: Stories, Ballads, and Traditions of the People*. New York: Crown Publishers, 1944.

Bourdieu, Pierre. *Distinction: A Social Critique of the Judgment of Taste*. Trans. Richard Nice. Cambridge: Harvard UP, 1984.

Brahen, Marilyn. "The Thin Line Between." Schweitzer, *The Neil Gaiman Reader*, 140–147.

Brickley, London E. "Ghouls in Cyberspace." *In The Hunt*, 263–274.

Brooker, Will. "Living on Dawson's Creek: Teen Viewers, Cultural Convergence, and Television Overflow." *The Television Studies Reader*. Eds. Robert Allen & Annette Hill. London & New York: Routledge, 2004. 569–580.

Brown, Simon and Stacey Abbott. "The Art of Sp(l)atter: Body Horror in *Dexter*." *Dexter: Investigating Cutting Edge Television*. Ed. Douglas L. Howard. London & New York: I.B. Tauris, 2010. 205–220.

Bruce, Melissa N. "The Impala as Negotiator of Melodrama and Masculinity in *Supernatural*." Tosenberger, ed. "Saving People, Hunting Things." <journal.transformativeworks.org/index.php/twc/article/view/154/157>.

Burns, Tom and Jeffrey W. Hunter, eds. "Gaiman, Neil — Introduction." *Contemporary Literary Criticism*, 195. Cengage, 2005. eNotes.com. 2006. <www.enotes.com/contemporary-literary-criticism/gaiman-neil>.

Busse, Kristina. "Fandom-is-a-Way-of-Life versus Watercooler Discussion; or, The Geek Hierarchy as Fannish Identity Politics." *Flow TV* 5.13 (November 18, 2006). <flowtv.org/2006/11/taste-and-fandom>.

Busse, Kristina and Karen Hellekson. "Introduction: Work in Progress." *Fan Fiction and Fan Communities in the Age of the Internet.* Eds. Karen Hellekson and Kristina Busse. Jefferson, NC: McFarland, 2006. 5–54.

Bussolini, Jeffrey. "Television Intertextuality After *Buffy*." Slayage International Conference on the Whedonverses. Henderson State University, Arkadelphia, AK. June 5–8, 2008. Featured presentation.

Carroll, Noël. "Notes on the Sight Gag." *Comedy/Cinema/Theory.* Ed. Andrew S. Horton. Berkeley: U of California P, 1991. 25–42.

—. *The Philosophy of Horror: or Paradoxes of the Heart.* London & New York: Routledge, 1990.

Carter, Bill. "Neither WB Nor UPN." *New York Times.* May 2, 2006: C1.

Carter, R.J. "Interview: Neil Gaiman: American God (By Way of Britain)." *The Trades.* January 1, 2002. <www.the-trades.com/article.php?id=1626>.

"Castiel." *Handwörterbuch des deutschen Aberglaubens.* 3rd ed. 2000. Eds. Bächtold-Stäubli, Hanns/Hoffmann-Krayer, Eduard place of publication: Berlin [u.a.].

Catlin, Roger. "Sci fi bubble on TV bursts." *Toronto Star.* May 26, 2006: C11.

Cavell, Stanley. *Pursuits of Happiness: The Hollywood Comedy of Remarriage.* Cambridge, MA: Harvard UP, 1981.

Chambers, Jamie. "Blue Collar Ghost Hunters." *In the Hunt,* 165–174.

Chan, Suzette. "*Supernatural* Bodies: Writing Subjugation and Resistance onto Sam and Dean Winchester." Tosenberger, ed. "Saving People, Hunting Things." <journal.transformativeworks.org/index.php/twc/article/view/179/160>.

Chandler, Daniel. "Intertextuality." *Semiotics for Beginners.* Online. Aberystwyth: Aberystwyth University, 1999. <www.aber.ac.uk/media/Documents/S4B/sem09.html>.

Chipman, Leigh N.B. "Adam and the Angels: An Examination of Mythic Elements in Islamic Sources." *Arabica* 49.4 (2002): 429—444.

Clifton, Jacob. "Spreading Disaster: Gender in the *Supernatural* Universe." *In the Hunt,* 119–143.

"A Closer Look: *Supernatural*: 'Bad Day at Black Rock,' with writer Ben Edlund." *Supernatural: The Complete Third Season.* DVD extra. Warner Home Video, 2008.

Clover, Carol J. *Men, Women and Chainsaws: Gender in the Modern Horror Film.* Princeton New Jersey: Princeton UP, 1992.

Cochran, C.P. "Supernatural Season Four News From Eric Kripke." *Chicago Tribune.* Online. April 26, 2008. <featuresblogs.Chicagotribune.com/ entertainment_tv/2009/08/Supernatural-season-5-eric-kripke-cw.html>. Accessed June 17, 2010.

Cohan, Steven and Ina Rae Hark, eds. *The Road Movie Book.* London & New York: Routledge, 1997.

Collins, Misha. "Misha Collins Talks About 'Apocalyptic' Finale of *Supernatural*" (interview with Yvonne Villareal). *Los Angeles Times.* May 13, 2009.

Cortese, Genevieve. "*Supernatural*'s Ruby: 'I Feel Like, Deep Down, She's in Love with Sam'" (interview with Matt Mitovic). *TV Guide.* Online. November 19, 2008. <www.tvguide.com/News/Genevieve-Cortese-Supernatural-3.aspx>.

Corner, John. *Critical Ideas in Television Studies.* Oxford: Oxford UP, 1999.

Creed, Barbara. *The Monstrous-Feminine: Film, Feminism, Psychoanalysis.* London & New York: Routledge, 1993.

Crosby, Sara. "The Cruelest Season: Female Heroes Snapped into Sacrificial Heroines." *Action Chicks: New Images of Tough Women in Popular Culture.* Ed. Sherrie Inness. Houndmills: Palgrave, 2004. 153–178.

Cuddon, J.A. *The Penguin Dictionary of Literary Terms and Literary Theory.* Fourth Edition. NY: Penguin, 1998.

"CWTV Store." The CW. The CW Television Networks Inc, 2010. Online. September 6, 2010. <store.cwtv.com/>.

Dale, Alan. *Comedy Is a Man in Trouble: Slapstick in American Movies.* Minneapolis and London: U of Minnesota P, 2000.

Dallenbach, Lucien. *The Mirror in the Text.* Chicago & Cambridge: Chicago UP, 1989.

Dampier, Charlotte, message board post on Cochran, C.P., "Supernatural Season Four News From Eric Kripke," *Chicago Tribune.* Online. April 26, 2008. <featuresblogs.Chicagotribune.com/entertainment_tv/2009/08/ Supernatural-season-5-eric-kripke-cw.html>.

Danielson, Larry. "Folklore and Film: Some thoughts on Baughman Z500–599." *Western Folklore.* 38.3 (1979): 209–219.

Danzico, Matthew. "Cult of less: Living out of a hard drive." BBC News. August 16, 2010. <www.bbc.co.uk/news/world-us-canada-10928032>.

Davisson, Amber and Paul Booth. "Reconceptualizing Communication and Agency in Fan Activity: A Proposal for a Projected Interactivity Model for Fan Studies." *Texas Speech Communication Journal* 23.1 (2007): 33–43.

Denison, Reyna and Mark Jancovich. Introduction to "Mysterious Bodies." *Intensities: The Journal of Cult Media Special Issue 4.* <intensities.org/ Essays/Jancovich_Intro.pdf>.

Derecho, Abigail. "Archontic Literature: A Definition, A History, and Several Theories of Fan Fiction." *Fan Fiction and Fan Communities in the Age of the Internet.* Eds. Karen Hellekson and Kristina Busse. Jefferson, NC: McFarland, 2006. 61–78.

Dilman, Ilham. *Free Will. An Historical and Philosophical Introduction.* London & New York: Routledge, 1999.

Doane, Mary Ann. "Film and the Masquerade: Theorising the Female Spectator." *The Sexual Subject: A SCREEN Reader in Sexuality.* London & New York: Routledge, 1992. 227–243.

Dorson, Richard. *American Folklore.* Chicago: U of Chicago P, 1959.

—. *Folklore and Fakelore: Essays Toward a Discipline of Folk Studies.* Cambridge: Harvard UP, 1976.

Dowd, Chris. "An Autopsy of Storytelling: Metafiction and Neil Gaiman." Schweitzer, *The Neil Gaiman Reader,* 103–120.

Dundes, Allen. *Interpreting Folklore.* Bloomington: Indiana UP, 1980.

Eco, Umberto. *The Open Work.* Cambridge: Harvard UP, 1989.

Edlund, Ben. "Foreword." Knight, *Supernatural: The Official Companion, Season 4,* 6–7.

Edwards, Mark Jr. "Apocalypticism Explained." PBS.org. <www.pbs.org/ wgbh/pages/frontline/shows/apocalypse/explanation/martinluther. html>.

Elder, Robert K. "Gods and Other Monsters: A *Sandman* Exit Interview and Philosophical Omnibus." Schweitzer, *The Neil Gaiman Reader,* 54–78.

Elliott, Stuart. "Next Season's Hit Shows? They're the Talk of the Web." *New York Times.* August 18, 2006: C5.

Ellis, John. *Seeing Things: Television in the Age of Uncertainty.* London & New York: I.B. Tauris, 2000.

"Engel." *Lexikon der christlichen Ikonographie.* 1st ed. 1968. Aurenhammer, Hans: Wien.

Engstrom, Erika and Joseph M. Valenzano III. "Demon Hunters and hegemony: Portrayal of religion on the CW's *Supernatural*." *Journal of*

Media and Religion 9 (2010): 67–83.

Erickson, Steve. "Dreamland." *Los Angeles Times.* September 3, 1995: 14.

Felschow, Laura. "'Hey, check it out, there's actually fans': (Dis) empowerment and (mis)representation of cult fandom in *Supernatural.*" Tosenberger, ed. "Saving People, Hunting Things." <journal. transformativeworks.org/index.php/twc/article/view/134/142>.

Fernandez, Maria Elena. "On the Road Trip from Hell." *The Age.* 2006. Online.

Fetcher, Mary. "Riding Down the Highway: Why the Impala is the Third Main Character." *In the Hunt,* 209–217.

Feuer, Jane. "HBO and the Concept of Quality TV." *Quality TV: Contemporary American Television and Beyond.* Eds. Janet McCabe and Kim Akass. London & New York: I.B. Tauris, 2007: 145–57.

Flegel, Monica and Jenny Roth. "Annihilating Love and Heterosexuality without Women: Romance, Generic Difference, and Queer Politics in *Supernatural* Fan Fiction." Tosenberger, ed. "Saving People, Hunting Things." <journal.transformativeworks.org/index.php/twc/article/ view/133/147>.

Forsyth, Neil. *The Old Enemy. Satan and the Combat Myth.* Princeton: Princeton UP, 1987.

Fox, Aaron A. "'Ain't It Funny How Time Slips Away?': Talk, Trash, and Technology in a Texas 'Redneck' Bar." *Knowing Your Place: Rural Identity and Cultural Hierarchy.* Eds. Barbara Ching and Gerald W. Creed. New York: Routledge, 1997. 105–130.

Francich, Darren. "Neil Gaiman's 'The Sandman' becoming a TV show?" *Entertainment Weekly Popwatch.* September 3, 2010. <popwatch. ew.com/2010/09/03/neil-gaimans-the-sandman-becoming-a-tv-show/>.

Friedman, Wayne. "Gambling With the New Fall Season." *Media Post* "TV Watch" weblog. August 23, 2005.

Frith, Simon. *Performing Rites: On the Value of Popular Music.* Cambridge, Mass: Harvard UP, 1996.

Gaiman, Neil. *American Gods.* New York: HarperCollins, 2001.

—. *Death: The High Cost of Living.* New York: DC Comics, 1994.

—. *Neverwhere.* New York: HarperCollins, 1996.

—. "Other People." In *Fragile Things.* New York: HarperCollins, 2006: 109–112.

—. *The Sandman: Endless Nights.* New York: DC Comics, 2003.

—. *The Sandman Volume Eight: World's End*. New York: DC Comics, 1994.

—. *The Sandman Volume Five: A Game of You*. New York: DC Comics, 1993.

—. *The Sandman Volume Four: Season of Mists*. New York: DC Comics, 1992.

—. *The Sandman Volume One: Preludes & Nocturnes*. New York: DC Comics, 1988.

—. *The Sandman Volume Nine: The Kindly Ones*. New York: DC Comics, 1996.

—. *The Sandman Volume Seven: Brief Lives*. New York: DC Comics, 1994.

—. *The Sandman Volume Six: Fables & Reflections*. New York: DC Comics, 1993.

—. *The Sandman Volume Ten: The Wake*. New York: DC Comics, 1997.

—. *The Sandman Volume Three: Dream Country*. New York: DC Comics, 1991.

—. *The Sandman Volume Two: The Doll's House*. New York: DC Comics, 1990.

Gaiman, Neil and Terry Pratchett. *Good Omens*. New York: HarperCollins, 1990.

Gans, Herbert J. *Popular Culture & High Culture: An Analysis and Evaluation of Taste*. New York: Basic Books, 1999.

García Martínez and Alberto Nahum. "El espejo roto: la metaficción en las series anglosajonas." *Revista Latina de Comunicación Social* 64 (2009): 654–667. April 30, 2010. <tinyurl.com/espejoroto>.

Gardella, Peter. *American Angels. Useful Spirits in the Material World*. Lawrence: UP of Kansas, 2007.

Gaudreault, André and François Jost. *Le récit cinématographique*. Paris: Nathan, 1990.

Gee, James. *What Video Games Have to Teach Us About Learning and Literacy*. New York: Palgrave MacMillan, 2003.

Genette, Gérard. *Nouveau discours du récit*. Paris: Editions du Seuil, 1983.

Geraghty, Lincoln. "A Network of Support: Coping with Trauma Through *Star Trek* Fan Letters." *Journal of Popular Culture* 39.6 (2006): 1002–1024.

Gerzon, Mark. *A Choice of Heroes: The Changing Faces of American Manhood*. New York: Houghton Mifflin Company, 1992.

"The Gideons." Lake Drummond Baptist Church. <www.ldbcva. org/?p=585>.

Goad, Jim. *The Redneck Manifesto: How Hillbillies, Hicks, and White Trash Became America's Scapegoats*. New York: Simon & Schuster, 1997.

Godwin, Michael. *Engel — eine bedrohte Art*. Frankfurt am Main: Zweitausendeins, 1990.

Good Omens and *Supernatural* Crossover Archive. <www.fanfiction.net/ Good_Omens_and_Supernatural_Crossovers/1182/2237/>. Accessed September 30, 2010.

Grantham, Dewey. *Recent America: The United States Since 1945*. Wheeling, IL: Harlan Davidson, 1987.

Gray, Jonathan, Cornell Sandvoss, and C. Lee Harrington, eds. *Fandom: Identities and Communities in a Mediated World*. New York: New York UP, 2007.

Gray, Melissa. "From canon to fanon and back again: The epic journey of *Supernatural* and its fans." Tosenberger, ed. "Saving People, Hunting Things." <journal.transformativeworks.org/index.php/twc/article/ view/146/149>.

Greenspahn, Frederick E. *When Brothers Dwell Together. The Preeminence of Younger Siblings in the Hebrew Bible*. New York: Oxford UP, 1994.

Grey Bard. "Becky Is Not Writing This Story." LiveJournal (May 15, 2010). August 6, 2010. <grey-bard.livejournal.com/79246.html>.

Grossman, Lev. "Interview: Neil Gaiman and Joss Whedon." *TIME Magazine*. 25 September 2005. <www.time.com/time/arts/ article/0,8599,1109313-1,00.html>. Accessed September 30, 2010.

Gwenllian-Jones, Sara. "The Sex Lives of Cult TV Characters." *Screen* 43 (2002): 79–90.

—. "Virtual Reality and Cult Television." *Cult Television*. Eds. Roberta E. Pearson and Sara Gwenllian-Jones. Minneapolis: U Minnesota P, 2004. 83–97.

Halberstam, Judith. *Skin Shows: Gothic Horror and the Technology of Monsters*. Durham: Duke UP, 1995.

Hannah-Jones, Avril. "Good and Evil in the World of *Supernatural*." *In the Hunt*, 53–66.

Hampp, Andrew. "OMFG! A show with few TV viewers is still a hit." *Advertising Age* 80. Online. May 18, 2009. LexisNexis. Accessed August 15, 2010.

Handler, Richard and Jocelyn Linnekin. "Tradition, Genuine or Spurious." *Journal of American Folklore* 97 (1984): 273–290.

Heinecken, Dawn. "The Warrior Women of Television: A Feminist Cultural Analysis of the New Female Body in Popular Media." *Intersections in*

Communications and Culture, Vol 7. New York: Peter Lang, 2003.

Hibberd, James. "The Big Sweeps; Ratings Period Key to Determining Success of New Networks and Emerging Leaders Alike." *Television Week*. November 6, 2006: 1.

—. "On Target; CW Affiliates, Pleased With New Network's Progress, Report Increased Revenue Despite Soft Rating." *Television Week*. November 27, 2006: 1.

—. "Q&A: CW's Ostroff talks pilots, 'Vampire Diaries' and more." *The Hollywood Reporter*. March 4, 2010. <www.hollywoodreporter.com/blogs/live-feed/qa-cws-ostroff-talks-pilots-53226>.

—. "Sophomore Slump at CW; Promising New Series Weak in Ratings." *Television Week*. October 22, 2007: 1.

Hills, Matt. *The Pleasures of Horror*. London & New York: Continuum, 2005.

—. *Triumph of a Time Lord: Regenerating Doctor Who in the Twenty-First Century*. London & New York: I.B. Tauris, 2010.

Hills, Matt and Rebecca Williams. "*Angel*'s Monstrous Mothers and Vampires with Souls: Investigating the Abject in 'Television Horror.'" *Reading Angel: The Spin-off With a Soul*. Ed. Stacey Abbott. London & New York: I.B. Tauris, 2005. 203–217.

Hobsbawm, Eric and Terence Ranger, eds. *The Invention of Tradition*. Cambridge: Cambridge UP, 1992.

Holt, Douglas B. *How Brands Become Icons: The Principles of Cultural Branding*. Boston: Harvard Business School P, 2004.

Holt, Jennifer and Alisa Perren, eds. *Media Industries: History, Theory, and Method*. Malden: Blackwell, 2009.

Horton, Andrew. "Introduction." *Comedy/Cinema/Theory*. Ed. Andrew S. Horton. Berkeley: U of California P, 1991. 1–21.

Huddleston, Kathie. "*Supernatural* surprise: More Winchester deaths coming." Sci Fi Wire. April 2, 2010. <blastr.com/2010/04/supernatural-surprise-mor.php>.

Hunter, Stephen. "Out in the West: Reexamining A Genre Saddled With Subtext." *Washington Post*. December 25, 2005. <www.washingtonpost.com/wp-dyn/content/article/2005/12/23/AR2005122300323.html>.

In the Hunt: Unauthorized Essays on Supernatural. Ed. Supernatural.tv. Dallas, TX: BenBella Books, 2009.

"Is glass half-empty or half-full?" *Daily Variety*. January 25, 2006: 18.

Jacob, Benjamin. "Los Angelus: The City of Angel." *Reading Angel: The TV*

Spin-Off with a Soul. Ed. Stacey Abbott. London & New York: I.B. Tauris, 2005. 75–87.

Jenkins, Henry. *Cultural Convergence: Where Old and New Media Collide.* New York: New York UP, 2006.

—. *Textual Poachers: Television Fans and Participatory Culture.* London & New York: Routledge, 1992.

Jester, Alice. "*Supernatural*: How a Show Manages to Succeed Despite Its Network." Blogcritics.org. March 4, 2008.

Johnson, Catherine. *Telefantasy.* London: BFI, 2005.

Johnson, Michael P. *A Typology of Domestic Violence: Intimate Terrorism, Violent Resistance, and Situational Couple Violence.* Boston: Northeastern UP, 2008.

Jones, Leslie. "'Last Week We Had an Omen': The Mythological *X-Files.*" *Deny All Knowledge: Reading the X-Files.* Eds. David Lavery, Angela Hague, and Marla Cartwright. London: Faber & Faber, 1996. 77–98.

Jowett, Lorna. "Biting Humor: Harmony, Parody and the Female Vampire." *The Literary* Angel: *Essay on Influences and Traditions Reflected in the Joss Whedon Series.* Eds. AmiJo Comeford and Tamy Burnett. Jefferson, North Carolina and London: McFarland P, 2010. 17–29.

—. "Plastic, Fantastic? Genre, Technology, Science and Magic in *Angel.*" *Channeling the Future.* Ed. Lincoln Geraghty. Lantham, MD: Scarecrow P, 2009. 167–181.

Jung, Leo. *Fallen angels in Jewish, Christian, and Mohammedan literature.* New York: Ktav Publishing House, 1974.

Karnick, S.T. "CW's Supernatural Presents Christian Ideas in a Dark Melodrama." *The American Culture.* May 14, 2009. <stkarnick.com/blog2/2009/05/post_246.html>.

Kermode, Mark. *The Exorcist.* London: BFI, 1997.

Kirshenblatt-Gimblett, Barbara. "Mistaken Dichotomies." *Journal of American Folklore* 101 (1988): 140–155.

Kissell, Rick. "'Betty' Turns Heads." *Daily Variety.* October 2, 2006: 3.

Kit Borys and James Hibbard. "Neil Gaiman's 'Sandman' being adapted . . . as a TV show." *The Hollywood Reporter.* September 1, 2010.

Klaassen, Abbey. "Buyers hope less means more as WB-UPN merge." *Advertising Age* 77.5. January 30, 2006. LexisNexis.

Klener, Julien. "Démonologie talmudique et ashkénaze." *Anges et Démons. Actes du colloque de Liège et de Louvain-la-neuve 25–26 novembre 1987.* Eds.

Julien Ries and Henri Limet. Louvain-la-neuve: Centre d'histoire des religions, 1989. 177–201.

Klitenic Wear, Sarah and John M. Dillon. *Dionysius the Areopagite and the Neoplatonist tradition. Despoiling the Hellenes.* Aldershot: Ashgate, 2007.

Knight, Nicholas. *Supernatural: The Official Companion, Season 1.* New York: Titan Books, 2007.

—. *Supernatural: The Official Companion, Season 2.* New York: Titan Books, 2008.

—. *Supernatural: The Official Companion, Season 3.* New York: Titan Books, 2009.

—. *Supernatural: The Official Companion, Season 4.* New York: Titan Books, 2010.

Koven, Mikel J. *Film, Folklore and Urban Legends.* Lanham, MD: Scarecrow P, 2008.

Kripke, Eric. "Eric Kripke Talks About Season 4 of *Supernatural.*" theinsider .com. April 6, 2008. Online. Accessed November 30, 2009.

—. "Eric Kripke interview part 2." *Supernatural: The Inside Scoop,* July 3, 2008. YouTube. Accessed August 22, 2010. <www.youtube.com/ watch?v=5gNgKkofupo>.

—. "Kripke's Guide to the Apocalypse." *Supernatural: The Complete Fifth Season.* DVD extra. Warner Home Video, 2010.

—. "Lucifer Rising" Commentary. *Supernatural: The Complete Fourth Season.* Warner Home Video, 2009.

—. "Pilot" Commentary. *Supernatural: The Complete First Season.* Warner Home Video, 2006.

—. *TV.com Q&A* (interview with Tim Surette). TV.com. January 10, 2008. Online. Accessed July 22, 2010.

—. "What Is and What Should Never Be" Commentary. *Supernatural: The Complete Second Season.* Warner Home Video, 2007.

Kripke, Eric and Jeremy Carver. "In the Beginning" Commentary. *Supernatural: The Complete Fourth Season.* Warner Home Video, 2009.

Kristeva, Julia. *Powers of Horror: An Essay on Abjection.* Trans. Leon S. Roudiez. New York: Columbia UP, 1982.

Kustritz, Anne. "Slashing the Romance Narrative." *Journal of American Culture* 26 (2003): 371–386.

Kylios, Blaine. "Should Neil Gaiman join 'Supernatural'?" *CinemaSpy.* April 27, 2010. <www.cinemaspy.com/Remote-View/Should-Neil-Gaiman-

join-Supernatural/4399>.

Langton, Emily. "Demon Terrorists and Amoral Women: The Upcoming Season of 'Supernatural.'" Classic-Horror.com. August 6, 2007. <classic-horror.com/newsreel/demon_terrorists_and_amoral_women_the_upcoming_season_of_supernatural>.

Lassiter. "Peanuts." LiveJournal. January 29, 2010. Online. Accessed August 6, 2010 <twoskeletons.livejournal.com/133201.html>.

Lavery, David. "God, Death, and Pizza: *Supernatural* and the Death of God." Critical Studies in Television. <www.criticalstudiesintelevision.com/index.php?siid=13794>.

—. "Serial" Killer: *Dexter*'s Narrative Strategies." In *Dexter: Investigating Cutting Edge Television* Ed. Douglas L. Howard. London & New York: I.B. Tauris, 2010. 43–48.

Lewis, C.S. *Mere Christianity*. San Francisco: HarperCollins, 1952.

Lichtenfeld, Eric. *Action Speaks Louder: Violence, Spectacle, and the American Action Movie*. Middletown, CT: Wesleyan UP, 2007.

Liebs, Chester H. *Main Street to Miracle Mile: American Roadside Architecture*. Baltimore, MD: Johns Hopkins UP, 1995.

Lisotta, Christopher. "CW Free to Be a Community; Promo Campaign Focuses on Adapting to Consumers." *Television Week*. September 4, 2006: 5. Online. Accessed September 15, 2010.

—. "Slamming for Time Slots: The CW's Programming Mix Should Leave Little Room for Newcomers." *Television Week*. February 6, 2006: 1. Online. Accessed September 15, 2010.

Lively, Robert L. "Remapping the Feminine in Joss Whedon's *Firefly*." *Channeling the Future: Essays on Science Fiction and Fantasy Television*. Ed. Lincoln Geraghty. Lanham: Scarecrow P, 2009. 183–197.

Lyotard, Jean-François. *The Postmodern Condition: A Report on Knowledge*. Trans G. Bennington & B. Massumi. Manchester: Manchester UP, 1984.

Mach, Michael. *Entwicklungsstadien des jüdischen Engelglaubens in vorrabbinischer Zeit*. Tübingen: Mohr, 1992.

MacKenzie, Carina Adley. "'Supernatural': Jason Manns on music, movies, and twisting Jensen Ackles' arm." Zap2It. August 7, 2010: <blog.zap2it.com/frominsidethebox/2010/08/supernatural-jason-manns-on-music-movies-and-twisting-jensen-ackles-arm.html>.

Manick, Mike. "Neil Gaiman on J.K. Rowling, Fair Use and The Flattery of Derivative Works." *Tech Dirt*. April 24, 2008. <www.techdirt.com/

articles/20080422/191917922.html>.

Marshall, Brenda. *Teaching the Postmodern: Fiction and Theory*. New York & London & New York: Routledge, 1992.

Martin, Aubert. "Les djinns dans le Coran." *Anges et Démons. Actes du colloque de Liège et de Louvain-la-neuve 25–26 novembre 1987*. Eds. Julien Ries and Henri Limet. Louvain-la-neuve: Centre d'histoire des religions, 1989. 355–65.

Martin, Wallace. *Recent Theories of Narrative*. London: Cornell UP, 1986.

McClellan, Steve. "Stewart, Rock Have Best 'Buzz.'" *Adweek*. September 1, 2005. <www.adweek.com/aw/esearch/article_display.jsp?vnu_content_id=1001053772>.

McConnell, Frank. "Epic Comics: Neil Gaiman's *The Sandman*." *Commonweal* 122.18 (October 20, 1995): 21–22.

McGee, Patrick. *From Shane to Kill Bill: Rethinking the Western*. Malden, MA: Blackwell Publishing Ltd, 2007.

McKay, J.W. "Helel and the Dawn-Goddess. A Re-Examination of the Myth in Isaiah XIV 12–15." *Vetus Testamentum* 20.4 (1970): 451–464.

McKeever, Bill. "An American Garden of Eden." Mormon Research Ministry. <mrm.org/eden>.

Meehan, Eileen R. "Why We Don't Count: The Commodity Audience." *Connections*. Ed. Michele Hilmes. Belmont: Wadsworth/Thomson, 2003. 63–82.

Meyer, Stephenie. *Twilight*. London: Atom, 2007.

Miller, April. "'The Hair that Wasn't There Before': Demystifying monstrosity and menstruation in *Ginger Snaps* and *Ginger Snaps Unleashed*." *Western Folklore* 64.3–4 (2005): 281–303.

Munoz, Jose. *Disidentifications: Queers of Color and the Performance of Politics*. Minneapolis: U of Minnesota P, 1999.

Murphy, Bernice M. *The Suburban Gothic in American Popular Culture*. New York: Palgrave MacMillan, 2009.

"The Mythologies of *Supernatural*: From Heaven to Hell." *Supernatural: The Complete Fourth Season*. DVD Extra. Warner Home Video, 2009.

"The Mythologies of *Supernatural*: The Sweet Song of Death." *Supernatural: The Complete Fourth Season*. DVD Extra. Warner Home Video, 2009.

Naremore, James. *More Than Night: Film Noir in its Contexts*. Berkeley: U of California P, 2008.

New American Standard Bible. Ed. Kenneth Barker. Michigan: Zondervan,

1999.

Newall, Venetia J. "The Adaptation of Folklore and Tradition (Folklorismus)." *Folklore* 98.2 (1987): 131–151.

Newitz, Annalee and Matthew Wray. "What is 'White Trash'? Stereotypes and Economic Conditions of Poor Whites in the United States." *Whiteness: A Critical Reader*. Ed. Mike Hill. New York: New York UP, 1997. 168–186.

O'Rourke, Fran. *Pseudo-Dionysius and the Metaphysics of Aquinas*. Leiden, New York: Brill, 1992.

Oliver, Kelly. *Subjectivity Without Subjects: From Abject Fathers to Desiring Mothers*. Lanham, Maryland: Rowman & Littlefield Publishers, Inc, 1998.

Pagels, Elaine. *The Origin of Satan*. New York: Vintage Books, 1996.

Pamer, Melissa. "TV, straight up." *Los Angeles Times*. August 27, 2006: <articles.latimes.com/2006/aug/27/entertainment/ca-binge27>.

Parks, Lisa. "Brave New *Buffy*: Rethinking TV Violence." *Quality Popular Television: Cult TV, the Industry, and Fans*. Eds. Mark Jancovich and James Lyons. London: BFI, 2003. 118–133.

Paul, William. *Laughing Screaming: Modern Hollywood Horror and Comedy*. New York: Columbian UP, 1994.

Pearson, Roberta. "Lost in Transition: From Post-Network to Post-Television." *Quality TV: Contemporary American Television and Beyond*. Eds. Janet McCabe and Kim Akass. London & New York: I.B. Tauris, 2007: 239–256.

Peirse, Alison. "Supernatural." *The Essential Cult TV Reader*. Ed. David Lavery. Lexington: UP of Kentucky, 2010. 260–267.

Petersen, Line Nybro. "Praxis: Renegotiating religious imaginations through transformations of 'banal religion' in Supernatural." Tosenberger, ed. "Saving People, Hunting Things." <journal.transformativeworks.org/index.php/twc/article/view/142/145>.

—. "Renegotiating religious imaginations through transformations of 'banal religion' in *Supernatural.*" Tosenberger, ed. "Saving People, Hunting Things." <journal.transformativeworks.org/index.php/twc/article/view/142/145>.

Piepke, Joachim G. "Die Engel — Gottes traditionelle Boten. Zur christlichen Engellehre in Tradition und Gegenwart." *Engel im Aufwind. Gottes Boten auf der Spur*. Ed. Hermann Kochanek. Nettetal: Verl. St. Gabriel; Steyler Verl., 2000. 47–70.

Poole, Carol. "Who Threw Momma on the Ceiling?: Analyzing *Supernatural*'s Primal Scene of Trauma." *In the Hunt*, 143–54.

Porter, Rick. "The Bubble Bursts for 'Everwood.'" Zap2It.com. May 19, 2006. <www.zap2it.com/tv/news/zap-cwupfront-everwood,0,4271583.story?coll=zap-news-headlines>.

Prudom, Laura. "CW Executive Session: *Supernatural, Vampire Diaries*, and More — TCA Report." TVSquad.com. July 29, 2010. <www.tvsquad.com/2010/07/29/cw-executive-session-supernatural-vampire-diaries-and-more>.

"Pseudonyms." Supernatural Wiki: A Supernatural Canon & Fandom Resource. June 27, 2010. <tinyurl.com/Winchwiki>.

Pyle, Max. "Supernatural." SciFi 411. <scifi411.com/Shows/supernatural.html>.

"Ratings." *Supernatural* Wiki: <www.supernaturalwiki.com/index.php?title=Ratings&oldid=48194>.

Rauch, Stephen. *Neil Gaiman's "The Sandman" and Joseph Campbell: In Search of Modern Myth*. Holicong, PA: Wildside P, 2003.

Reed, M.R. "*Supernatural* Series Creator Eric Kripke Discusses the Third Season." October 1, 2007. Online associated content. <www.associatedcontent.com/article/397976/supernatural_series_creator_eric_kripke_pg4.html?com=2>. Accessed June 15, 2010.

Reiss, Jana. *What Would Buffy Do? The Vampire Slayer as Spiritual Guide*. San Francisco: Jossey-Bass, 2004.

Riviere, Joan. "Womanliness as Masquerade." *Psychoanalysis and Female Sexuality*. Ed. Hendrik M. Ruitenbeck. New Haven: New Haven UP, 1966: 209–220.

Roberts, Shari. "Western Meets Eastwood: Genre and Gender on the Road." *The Road Movie Book*. Eds. Steven Cohan and Ina Rae Hark. London & New York: Routledge, 1997. 45–69.

Rose, Margaret A. *Parody//Meta-fiction: An Analysis of Parody as a Critical Mirror to the Writing and Reception of Film*. London: Croom Helm, 1979.

Rosenberg, Alfons. *Engel und Dämonen. Gestaltwandel eines Urbildes*. München: Kösel, 1986.

Ross, Sharon Marie. *Beyond the Box: Television and the Internet*. Boston: Wiley-Blackwell, 2008.

Roush, Matt. "My *Supernatural* Summer." *TV Guide*. September 3, 2009. <devotedfansnetwork.com/forum/archive/index.php/t-13451.html>.

—. Personal Interview with Karen Petruska. September 24, 2010.

Ryan Maureen. "'It's the fun apocalypse': Creator Eric Kripke talks 'Supernatural.'" *Chicago Tribune*. August 26, 2009. <featuresblogs. chicagotribune.com/entertainment_tv/2009/08/supernatural-season-5-eric-kripke-cw.html>.

—. Personal Interview with Karen Petruska. September 7, 2010.

—. "Shows You Should Be Watching: *Supernatural* and *Privileged*." *The Watcher* weblog. *Chicago Tribune*. October 22, 2008. <featuresblogs. chicagotribune.com/entertainment_tv/2009/08/supernatural-season-5-eric-kripke-cw.html>. Accessed June 30, 2010.

—. "A 'Supernatural' holiday mystery and a question for you, dear readers." *The Watcher* weblog. *Chicago Tribune*. December 12, 2007. Accessed June 30, 2010.

Sablegreen. "Crowley — Good Omens?" The Winchester Family Business. May 26, 2010. <www.thewinchesterfamilybusiness.com/articles/9-misc/8049-crowley-good-omena.html>.

Sacchi, Paolo. *Jewish apocalyptic and its history*. Sheffield: Sheffield Academic P, 1990.

Sanders, Joe, ed. *The Sandman Papers*. Seattle, WA: Fantagraphics Books, 2006.

Savorelli, Antonio. *Oltre la sitcom. Indagine sulle nuove forme comiche della televisione americana*. Milano: FrancoAngeli, 2008.

Schäfer, Peter. *Rivalität zwischen Engeln und Menschen. Untersuchungen zur rabbinischen Engelvorstellung*. Berlin: de Gruyter, 1975.

Schmidt, Lisa. "Monstrous Melodrama: Expanding the Scope of Melodramatic Identification to Interpret Negative Fan Responses to *Supernatural*." Tosenberger, ed. "Saving People, Hunting Things." <journal.transformativeworks.org/index.php/twc/article/view/152/155>.

Schneider, Michael. "CW's Theme Scheme." *Daily Variety*. May 22, 2009: 5. LexisNexis. Online. August 15, 2010.

—. "'Ghost' in the Machine." *Daily Variety*. January 26, 2010: 6.

—. "WBTV Deal a Natural." *Daily Variety*. June 23, 2008: 5.

Schweitzer, Darrell, ed. *The Neil Gaiman Reader*. Holicong, PA: Wildeside P, 2007.

"Seth" message board post on, Reed, M.R. "*Supernatural* Series Creator Eric Kripke Discusses the Third Season." October 1, 2007.

ShatteredSiren. Becky the Castiel Fangirl chapter 1. Fanfiction.net February

11, 2010. Online. <www.fanfiction.net/s/5736895/1/Becky_the_Castiel_
Fangirl>. Accessed August 13, 2010.

—. Becky the Castiel Fangirl chapter 2. Fanfiction.net. February 11, 2010.
Online. <http://www.fanfiction.net/s/5736895/2/Becky_the_Castiel_
Fangirl>. Accessed August 13, 2010.

—. Becky the Castiel Fangirl chapter 3. Fanfiction.net. February 11, 2010.
Online. http://www.fanfiction.net/s/5736895/1/Becky_the_Castiel_
Fangirl>. Accessed August 13, 2010.

Simmons, Darryn. "Viewers Welcome UPN-WB Merger." *Knight-Ridder
Tribune Business News.* January 25, 2006.

Slotkin, Richard. *Gunfighter Nation: The Myth of the Frontier in Twentieth-
Century America.* Norman, OK: U of Oklahoma P, 1998.

Stam, Robert. *Reflexivity in Film and Literature.* New York: Columbia UP,
1992.

Stam, Robert, Robert Burgoyne, and Sandy Flitterman-Lewis. *New
Vocabularies in Film Semiotics: Structuralism, Post-Structuralism and
Beyond.* London & New York: Routledge, 1992.

Stein, Louisa. "'What you don't know': *Supernatural* fan vids and millennial
theology." Tosenberger, ed. "Saving People, Hunting Things." <journal.
transformativeworks.org/index.php/twc/article/view/192/158>.

Steinberg, Brian. "CW attempts to get fans 'cwinging' between TV and web."
Advertising Age 79.21 (May 26, 2008). LexisNexis. Online. Accessed
August 15, 2010.

—. "CW shatters the TV-ad-as-usual mold." *Advertising Age* 78.30 (July 30,
2007). LexisNexis. Online. Accessed January 17, 2010.

—. "Nets try to get fans to go where the money still is: TV." *Advertising Age*
79.18 (May 5, 2008). LexisNexis. Online. Accessed August 15, 2010.

—. "Young CW still striving for popularity." *Advertising Age* 79.33
(September 8, 2008). LexisNexis. Online. Accessed August 15, 2010.

Stepakoff, Jeffrey. *Billion Dollar Kiss: The Story of a Television Writer in the
Hollywood Gold Rush.* New York: Gotham Books, 2007.

Sullenberger, T.E. "Ajax Meets the Jolly Green Giant: Some Observations on
the Use of Folklore and Myth in American Mass Marketing." *Journal of
American Folklore* 87 (1974): 53–65.

The Supernatural Neil Gaiman Crossover Ficathon. <community.
livejournal.com/spn_gaiman>. Accessed September 30, 2010.

"Supernatural: More TVGuide.com Reader Questions Answered!" *TV Guide.*

Online. January 29, 2009. <www.tvguide.com/News/Supernatural-Questions-Answered-1002240.aspx>. Accessed March 23, 2010.

"*Supernatural*: Sexy. Scary. Over?" *Entertainment Weekly*. April 8, 2009. Online. Accessed July 25, 2010. <tinyurl.com/ewkripke>.

Supernatural. The CW Lounge Message Boards. Cwtv.com, 2007–2010. Online. Accessed July 22, 2010.

Supernatural Wiki: A *Supernatural* Canon and Fandom Resource. <www.supernaturalwiki.com>.

Surette, Tim. "TVs Craziest Fanbases . . . With Video Proof." TV.com News. March 10, 2010. <www.tv.com/tvs-craziest-fan-bases...-with-video-proof/story/21826.html>.

Swendson, Shanna. "Keepers of the Lore." *In the Hunt*, 251–261.

Thompson, Stith. *The Folktale*. Berkeley: U of California P, 1977 [1946].

Tompkins, Joseph. "What's the Deal with Soundtrack Albums? Metal Music and the Customized Aesthetics of Contemporary Horror." *Cinema Journal* 49.1 (2009): 65–81.

Tosenberger, Catherine. "'The epic love story of Sam and Dean': *Supernatural*, queer readings, and the romance of incestuous fan fiction." *Transformative Works and Cultures*, no. 1 (2008). <journal.transformativeworks.org/index.php/twc/article/view/30>.

—. "'Kinda like the folklore of its day': *Supernatural*, Fairy Tales, and Ostension." Tosenberger, ed. "Saving People, Hunting Things." <journal.transformativeworks.org/index.php/twc/article/view/174/156>.

—. "Love! Valor! *Supernatural!*" Tosenberger, ed. "Saving People, Hunting Things." <journal.transformativeworks.org/index.php/twc/article/view/212/167>.

—, ed. "Saving People, Hunting Things." *Transformative Works and Cultures* 4 (2010): <journal.transformativeworks.org/index.php/twc/issue/view/5>.

Tropp, Martin. *Images of Fear: How Horror Stories Helped Shape Modern Culture (1818–1918)*. Jefferson, NC: McFarland & Company, Inc., Publishers, 1990.

Tudor, Andrew. "Unruly Bodies, Unquiet Minds." *Body & Society* 1.1 (1995): 24–41.

TV Guide.com. *Supernatural* Episode Recaps. <www.tvguide.com/tvshows/supernatural/episodes-season-1/192272>.

Tyler, Carole-Anne. "Boys Will Be Girls: Drag and Transvestic Fetishism."

Camp: Queer Aesthetics and the Performing Subject. Ed. Fabio Cleto. Ann
    Arbor: U of Michigan P, 1999. 369–392.

Udovitch, Mim. "What Makes Buffy Slay." *Rolling Stone.* May 11, 2000.

Van de Ven, Katherine Lawrie. "'Just an Anonymous Room': Cinematic
    Hotels and Motels as Mnemonic Purgatories." *Moving Pictures/Stopping
    Places: Hotels and Motels on Film.* Eds. David B. Clarke, Valerie Crawford
    Pfannhauser, Marcus A. Doel. Lanham, MD: Lexington Books, 2009.
    235–53.

"A Very Supernatural Christmas": A Closer Look. *Supernatural: The Complete
    Third Season.* DVD extra. Warner Home Video, 2008.

Vorgrimler, Herbert, Ursula Bernauer, Thomas Sternberg. *Engel.
    Erfahrungen göttlicher Natur.* Freiburg, Basel, Wien: Herder, 2001.

Waugh, Patricia. *Metafiction. The Theory and Practice of Self-Conscious Fiction.*
    London & New York: Routledge, 1984.

Weeks, Jeffrey. *Sexuality and its Discontents: Meanings, Myths and Modern
    Sexualities.* London & New York: Routledge, 1985.

Wheatley, Helen. *Gothic Television.* Manchester: Manchester UP, 2006.

Whedon, Joss. *Firefly: The Official Companion, Volume 1.* New York: Titan
    Books, 2006.

White, Josh. "Soldiers Facing Extended Tours: Critics of Army Policy Liken
    It to a Draft." *Washington Post.* June 3, 2004: A01.

Wilkinson, Jules. "Back in Black." *In the Hunt,* 197–207.

—. "A box of mirrors, a unicorn and a pony." Tosenberger, ed. "Saving
    People, Hunting Things." <journal.transformativeworks.org/index.php/
    twc/article/viewArticle/159/138>.

Williams, Raymond, *Television: Technology and Cultural Form.* London:
    Fontana, 1974.

Williams, Tony. *Hearths of Darkness.* London: Associated UP, 1996.

Woledge, Elizabeth. "Intimatopoia: Genre Intersections Between Slash
    and the Mainstream." *Fan Fiction and Fan Communities in the Age of
    the Internet.* Eds. Karen Hellekson and Kristina Busse. Jefferson, NC:
    McFarland, 2006. 97–114.

Wollen, Peter. *Signs and Meaning in the Cinema.* London: Thames &
    Hudson, 1970.

Wood, Robin. *Hollywood from Vietnam to Reagan.* New York: Columbia UP,
    1986.

Woolf, Virginia. "Professions for Women" (1931). *The Death of the Moth and*

Other Essays. London: Hogarth, 1942. 149–154.

Wright, Julia M. "Latchkey Hero: Masculinity, Class and the Gothic in Eric Kripke's *Supernatural*." *Genders* 47 (2008). <www.genders.org/g47/g47_wright.html>.

Zhang, Juwen. "Filmic Folklore and Chinese Cultural Identity." *Western Folklore* 64.3–4 (2005): 263–280.

Zipes, Jack. *Happily Ever After: Fairy Tales, Children and the Cultural Industry*. London & New York: Routledge, 1997.

Index

28 Days Later, 151
"99 Problems" (episode), 40, 166,
    172, 237, 240, 268
"Abandon All Hope . . ." (episode),
    29, 83, 102, 239, 267
*Abbott and Costello Meet Franken-
    stein*, 4
abjection, 11–13, 15, 48, 57, 58
AC/DC, 22, 65–66, 197
Ackles, Jensen (actor), 5, 15–16,
    80, 86, 121, 126, 128, 130,
    158, 194, 250–51, 269, 271,
    273–274n
Adventures of Huckleberry Finn, The,
    43
Aerosmith, 195
"After School Special" (episode), 113,
    149, 195–196, 264, 275n
Alastair (character), 7–9, 12–13, 79,
    99, 148
Alias, 91
"All Dogs Go to Heaven" (episode),
    250, 270
"All Hell Breaks Loose, Part 1" (epi-
    sode), 79, 81, 139, 260
"All Hell Breaks Loose, Part 2" (epi-

sode), 24, 98, 165, 260
allusion, 4, 63, 125–127, 150–151,
    154, 193, 195–199, 242, 282n
alternate realities, 148–149, 170,
    265
Althusser, Louis Pierre, 190
Alvey, Mark, 83
American dream, xv, 51, 61, 63,
    69–70
American frontier, 56, 78
American Gods, 230, 232–233, 236,
    240–242
American Nightmare, The, 61–62, 74
American Psycho, 37, 275n
American Werewolf in London, An,
    123, 196, 233
anachronistic music, 19–20, 22, 24
"And Then There Were None" (epi-
    sode), 250, 271
Andy Griffith Show, The, 83
Angel, xi–xii, 4, 87–88, 91, 95, 128,
    248
angels, xii, xvi, 12, 14, 18, 30, 35,
    78–79, 89, 91–93, 129,
    139–140, 163–164, 166–169,
    171, 173, 176–186, 236–240,

264, 266, 268–269, 281n
Anger, Kenneth, 196
"Appointment in Samarra" (episode), 250–251, 270
archangels, x, xii, 81, 139, 163–164, 167, 173, 178–181, 183, 195, 216, 237, 266, 269, 279n
archontic literature, 204–205, 209–210, 217–218
"Are You There, God? It's Me, Dean Winchester" (episode), 72, 99, 176, 196, 263
Armageddon/Apocalypse, ix–x, xvi, 18, 22, 89, 133, 139–142, 144–145, 164–164, 167, 172–174, 181, 183, 186, 229, 236–237, 239, 240–241, 245, 247
Assault on Precinct 13, 64, 151
"Asylum" (episode), 121, 128, 138–139, 151, 254–255
audiences, xiv, xvi, 6, 18–19, 21–22, 25–27, 30, 37, 49, 51, 53–55 61, 67, 120, 124–131, 142, 150, 154–155, 157–158, 160, 187, 192, 194–195, 197–200, 222–224, 227–229, 230, 274n, 281n, 284n
Ausiello, Michael, xiv, 210
Azazel (character), 77–79, 81–82, 93, 97–98, 103, 119, 165–166, 257n
Back to the Future, 151
Bad Day at Black Rock, 194
"Bad Day at Black Rock" (episode), 3, 14–15, 91, 100, 194, 260
Balthazar (character), 251, 271
Barnes, Pamela (character), 83, 86, 105, 114–115, 207–208,
Batman, 88, 232
Battlestar Galactica, 154
Bauman, Richard, 281n
Beaver, Jim (actor), 274n
"Bedtime Stories" (episode), 123, 126, 151, 261
Beeson, Charles, 258–259, 261–268, 271
Being Human, 95, 247
Ben-Amos, Dan, 281n

"Benders, The" (episode), 8, 42, 63–64, 70, 151, 255, 275n
Bendix, Regina, 281n
Benedict, Rob (actor), 129
Berry, Chuck, 193
Beverly Hillbillies, The, 47
Bible, The, 176–180, 183, 186, 225
Bird, Sharon, 55
Black Peter [Zwarte Piet], 192
Black Sabbath, 21, 66, 194
Blade Runner, 87
Blair Witch Project, The, 151
"Bloodlust" (episode), 7, 95, 257
"Bloody Mary" (episode), 24, 26, 70, 94, 140, 143, 151, 191–192, 234, 254
Blume, Judy, 196
Bonanza, 83
Bones, 205, 207
Boogeyman, 155
borders, 11–12, 34, 81–82, 84, 128, 154
"Born Under a Bad Sign" (episode), 23, 194, 259
Botkin, Benjamin, 189
Bradbury, Ray, 193, 282n
Braeden, Ben (character), xiii, 71, 260, 269, 272
Braeden, Lisa (character), xiii, 71, 103, 215, 260, 269, 272, 276n, 278n
Bruce, Melissa N., 35, 39, 84
Buckner, Brad, 248, 255
Buffy the Vampire Slayer, xi–xii, xiv, 4, 7, 38, 54–55, 91, 94–95, 128, 133, 207, 225–226, 238, 277n
"Bugs" (episode), 5, 70, 85, 107, 122, 192, 234, 254
Burton, Terri Hughes, 248, 253–254
Busse, Kristina and Karen Hellekson, 218
"Caged Heat" (episode), 250, 270
Californication, 19
Callaway, Trey, 248, 256
cameos, 153–154
camp, xvi, 61, 103, 111, 114–115, 119, 123–128, 131

Campbell, Bruce, 196
Campbell, Gwen (character), 271
Campbell, Samuel (character), 251
Car, The, 64
Carver, Jeremy, 236, 247, 261–268
Casablanca, 282n
Cash, Johnny, 23–24, 194
Cassidy, Katie (actress), 276n
Castiel (character), x, xiii, 13, 16,
    38, 103, 106, 125, 129, 144,
    159, 163, 167–170, 173–174,
    176, 179, 181, 183, 204, 209,
    214–217, 236–240, 250–252,
    263, 265–272
Cat and Canary, The, 4
Catholic, 62, 172–173, 178–180, 186,
    278n, 280n
celebrity, 209, 212
Charmelo, Eric, 270–71
"Changing Channels" (episode), 34,
    40, 129, 142, 151, 153, 183,
    247, 267
*Children Shouldn't Play With Dead
    Things*, 193
"Children Shouldn't Play with Dead
    Things" (episode), 151, 193,
    257
Christianity, 30, 163–164, 167, 174,
    176–185, 241, 245, 247
Christine, 64
city, the/the metropolis, 87–88
"Clap Your Hands If You Believe"
    (episode), 250–251, 270
Clark, Bob, 193
classic rock, xv, 18, 20, 22–23,
    26–28, 193–196, 198–199
class-passing, 166, 169
Cliff, Jimmy, 195
Coakley, Bill, 248, 254
Cohan, Lauren (actress), 276n
Cohan, Steven, 34–35, 37, 39, 41
Cohen, Matt (actor), 55
Cold Case, 207
Collins, Misha (actor), 209
Colt revolver, 29, 77–78, 88, 256,
    260, 267, 271
Comeback, The, 157
comedy, xv, xix, 3–16, 100, 124, 147

communities, 30, 37, 55, 123, 193,
    205, 210, 213
Conway, James L., 265–267
Corbett, Alan, 105, 109–113, 115,
    278n
Cortese, Genevieve (actress), 276n–
    277n
costuming, 61, 77, 88, 103, 120–130,
    207, 267, 282n-283n
Creed, Barbara, 11
"Criss Angel Is a Douchebag" (epi-
    sode), 41, 113, 264
"Croatoan" (episode), 64, 151, 170,
    195, 258
"Crossroad Blues" (episode), 98,
    194, 258
Crowley (character), x, 29, 236,
    239–240, 250–251, 267–272
CSI: Miami, 153, 207
cult fans, 23, 30
cultural ownership, 213, 218
Curb Your Enthusiasm, 154
*Curious Case of Benjamin Button,
    The*, 151
"Curious Case of Dean Winchester,
    The" (episode), 14, 151, 194,
    249, 267
CW, the, ix, xiv, 16, 26, 49–50, 128,
    130, 153, 198, 220–229, 233,
    246, 276n, 284n
Dabb, Andrew, 263–271
damsels, 90–104
Danielson, Larry, 188
Dante, Joe, 123, 196
Dark Angel, 91, 286
"Dark Side of the Moon" (episode),
    13, 67, 73, 84, 149, 165, 169,
    171, 174, 179, 183, 194, 237,
    249, 268
Davis, Stephen, 195
Davisson, Amber and Paul Booth,
    206
Dawson's Creek, 128, 274n
"Dead in the Water" (episode), 93,
    134, 137, 151, 249, 253
"Dead Man's Blood" (episode), 78,
    88, 256
"Dead Men Don't Wear Plaid" (epi-

sode), 72, 83, 122, 195, 268
Death Takes a Holiday, 194
"Death Takes a Holiday" (episode),
    13, 74, 83, 85, 194, 265
Death (character), x, 235, 245–246,
    267, 269–270
Deliverance, 53
Derecho, Abigail, 204
Dessertine, Rebecca, 267
deus ex machina, 159
"Devil You Know, The" (episode),
    98, 239, 248, 268
"Devil's Trap" (episode), 98, 256
Dexter, 141, 145
diegetic music, 24
djinn, 73, 148, 166, 250, 269
Doctor Who, 4, 152
domestic violence, 56–58
domestic, the, 37, 39, 43, 56–58, 69,
    82–85, 87, 92, 103
Don't Look Now, 4
Doors, The, 194
Dorson, Richard, 189
Dr. Jekyll and Mr. Hyde, 87
Dracula, 61, 122, 153, 188
Dracula: Dead and Loving It, 6
drag, 45, 50–51, 53, 59, 119–124,
    126–131
"Dream a Little Dream of Me" (epi-
    sode), 13, 23, 72, 261
Duel, 64
Dundes, Alan, 190
Edlund, Ben, xi, 5, 68, 91, 114,
    129, 146, 216, 247–249, 251,
    257–271
Ehrman, David, 248, 256
Eliasberg, Jan, 270
Ellis, Peter, 254
"End, The" (episode), 170, 195, 237,
    248–249, 266
Englund, Robert (actor), 251
Entourage, 154
Everwood, 222–23
"Everybody Loves a Clown" (epi-
    sode), 101–103, 257
Evil Dead, The, 151, 196
Evil Dead 2, The, 196
excessive consumers, 204

"Exile on Main Street" (episode),
    194, 250, 269
Exorcist, The, 61–64, 154, 275
Extras, 154
"Faith" (episode), 42, 94–95, 172,
    255
fakelore, 187, 189–192, 199
fallen angels, x, 176, 180–182, 195
"Fallen Idols" (episode), 65, 123,
    142, 154, 206, 208, 266
family, xiii–xiv, 36–46, 51, 54,
    58–59, 6–74, 83–87, 102–103,
    136–137, 140, 142, 165, 167–
    168, 171, 173, 175, 184–185,
    234
"Family Matters" (episode), 250–251,
    270
"Family Remains" (episode), 64, 151,
    196, 264
fandom, ix, xiv, 22, 50, 155, 203–218,
    221, 275n, 278n, 282n
fanfic, 40, 204, 213–215, 217–218,
    236, 282n, 283n
Fedor, Harvey, 267
Fight Club, 37, 275n
film noir, 35, 88, 100
filmic folklore, 190–191, 199–200
Firefly, 91, 248
Firestarter, 120
flashbacks, 19, 28, 43–45, 51, 101,
    119, 275n
flexi-narrative, 142–144
folklore, xiv, xvi, 41, 81, 131, 133–134,
    136, 161, 185, 187–200
"Folsom Prison Blues" (episode), 23,
    194, 259, 280n
fourth wall, 125, 148, 155–158
Fox, Aaron A, 50
Freddy vs. Jason, 25
"Free to Be You and Me" (episode),
    38, 125, 196, 266
free will, xii, 14, 74, 174, 176, 181,
    183–184, 239
"French Mistake, The" (episode),
    250–252, 271
"Fresh Blood" (episode), 261
Freud, Sigmund, 86
Friends, 38

frontier masculinity, 82
"Frontierland" (episode), 250–251, 271
Frye, Northrop, 87
Fugitive, The, 83
fundamentalists, 172
Gabriel (character), 139, 173, 179, 181, 183–184, 216, 268, 279n
Gaiman, Neil, 230–243, 284n
Gamble, Sera, xiv, 106–107, 145, 159, 211, 229, 246, 249, 252–253, 255–267, 269–270, 272
gay, 39, 86, 105–109, 111–113, 115, 119–131, 277n, 278n
genre hybridity, 4, 91–92
Geraghty, Christine, 210
Gewertz, Eric "Giz," 269
Ghost Whisperer, The, 128
Ghost, 127
"Ghostfacers" (episode), 105, 108–109, 111, 115, 147, 153, 157, 196, 206–207, 248, 262, 278n–279n, 284n
Ghostfacers, the (characters), 109–113, 148, 207, 212
Ghostfacers!, xi, 262
Gilmore Girls, 128, 155, 228, 283n, 284n
Ginger Snaps, 281n, 308
Girl, Interrupted, 152
Girotti, Ken, 254
Glass, Adam, 269–271
Goad, Jim, 54
God, xi, xiii, 74, 129, 163, 173–174, 176–186, 215, 217, 238–239, 245–246, 266n, 280n, 284n
Godzilla, 87
"Good God, Y'all!" (episode), 266
Good Omens, 230, 232, 236, 239–240, 242, 284n
Gossip Girl, 223–225, 284n
Gotham City, 87
Gray, Melissa, 190
Gray, Jonathan, Cornell Sandvoss, and C. Lee Harrington, 213
Grimm, Jacob & Wilhelm, 189
gross-out comedy, 11
Groundhog Day, 86, 151, 247, 262

Gumenick, Amy, 103
Gwenllian-Jones, Sara, 20, 106–108, 274n, 278n
Halberstam, Judith, 53
"Hammer of the Gods" (episode), 89, 173, 184, 195, 240–241, 268, 279n
Happy Days, 197
Hardy, Rod, 269
Harvelle, Ellen (character), 53, 83, 96, 101–103, 257
Harvelle, Jo (character), 53, 100–103, 257–258, 277n
Hatem, Richard, 248, 254
Haunting of Hill House, The, 282
Heart, 95, 97, 123, 196, 249, 259
Heaven, 7, 67, 72, 99, 148–149, 167–168, 171–174, 176–177, 179–180, 182–184, 186, 236, 249, 268n
"Heaven and Hell" (episode), 99, 180, 182, 194, 237, 264
heavy metal, 26–27, 66, 194
Hein, Jon, 197
Hell, x–xiv, 8, 13–14, 24, 29, 34, 67–69, 74, 79–80, 86, 89, 103, 136, 165, 171, 177, 180, 182, 185, 237, 263, 269, 272, 274n, 276n
"Hell House" (episode), 9–10, 70, 110, 193, 206–208, 234, 256
hellhounds, 83, 85, 100, 102, 207, 262
Henriksen, FBI Agent Victor (character), 259, 262
hermeneutics, 30, 274n
heroes/heroism, xii, 8, 12, 16, 35, 47, 49, 53–55, 58–59, 88, 92, 102, 115, 123, 130, 185, 232, 241
Heyerdahl, Christopher (actor), 276n
Hills Have Eyes, The, 12, 151
Hills, Matt, xiv, 4, 11–12, 15, 144, 273n
Hilton, Paris (actress), 154, 209
history, 41–43, 51, 53, 138, 232–233, 247, 251

"Hollywood Babylon" (episode), 152, 155, 196, 248, 259

homage, 63, 68, 123, 188, 231, 240, 242, 247, 252, 275

"Home" (episode), 63, 68, 72, 151, 254

homoeroticism, xvi, 86–87, 107

homosexual, xvi, 61, 85, 106, 108, 111–113, 115, 126, 277n, 78n

homosocial genres/homosociality, 84, 87

"Hook Man" (episode), 94, 96, 143, 192, 234, 254

Hook Man, the, 140, 254

horror film, 6–7, 12, 25–26, 53, 61, 63, 69–70, 94, 144, 150, 152, 188, 194, 259

horror TV, xi, xiii–iv, 3–4, 6–7, 15, 17, 144, 193, 273n

House of Wax, 154, 288

House on Haunted Hill, 151

"Houses of the Holy" (episode), 23, 42, 139, 172, 259, 276n

Houston, Whitney, 194–195

Howling, The, 123

humanism, 140, 173, 280n

Humphris, Cathryn, 256, 258–259, 261, 263–264

"Hunted" (episode), 258

hunters, xi, 7–8, 13, 37, 40, 42, 47, 49–50, 55, 58, 78, 81, 96, 103, 109, 114, 143, 163, 165, 169, 256–57, 262–63, 266, 268, 270, 280n

hypermasculine, 105, 108, 112–113, 115, 278n

"I Believe the Children Are Our Future" (episode), 195, 238, 266

"I Know What You Did Last Summer" (episode), 98, 193, 264, 274n

Iacofano, Tim, 257

identity, 5, 11, 14, 33–35, 37, 47–50, 55–56, 81–82, 112, 125, 127, 130–131, 150, 154, 159, 199, 203, 206, 209, 214, 218, 235, 276n, 277n

illusionism, 146–48

Impala, the, ix–x, 20, 34, 37–39, 46, 60, 64–66, 68, 78, 84–85, 87, 89, 131, 158, 174, 259, 274n, 275n

"In My Time of Dying" (episode), 13, 80–82, 97–98, 127, 257

"In the Beginning" (episode), 19, 43, 67, 71, 98, 103, 149, 151, 247, 263, 276n, 280n

Incredible Hulk, The, 267

Incredible Hulk, The, 33

Indiana Jones and the Kingdom of the Crystal Skull, 282n

intertextuality of casting, 276

intertextuality, xvi, 4, 128, 148, 150, 197–198, 218, 276n

intimacy, 39–40, 282n

intimatopic fic, 205

Invasion, 220

Iron Maiden, 194

Islam, 176, 181, 281n

"It's a Terrible Life" (episode), 15, 36, 148, 151, 169, 206, 249–250, 265, 277n

It's a Wonderful Life, 151

"It's the Great Pumpkin, Sam Winchester" (episode), 195–196, 263

Jack the Ripper, 87

Jackson, David, 254

Jackson, Shirley, 88

Jacob, Benjamin, 88

Jaws, 135, 151

Jenkins, Henry, 210, 218

Johnson, Robert, 194

Jones, Leslie, 189

Jowett, Lorna, 4–7, 84, 273n, 274n, 275n

Judaism/Jewish, 177–182, 282n

Judeo-Christian tradition, 186, 241

"Jump the Shark" (episode), 40, 67, 71, 197, 265, 279n, 282n

"Jus in Bello" (episode), 35, 64, 151, 262, 279n, 280n

Just Legal, 228, 283n

Kafka, Franz, 196

Kane, Adam, 264

"Kids Are Alright, The" (episode),

23, 40, 65, 80, 85, 194, 260
Kinder un hausmarchen, 189
King, Albert, 23, 194
KISS, 121, 195
Klein, Jenny, 267, 270
Knauf, Daniel, 248, 256
Kolchak: the Night Stalker, xi
Koven, Mikel J., 189
Kripke, Eric, xiv, xvi–xvii, 5, 18–19,
    33, 43–44, 49, 68, 70, 77–78,
    85, 90–91, 101, 106, 132, 140,
    143, 145, 153, 155, 158–159,
    168, 171, 173, 175, 187, 195,
    210–211, 213, 217, 219, 225,
    229–230, 233–34, 236, 242–
    243, 246–249, 252, 253–257,
    260, 262–267, 269, 272,
    273n, 276n, 284n, 285n
Kristeva, Julia, 11–12, 48, 58
Kroeker, Allan, 255
Kubrick, Stanley, 63, 289
Kustritz, Anne, 320
Landis, John, 123, 196
Last House on Left, The, 61–62, 64
Lavery, David, xiii–xiv, xvii, 141–142,
    145, 273n
Lawrence, Kansas, 71, 78, 159, 174,
    254, 263
"Lazarus Rising" (episode), 27, 66,
    83, 165, 179, 263
Leave it to Beaver, 83
Led Zeppelin, 23, 66, 195
Legend of Hell House, The, 193
Legion, 186
leprechauns, 241
"Let It Bleed" (episode), 250, 272
"Like a Virgin" (episode), 250, 270
Lilith (character), 13, 144, 238, 262,
    265, 276n, 280n
"Live Free or TwiHard" (episode),
    250–251, 264
Loflin, Daniel, 263–271
Long, Chris, 256
"Long-Distance Call" (episode), 42,
    196, 247, 262
Lordsburg, 77, 89
Lost, 144
love, xv, 39, 105–109, 111–112

Lucifer (character), x, xii–xiii,
    xvi, 14, 65, 69, 74, 81, 89,
    129–130, 142, 159, 164–167,
    169–171, 174, 176, 180–186,
    195, 232, 237–238, 241, 245,
    266–268, 270, 276n, 277n,
    279n
"Lucifer Rising" (episode), xiii, 22,
    98–99, 174, 182, 196–197,
    237, 265, 276n–277n, 279n
Lucy Show, The, 83, 287
Lyotard, Jean François, 133, 136
"Magnificent Seven, The" (episode),
    40, 46, 83, 260
"Malleus Maleficarum" (episode),
    80, 196, 261
"Man Who Knew Too Much, The"
    (episode), 250–252, 272
"Man Who Would Be King, The"
    (episode), 250, 271
"Mannequin 3: The Reckoning" (epi-
    sode), 250, 271
Manners, Kim, xi, 253–257, 259–263
Manson, Charles, 197
Marley, Bob, 195
masculinity, xv–xvi, 37, 39, 55,
    77–89, 91–92, 105–115, 126
Mask, The, 9
Masters, Meg (character), 12, 98–
    99, 103, 139, 144, 255–256,
    270, 276n, 277n
Matheson, Richard, 193
Mathis, Johnny, 193
Matthews, Brett, 269–271
McLaughlin, Emily, 262
McNeill, Robert Duncan, 254
Medium, 128
melodrama, xv, 4, 27, 30, 36, 44,
    84, 194
metafiction, 128, 146–160, 231–232,
    248
"Metamorphosis" (episode), 80–81,
    85, 196, 263, 281n
metatext, 46, 149, 155, 188, 206–
    207, 210–211, 214, 216, 218,
    247
Michael (character), x, xii, 12, 14,
    74, 81, 89, 129–130, 164,

167, 169, 174, 176, 179, 181, 183–186, 195, 237, 266, 268
micro-narratives, 132–145
Midnight Run, 125
Milbauer, Ron, 248, 253–254
Millennium, 36
Miller, Frank, 151, 232
Milligan, Adam, 265
Milton, Anna (character), 72, 180–182, 217, 237, 264, 267
miscegenation, 79
Moby-Dick, 43
mockumentary, 79
Modern Times, 9
Mommy Dearest, 271
"Monster at the End of This Book, The" (episode), xvi, 40, 43, 68, 86, 129, 144, 146, 155–156, 163, 196, 203, 205, 237, 265
"Monster Movie" (episode), xi, 63, 147, 152–153, 188, 193, 248, 263
monsters, ix, xi, xiii, 6, 10, 12–14, 44–45, 47, 49, 52–55, 59, 63, 74, 77, 87, 91, 95–97, 99, 108, 137, 140, 145, 153, 187–188, 190, 193, 248
monstrous, 48, 87, 95, 98, 114
Moore, Jessica (character), 21, 90, 92–94, 120, 122, 234, 260
Moore, Michael T., 260
Morgan, Jeffrey Dean (actor), 274
motels, xv, 37–46, 65, 72, 172, 280n
mother figures, 71–72
Murphy, Bernice, 54
My Bloody Valentine (1981), 194, 282n
My Bloody Valentine (2009), 194
"My Bloody Valentine" (episode), 194, 248, 268, 285n
"My Heart Will Go On" (episode), 250–251, 271
"Mystery Spot" (episode), xvi, 15, 85–86, 151, 247, 262
Naremore, James, 88
Nave, Rachel, 248, 254
Neverwhere, 230, 232, 236–37

Newall, Ventia, 281n
Newitz, Annalee, 49–51
Night of the Living Dead, 12, 63
"Nightmare" (episode), 121, 195, 255
Nightmare on Elm Street, 7, 120
"Nightshifter" (episode), 42, 258, 280n
Nip/Tuck, 119
"No Exit" (episode), 42, 101, 257
"No Rest for the Wicked" (episode), 85, 262
non-diegetic music, 188
Numb3rs, 207
Nutter, David, xi, 253
Office, The, 157
Oliver, Kelly, 58
Omen, The, 61–62, 64, 242
"On the Head of a Pin" (episode), 8, 13, 79, 237, 265, 276n
Oring, Elliott, 281n
Others, The, 151
Padalecki, Jared (actor), 5, 15–16, 86, 126, 128, 130, 145, 154–155, 251, 271, 283n
parody, 6, 40, 113, 115, 152, 154, 156, 196
performance, xvi, 15–16, 115, 119–131, 190–191, 199, 215, 218
Pestilence (character), 269
"Phantom Traveler" (episode), 121–122, 234, 254
"Pilot" (episode), ix, xiii, 8, 21, 33, 36, 38, 64–65, 67–68, 79, 90, 92–93, 103, 109, 119–121, 166, 234, 253
Pink Floyd, 194
plagiarism, 230–43
"Playthings" (episode), 39, 63, 107, 151, 258
"Point of No Return" (episode), 39, 168–169, 237, 239, 247, 268
Point Pleasant, 248
Poltergeist, 4, 39, 64, 119
postmodernism, xvi, 4–5, 132–133, 136, 140, 199, 232, 235
Pratchett, Terry, 230, 236, 240, 242
private space, 38
projected interactivity, 206, 212–

214, 218
Protestants/Protestantism, 172,
179–180, 186
"Provenance" (episode), 119, 256
Psych, 119
Psycho, 61, 151
Queer As Folk, 119
queer subject, the, 86
queer/queerness, 46, 86, 105–109,
113–114, 119, 277n, 278n
Raimi, Sam, 196
Raise the Red Lantern, 281
Ransick, Whitney, 256
Raphael (character), 174, 179,
181–182, 237, 250, 266, 271
"Rapture, The" (episode), 167, 265
"Real Ghostbusters, The" (episode),
43, 84, 86, 105, 108, 114–115,
129, 155–156, 207, 209, 215,
247, 267, 278n
Red River, 86
"Red Sky at Morning" (episode), 5,
100, 261
Reed, David, 268
reflexivity, 86, 114, 144, 147, 159,
211, 241
religion, xiv, 133, 164, 168, 171–173,
175–177, 181, 184, 234, 241,
279n, 280n
Ringu, 151
rite of passage, 89
road movie, ix–x, xvii, 34, 39, 78, 82,
84–87, 89, 91
"Roadkill" (episode), 94–95, 149–
150, 154, 259
Rodriguez, Robert, 197, 252
Rohl, Mike, 258–259, 261, 265, 268,
270–271
Rolling Stones, The, 23, 193–194
Rosen, Becky (character), xvi, 56,
114, 203–218, 267, 278n, 283n
Ross-Leming, Eugenie, 248, 255
Roth, Jenny, 85
Route 66, ix–x, 33, 83–84, 123, 273n
"Route 666" (episode), 8, 40, 42,
64, 70, 84, 192–193, 255
Ruby (character), 7, 12, 29, 72,
80–81, 98–99, 103, 108, 236,

238, 261–265, 276n–277n
Rush, 66, 195
"Salvation" (episode), 64, 77, 85,
93, 256
"Sam, Interrupted" (episode), 152,
194, 267
Sandman, The, 230–232, 235, 238,
240–241, 243
Sands, Trevor, 264
"Scarecrow" (episode), 94, 96, 139,
151, 255
science fiction, xiv, 4, 220, 230
science, 139, 181, 207
Scream, 248
Searchers, The, 79, 82, 84
self-referentiality, 109, 155, 209,
212, 252, 279n
serialization, 141, 144, 278n
Sesame Street, 196
sex, 35, 40–41, 46, 106, 112, 119,
207
"Sex and Violence" (episode), 22,
123, 264, 280n
sexual freedom, 40
Sgriccia, Phil, 255–260, 262–271
"Shadow" (episode), 127, 255
Shakespeare, William, 231
Shapiro, Paul, 255
Shaun of the Dead, 6
Shiban, John, xi, 254–259
Shining, The, 4, 63, 150
Showalter, John F., 268–272
shtriga, 44, 256
Shurley, Chuck (character), xvi,
5, 13, 43, 106, 114, 117, 129,
155–156, 158–159, 174–175,
185, 193, 211–213, 215–217,
245, 247–248, 265, 269, 278n
Siege, Julie, 211, 263–266, 268
Silence of the Lambs, 7, 151
"Simon Said" (episode), 73, 257
Sin City, 151
"Sin City" (episode), 42, 151, 197,
247, 261
Singer, Bobby (character), x, xii–
xiii, 7, 42, 53, 62, 69, 72, 82,
89, 98, 102–103, 122, 125,
144, 159, 164, 169, 251, 256,

259–261, 263–266, 268–269, 271–272, 274n, 276n
Singer, Robert, 254, 256–258, 260–270, 272
Singing Detective, The, 19
sitcom, 34, 38, 40, 83, 153
Six Feet Under, 119
"Skin" (episode), 56, 58, 70, 167, 254
slapstick, 3–5, 9–10, 100
slash fiction, 85, 106–108, 114, 205, 209–210, 217, 278n
slash, xvi, 6 108, 155, 203–205, 211, 213, 215, 217, 278n
slasher film, 194
Slotkin, Richard, 78–79, 82, 89
Smallville, 128, 222–224, 227–228, 284n
Smith, Patrick Sean, 255
Snyder, Nicole, 270
soap opera, 36, 143
"Something Wicked" (episode), 39, 43–44, 107, 124, 193, 256
Something Wicked This Way Comes, 193, 282n
"Song Remains the Same, The" (episode), xii, 19, 43, 55, 92, 239, 267, 276n
Spade, Sam, 88
Spangler, Harry (character), 256, 262
Stagecoach, 77
Stanwyck, Barbara, 196
Star Wars, 125, 159, 233
Stay Tuned, 151
Stein, Louisa, 198
storytelling, xiv, xvi, 117, 119, 128–130, 133, 141–142, 149, 158, 187, 200, 232–234, 281n
Sturges, John, 194
suburbia, 47, 56–57, 59, 103
subversive, 106, 113, 115
Surette, Tim, 203–205, 218
Surface, 220
"Swan Song" (episode), x, xiii, 65, 89, 141, 147, 156, 158, 165, 173–174, 183–184, 195, 215, 237, 269, 275n, 278n

"Swap Meat" (episode), 14, 267
"Sympathy for the Devil" (episode), 13, 43, 81, 144, 164, 194, 207, 237, 266, 278n
Szwarc, Jeannot, 271
Tal, Alona (actress), 103
Talalay, Rachel, 258
Talbot, Bela (character), 100–101, 122, 260–263, 276–277
"Tall Tales" (episode), xvi, 10, 139, 147, 149, 259
Tarantino, Quentin, 199
target audience/demographic, xiv, 19, 21, 26, 77, 198, 223–224, 227, 274n
televisual folklore, 187, 190–191, 199–200
Tessa (character), 80
Texas Chainsaw Massacre, 8, 12, 53, 61–63, 72, 151, 275n
Thing, The, 64
"Third Man, The" (episode), 250, 269
Threshold, 220
"Time Is on My Side" (episode), 23–24, 68, 100, 151, 194, 262
Titan AE, 248
Tobin, J. Miller, 259, 261, 264, 266
Tosenberger, Catherine, 81, 106–108, 122, 132, 134, 136
trash drag, 50–51, 53, 59
Trickster, the (character), 10, 34, 40, 85, 129, 139, 149, 153, 234, 267
Tucker, Raelle, 253, 255–260
Turner, Rufus (character), 68, 266, 269, 271
Twilight, 95
"Two and a Half Men" (episode), 250, 269
"Two Minutes to Midnight" (episode), x, xii, 194, 237, 239, 245, 249, 269, 280n
"Unforgiven" (episode), 250, 270
Up in the Air, 37
urban myth/legend, ix, xiii, xvi, 4, 41, 132–133, 137, 139–140, 142–143, 150, 170, 187–189,

191–192, 234, 273n
Uriel (character), 8, 179–182, 237, 265
Usual Suspects, The, 194
"Usual Suspects, The" (episode), 35, 63, 154, 194, 258, 280n
Vampire Diaries, The 131
vampires, x, xii, 6–7, 13, 79–80, 88, 95–96, 104, 146, 150, 191, 234, 247–248, 251, 256–257, 261, 263, 270, 277n
Van Halen, 195
Van Wilder, 11
"Very Supernatural Christmas, A" (episode), 8, 28, 37, 44, 46, 51–52, 85, 165, 192, 196, 247, 261
vessels, xii, 12, 74, 89, 129, 164–171, 174, 179, 184, 265, 268
Walker, Gordon (character), 7, 95–96, 258, 261
Ward, Marcy (character), 269
Wayne, John, 77
"Weekend at Bobby's" (episode), 194, 250, 269
Weiner, Nancy, 265, 267
"Wendigo" (episode), x, 134, 136, 192, 234, 253
wendigos, x, xvi, 74, 136, 141, 191, 253
Westerns, 77–80, 82, 84–89, 279n
Wharmby, Tony, 256
"What Is and What Should Never Be" (episode), 36, 73, 85, 148, 166, 250, 260
white trash, 47–59, 62, 275n
"When the Levee Breaks" (episode), 7, 23, 148, 163, 237, 265
Who, The, 23, 194

Wicker Man, The, 281n
Wilkinson, Jules, 38, 209
Wincest, 39–40, 86, 106, 108, 204, 217, 278n
Winchester, John (character), 19, 21, 40, 43–45, 47, 52, 55, 64–65, 67–68, 72, 74, 77–78, 81–82, 88, 93, 102, 122, 174, 189, 256–257, 263, 267 274n, 280n
Winchester, Mary (character), 36, 38, 55, 64–65, 67–69, 71–74, 82, 90, 92–94, 102–103, 253, 256, 263, 267, 276n–277n, 280n
"Wishful Thinking" (episode), 71, 86, 128, 151, 248, 264, 280n
witchcraft, 196, 281n
Witten, Matt, 257–58
Woolnough, Jeff, 268
working class, 48–50, 55, 208
Wray, Matthew, 49–51
Writers' Guild of America, 157
X–Files, The, xi, xiv, 4, 33, 39, 63, 120, 128, 133, 144, 151, 187, 189, 191, 197, 248, 281n
"Yellow Fever" (episode), ix, 3, 14–16, 124, 158, 195, 250, 263
"You Can't Handle the Truth" (episode), 250, 270
Zachariah (character), 12, 16, 39, 163–64, 166, 168–171, 179, 182, 237, 268, 277n
Zeddmore, Ed (character), 207, 256, 262
Zeddmore, Maggie (character), 110
Zhang, Juwen, 190
Zhang, Yimou, 281
ZZ Top, 125